THE OXFORD BOOK OF
SEA SONGS

THE OXFORD
BOOK OF
SEA SONGS

CHOSEN AND EDITED BY
ROY PALMER

Oxford   New York
OXFORD UNIVERSITY PRESS
1986

Oxford University Press, Walton Street, Oxford OX2 6DP

Oxford New York Toronto
Delhi Bombay Calcutta Madras Karachi
Kuala Lumpur Singapore Hong Kong Tokyo
Nairobi Dar es Salaam Cape Town
Melbourne Auckland
and associated companies in
Beirut Berlin Ibadan Nicosia

Oxford is a trade mark of Oxford University Press

Introduction, selection, and editorial matter © Roy Palmer 1986

British Library Cataloguing in Publication Data
The Oxford book of sea songs.
1. Sea songs
I. Palmer, Roy
784.6'86238 M1977.S2
ISBN 0-19-214159-7

Library of Congress Cataloging in Publication Data
Main entry under title:
The Oxford book of sea songs.
Includes index. Bibliography: p.
1. Sea songs. 2. Folk-songs, English.
I. Palmer, Roy, 1932–
M1977.S2095 1986 85-753420
ISBN 0-19-214159-7

Set by Wyvern Typesetting Ltd.
Printed in Great Britain by
Richard Clay (The Chaucer Press) Ltd.
Bungay, Suffolk.

For my wife, Pat

CONTENTS

The Marlborough

INTRODUCTION

JOHN MASEFIELD, pointing out that the literature of the sea in English has 'no great epic poem on the deeds of our sailors', added that 'the ballad singers have done their best for us'. Their work, he observed, included 'ballads which illustrate naval history; or ballads of sea life, its dangers, wonders and delights; or ballads of tragical disaster or poetical justice'. Finally, 'many of them, and some of these are among the best, are love ballads'.[1]

The first anthology of such ballads seems to have been J. O. Halliwell's *Early Naval Ballads of England* (1841), after which there was a gap of fifty years before John Ashton's *Real Sailor Songs*. In the early years of this century Masefield's collection, *A Sailor's Garland*, which was partly culled during his own time at sea, and Christopher Stone's *Sea Songs and Ballads* (both 1906) were quickly followed by the monumental (and now indispensable) *Naval Songs and Ballads* (1908), edited by C. H. Firth. None of these works included tunes. The first collection of sea songs to do so was Laura Alexandrine Smith's *Music of the Waters* (1888), though this was only partly concerned wth material in the English language. For the first time, shanties, the work songs of the sea, were considered, and as the title indicates these also appeared in W. B. Whall's *Ships, Sea Songs and Shanties* (1910).

Whall, who had gone to sea in 1861, was a retired captain with clear-cut views. His introduction begins with the unequivocal statement that: 'The romance of the sea is gone, and with it are gone sea songs.' Of shanties he says: 'Remains of them there are, it is true, but the character has all gone out of them.' The books by Masefield, Stone, and Firth (the last of whom Whall cannot even bring himself to name, but merely refers to as 'an Oxford professor') 'smell of the British Museum', and their lack of music is a serious detriment since 'the words of a song without music are very like dry bones'. Whall's definition of sea songs excludes 'imitations by landsmen' such as 'Hearts of Oak' and 'The Death of Nelson'. He is not happy with street ballads ('chiefly written by some

---

[1] *Garland*, pp. ix and xiii. (Abbreviated references throughout the Introduction can be found in full on p. 313 (Sources) or pp. 327–32 (Bibliography).

half-educated printer's tout'), and although he grudgingly concedes that 'some of these may be rightly termed real sailor songs, as, probably, sailors sang them', he dismisses them for the most part as 'poor stuff, and most wearisome to a modern'.[2]

While agreeing with Whall on excluding imitations and including tunes, I believe that he is shortsighted in his view of street ballads and unduly narrow in his definition of sea songs as only those which can be proved to have been sung at sea. The landsman's and landswoman's songs of sea and sailors must surely be admissible, providing they are not merely the pseudo-sea songs which Whall rightly despised.

The present collection includes 159 songs, chiefly from England, but also from Ireland, Scotland, Wales, Canada, New Zealand, Australia, and America. The idiom is broadly (and often narrowly) traditional, and tunes are included where they are known. Although there are fine songs of earlier date, such as 'Sir Patrick Spens' and 'Andrew Barton', this selection starts with 'John Dory', which was circulating in the 1560s, and ends with 'The Final Trawl', which was written in 1979. The wide range of nautical themes treated includes battles, storm and shipwreck, pressgangs and crimps, mutiny, slavery, privateering and piracy, smuggling, shipboard life and conditions, fishing, whaling, trading, emigration and exploration, separation and celebration, Jack Tar on shore as well as afloat. The viewpoint, on the whole, is that of lower-deck seamen, their wives and loved ones, and the communities from which they came.

Men went to sea for a whole range of reasons. Fishing for food was perhaps the earliest. Then came exploration, for living space, for markets, for conquest. Fighting was often a concomitant, and battle is a major theme of sea song. Men were lured to sea by songs which described the adventures, the riches, the fame, the sexual good fortune which might accrue to seafarers, but it is fair to add that hardship and disaster were also staple topics. Some songs made direct attempts to persuade men to join particular ships or noted captains; others made a general appeal to patriotic sentiments in time of war.

For some, there was no choice. Either they were driven by necessity, or they were taken by force. Impressment in wartime was carried out originally under the royal prerogative, but its legality was confirmed by an act of 1556 and much subsequent legislation. Although it was used only until 1815 the power remained up to 1853, when permanent service in the navy was instituted. Impressment makes its appearance in ballads early in the seventeenth century, but it is mentioned as a regrettable necessity, almost a fact of life, often in set pieces in which a man bids farewell to his wife or sweetheart:

[2] Introduction.

Sweet Margery I am prest to the sea;
with gold and silver in my hand
I come to take my leave of thee,
and bid adieu to fair England.[3]

However, resentment grew at the arbitrary and often violent razzias of 'the impress service', which by 1797 employed one admiral, 47 captains, 80 lieutenants, and a large number of seamen. In addition there were 32 tenders and a considerable number of 'receiving ships'. The pressgang was feared and hated, and in some places there was strong resistance. Christopher Thomson was born at Hull in 1799, and later went on a whaling voyage to Greenland. During his apprenticeship as a shipwright he was expected to keep a lookout for the pressgang in order to warn journeymen. He describes several fierce fights, including a pitched battle between the gang and navvies working on repairs to one of the docks. Despite the reading of the Riot Act, and an appeal by the Mayor, the naval rendezvous was stormed, and 'kidnapped wretches' liberated. Thomson adds that he could 'detail a score of such heart-harrowing scenes' and bitterly attacks the law 'which sanctions this kidnapping' and under which 'whenever it suits the ambition of war-spirits to light their brand, freeborn Englishmen may be stolen from their homes again, again torn from the embrace of their wives, even while "on downy beds lying"; entrapped for "blood-money" by vulture Judases, immediately after landing from a long voyage . . . This is part of our boasted "Constitution". This is the law in happy England, where "every man's house is his castle".'[4] Songs moved from resignation to rejection of pressganging. The mutineers of 1797 asked how a denial of liberty could help the cause of liberty for which the country was at war. The point was made in a song of the time (74), and it has a familiar ring today.

Such memories were slow to fade, and songs dealing with the pressgang continued to circulate for decades after its abolition. Until well within living memory merchant seamen also were subjected to forcible recruitment or shanghaiing, and were carried on to ships insensible from drugs, drink, or blows. In this way a ship got a crew and the crimp cashed the sailor's advance note for wages.

Once on board a man was immediately caught up in the rules and routines governing the small world of the ship. All aspects of this life are explored in ballads, from diet to discipline, from the details of working the ship to the occasional diversion or recreation. The people on board frequently appear in song. The hated purser is wellnigh ubiquitous, and there are captains and commanders, detested or admired as the case may be, and also shipmates, some of whom miraculously turn out to be

---

[3] 'Sweet Margery', Euing, no. 326.
[4] Thomson, pp. 69–71.

female. One of the conventions of sea songs is the dialogue between a lover and his lass in which the woman threatens to disguise herself as a sailor so as to accompany him to sea. The man usually dissuades her on the grounds of danger and hardship, and they reluctantly part. In some songs, however, the woman does dress as a seaman and follows her lover to sea. Much of this is fantasy or wishful thinking, and not necessarily any the worse for that, but there are documented instances of such masquerades.

A late seventeenth-century ballad, 'The Maiden Sailor', purports to be 'a true relation of a young damsel who was pressed on board the *Edgar* man-of-war, being taken up in seaman's habit'. Her sex was revealed when a sailor 'who thought she like a maid did speak' 'strove to feel her knee'. She rejected the liberty and confessed her imposture, whereupon she was freed by the captain and allowed to return to her native town of Maidenhead. The coincidence is too good to be true, but there are reports which, while they leave a great many questions unanswered, seem to provide firm evidence. In 1800 the *Liverpool Advertizer* printed news of 'a fine girl, about 18 years of age', who had served as a seaman for 'upwards of seven weeks' aboard HMS *Actaeon* before her sex was discovered through a letter sent to friends. She 'conducted herself with the greatest propriety' during her time at sea, and was sent ashore 'with a handsome collection made for her by officers and ship's company'.[5] As late as the 1860s one Charlotte Petrie, who was born at Aberdeen in 1846, 'abandoned her home for the roving life of a sailor' and managed several voyages on merchant vessels before her identity was revealed by unspecified means while her ship, the *Expedient* of Newcastle, was in harbour at Palermo. Until then she had performed her duties as ordinary seaman 'without the least suspicion having arisen among my mates during the whole voyage'.[6]

Shipboard life may have been sweetened by such stories and songs, but it was threatened from time to time by extreme danger. Sailors fought in a long series of wars, against the Spanish, the Dutch, the French, the Americans, the Russians, the Germans, and for that matter a host of other nations. Conflict at sea was part of the stock in trade of ballad makers from Laurence Minot's 'Sea Fight at Sluys' of 1340 to 'The Sinking of the *Graf Spee*' (149) of 1940, and beyond that, though the highpoint of the heroic naval song was probably Trafalgar. Merchant ships were by no means immune from fighting; they were a prey to warships and privateers during hostilities, and in certain waters to pirates at any time. The Thai navy is currently (1985) being strengthened in order to combat piracy in its waters. Anything from a duel

[5] Issue dated 12 May 1800. Quoted Williams, p. 378.

[6] *Sunderland Herald*, 8 December 1865. I am indebted to Keith Gregson for this reference.

between a pair of ships to a major fleet action provided a potential subject. Jerrold's remark on the French Wars that 'no battle was fought, no vessel taken or sunken, that the triumph was not published, proclaimed in the national gazette of the ballad singer'[7] could be extended to cover many centuries of naval history.

Storms and shipwrecks inspired ballads as readily as did battles, for the sea is a far more powerful and implacable enemy than man. The loss of a single fishing boat from Donegal with its six men was commemorated as recently as 1975 in a song (158) which has all the appearances of being traditional. It stands at the end of a long line of disaster ballads, many of which deal with the heavy casualties sustained by passengers as well as crews.

On sailing ships there were frequent occasions when because of adverse winds, storm damage, or shipwreck, those on board or in boats found themselves totally without food, and with no likely prospect of relief. In such cases, after the lapse of a decent space it was the custom of the sea that the bodies of those who died might be eaten, and even that some people might be killed to feed the rest. In the latter event, lots would be drawn to select the victims, though there is a suggestion that the process was rigged to choose the weakest or most suitable person. The subject has recently been examined in depth in a fine study by Professor A. W. B. Simpson, *Cannibalism and the Common Law* (1984), where dozens of instances are documented. One case not included is that of Thomas Moorhead, who subsisted for fifty-one days on the bodies of dead shipmates in the storm-battered *Acorn* of Stockton until he was taken off the wreck and eventually landed at New York in May, 1809. His story was made the subject of a ballad,[8] which was one of so many on cannibalism that the sardonic claim was made that

> To read of a shipwreck is fine,
> When every soul of 'em's lost,
> Or a few cast on rocks is divine,
> And to eat one another are forced.[9]

Eventually, this custom of the sea, at least in so far as it related to killing people to eat so that others might survive, was placed outside the law, after the celebrated case of the *Mignonette* in 1884, which inspired ballads, and is studied at length by Simpson.

Rex Clements wrote that 'Storm, battle and sea-robbery were the favourite themes of his [the sailor's] ballads; love and 'longshore life of his lighter pieces'.[10] It is true that sailors frequently expressed their

[7] D. Jerrold, *Heads of the People*, 1840, p. 294.

[8] 'Thomas Moorhead', Thomas, no. 269.

[9] Ballad entitled 'An Horrible Taste' in Baring-Gould Ballad Collection, Vol. I, p. 171, BL, LR 271 a 2. I am indebted to Professor A. W. B. Simpson for this reference.

[10] Clements, p. 28.

thoughts about those on shore, and *vice versa*. These relationships, cast into relief by the enforced separation, are full of the conflicting qualities of fidelity and fickleness, honesty and deception, celebration and sorrow. Exploration in remote areas is also well-represented in this collection, and nearer home, the coasting trade of colliers and sailing barges. The hopes and tribulations of emigrants travelling between Britain and North America or Australia provide another theme for prolific writing. Smuggling, slavery, the supernatural, sailortowns; the rise and decline of fishing and whaling; lifeboats; the sailor as hero and victim: all these repeatedly feature in songs.

The sources of these songs are oral tradition, street ballads, manuscripts and memoirs, compositions of recent date. The most important (*pace* Captain Whall) is that of street ballads, from Deloney's piece on the Spanish Armada of 1588 (6) to the anonymous 'Sorrowful Lines on the Loss of . . . the *Titanic*' of 1912.[11] Until roughly 1700, ballads were quarto sheets in the old black-letter or gothic type. The white-letter or Roman print was sometimes used instead of italics, and later became universal. One of the major seventeenth-century collections is that of Samuel Pepys, with over 1,600 sheets, of which more than half are unique. Not surprisingly for a man with such a close association with the navy, a great many are on nautical subjects. For the eighteenth century the collection assembled by Sir Frederic Madden is very important, particularly for its slip-songs. As the name implies, these are printed on slips of paper. They measure roughly three inches by anything up to sixteen, and are usually without imprint. (One of the consequences of the naval mutinies of 1797 was that all publications were required by law to bear an imprint.) They were sold at ½d. each. As both metropolis and major port, London was inevitably the main centre for the printing of street ballads, as of other things, but provincial entrepreneurs gradually entered the trade until in the nineteenth century sheets were being produced almost all over the country. Herman Melville's novel, *Redburn* (1849), is based on his experiences as a nineteen-year-old hand aboard the packet ship, *St Lawrence*, in 1839. Round Liverpool docks he noticed 'the number of sailor ballad-singers, who, after singing their verses, hand you a printed copy, and beg you to buy'. Country printers sometimes merely reissued material from elsewhere, but often printed original songs relating to, say, a privateer from a local port (42), a smuggling affray (89) or a raid by the pressgang (68).

There was an extraordinary outpouring of ballads during the Revolutionary and Napoleonic Wars. Gavin Greig wrote that 'The twenty years that ended with Waterloo have left more traces on our popular minstrelsy than any other period of history has done',[12] and Douglas

[11] Scrapbook J1, p. 57, Bigger Collection, Belfast Public Library. I am indebted to John Moulden for this reference.   [12] Greig, article XXV, p. 2, col. 1.

Jerrold observed of the same time that it was the ballad seller's 'peculiar province to vend half-penny historical abridgements to his country's glory; recommending the short poetic chronicle by some familiar household air that fixed it in the memory of the purchaser'. He went on:

No battle was fought, no vessel taken or sunken, that the triumph was not published, proclaimed in the national gazette of our ballad singer. . . . It was he who bellowed music into news, which, made to jingle, was thus, even to the weakest understanding rendered portable. It was his narrow strips of history that adorned the garrets of the poor; it was he who made them yearn towards their country, albeit to them so rough and niggard a mother.[13]

Much of this applies equally well to other times, but there was a rich flowering of this popular art-form at the time of the great struggles with France. Jerrold believed that this was a watershed: 'with the fall of Napoleon declined the English ballad singer', he wrote; and again: 'The sailor ballad singer has died with the long peace; he no longer attacks our sympathies with one arm and a wooden leg.' Yet as late as the 1860s William Pratt, a ballad printer in Birmingham, which is as far away from the sea as it is possible to go in Britain, had ten per cent of his 500 titles on maritime subjects. These included 'The Death of Nelson', 'The Golden Vanity' (22), 'The Lowlands of Holland', 'On Board the *Victory*' (81), 'The Saucy Sailor Boy', and 'William of a Man-of-War'.

Street ballads are by no means a watertight category; on the contrary, they were open to material from almost any source, though a central core was invariably traditional in character. On occasion, songs originally from oral tradition were printed in this form. For example, 'England's Great Loss by a Storm of Wind' (28), which refers to events of 1691, did not apparently find its way into print until at least a generation afterwards; and although it is possible that a now-lost sheet intervened, one can see the influence of oral tradition in the blurring of some details such as ships' names which are not fundamental to the message of the song. On the other hand, the printing of the early eighteenth century might well have assisted the song to survive and to travel. Certainly, many songs on British broadsides travelled great distances in space and time. Many not only went to North America, but continued to circulate orally there long after they had disappeard from Britain. A descendant of the song on the storm of 1691 was still being sung in Nova Scotia in 1929, and such instances could be multiplied. Tunes perforce had to be transmitted orally, since they were rarely printed on ballad sheets, and in addition, certain songs seem to have circulated without benefit of print. The *Ramillies* was lost in 1760 yet the song on the subject (47) was not taken down until almost a century and a half later.

[13] Op. cit., pp. 289 and 294–5.

In the late sixteenth and early seventeenth centuries a number of well-known writers specialized in street ballads. Copies of the work of Thomas Deloney, Laurence Price, and Martin Parker have survived in this form, and in some cases have enjoyed long histories of their own. Parker's ballad, 'Sailors for my Money' (13) was originally published in about 1635. A decade or so later it reappeared with some changes as 'Neptune's Raging Fury'. In 1800 it was adapted for singing in the parlour and the concert hall by Thomas Campbell as 'Ye Mariners of England', but also continued to circulate in something approaching its original form as 'When stormy winds do blow'. In addition, it served as a pattern for many other songs.

Most writers whose work appeared on ballad sheets remained anonymous. Some were employed by printers for a fee of a shilling or two a time to knock into verse noteworthy events, but they drew on traditional phraseology and traditional models. The basic information seems sometimes to have been provided by eyewitnesses, sometimes to have been obtained from newspaper reports. Such ballad narratives sold because they were cheaper than newspapers and more accessible to those with a low level of reading skills. Their editorial standpoint was more congenial to ordinary people and their idiom more memorable.

Sailors themselves often seem to have written ballads which found their way on to broadsides. There were times, no doubt, when sailor authorship was falsely claimed in the belief that it would help sales, just as ballad sellers often assumed the dress of sailors in an effort to enlist the sympathy of the public and thus to help dispose of their wares. Such impostors were known in the nineteenth century as 'turnpike sailors'. Nevertheless, the density and authenticity of detail provides internal evidence that certain ballads must have been written by sailors or ex-sailors, even when such authorship is not claimed. One thinks, for example, of 'Cordial Advice' (34), a graphic account from the late seventeenth century of the hardships of a whaling voyage, and of 'The Jolly Sailor's True Description of a Man-of-War' (49) from the late eighteenth century. In other cases attribution to sailors is difficult to dispute, because of the depth of knowledge and strength of feeling displayed.

In addition there is a good deal of evidence from memoirs and manuscripts that sailors aboard ship wrote ballads to suit their needs as though it were the most natural thing in the world to do, as indeed it was to them, for it is we who have lost sight of popular creativity. James Gardner went to sea unofficially in his father's ship at the age of five, in 1775; his father was a commander in the navy. Gardner later served as a midshipman on several ships, and became a lieutenant in 1795. In his *Naval Recollections* he mentions songs and singing on many occasions. The subject matter includes conditions aboard, battles, and even the idiosyncracies of shipmates. The purser of the *Gorgon*, Jerry Hacker, had a song, to the tune of 'The Black Joke', which reflected adversely on midshipmen, to which Gardner riposted with a verse tilting at pursers:

> Our b--- of a purser he is very handy,
> He mixes the water along with the brandy;
> Your anchors a-weigh and your topsails a-trip;
> The bloody old thief he is very cruel:
> Instead of burgoo he gives us water gruel;
> A lusty one and lay it well on,
> If you spare him an inch you ought to be damned,
> With your anchors a-weigh and your topsails a-trip.

Gardner heard another song on board the *Blonde* from an Irish singer called Gibson, which concerned 'a countryman of his by the name of Fegan, who, in the American War [of Independence] was sent by Sir John Fielding (the celebrated magistrate of Bow Street) [and brother of the novelist] on board the *Conquistador*. . . . This Fegan was a shrewd, keen fellow, and made a song on being sent on board a man-of-war.' On the *Barfleur* in 1790 Gardner heard a further song from the time of the American War which was 'made by a seaman of the *Princess Amelia*'. It tells the story of the Battle of the Dogger Bank, fought in 1781 between the English and Dutch fleets. The singer was Billy Culmer, who at the age of thirty-five was reputed to be the oldest midshipman in the navy.[14]

Exactly a century after Gardner's first voyage, Sam Noble left his work as oiler in a Dundee jute mill and joined the navy. He was sixteen. His first sea-going ship was the *Swallow*, in which he spent most of his active naval career, from 1877 to 1881. Songs still played an important part in the men's leisure time aboard ship, and Noble mentions a large number of them, from 'The Rocky Road to Dublin' to 'The Hills of Chile'. Those on nautical themes include 'Ratcliffe Highway' (94), to the tune of 'The Ash Grove', 'Sunday at Sea', 'The Lowlands Low' (22), 'The Dark-eyed Sailor', 'My love, William' (71), 'Windy Weather' (70), 'Around Cape Horn' (127), and among Noble's own songs, 'The Boatie Rows' (77).

On one occasion Noble wrote a song himself. The first lieutenant, known behind his back as Billy, promised a boat's crew a glass of grog apiece, and then found a series of good reasons why the men should not receive their due. The song went to the tune of 'The Sunny Fields of Spain', which was also used for another song Noble mentions, 'The Female Cabin Boy' (97), and 'turned out a rare focsle ditty, and caused quite a furore in the ship'. Noble continues: 'These were the days of the "long song". Some of them like "Windy Weather" had twenty or thirty verses, and, if they were extra good, as this old favourite

[14] Gardner, pp. 166, 214, and 103.

was, would be sung and re-sung over and over again. We never seemed to tire of them. Mine had eleven, and a rolling, one-line chorus. This is how it went:

> Ye toilers on the briny with loyal hearts and true,
> Come give me your attention and a tale I'll tell to you.
> 'Tis of the good ship, *Swallow*, who merrily doth sail,
> And before the fiercest hurricane can wag her pretty tail.
> *Oh, Billy. Billy, Billy boy.*

The concluding verse is:

> So now, my poor old comrades, I pray you do not frown,
> Nor give your hearts to sorrow, though Billy's turned you down;
> But think upon the moral: that promises are vain,
> And never trust an officer who wears a window pane [monocle].
> *Oh, Billy. Billy, Billy boy.*[15]

The successors of Sam Noble, AB, in the Royal Navy of the twentieth century were just as ready to express themselves in song. Their considerable repertoire has yet to be fully explored, though Cyril Tawney has done a great deal of work on it which still awaits publication. Extracts from some songs, often obscene, appeared in Tristan Jones' recent account of his experiences in the Second World War, *Heart of Oak* (1984). Jones was an eyewitness of the sinking of HMS *Hood*, which went down in 1942 with the loss of 1,400 lives. An unknown sailor made this song, to the tune of 'Silent Night'. It is too close to its model for artistic comfort, but is nevertheless moving:

> When HMS *Hood* went down in the deep,
> That was the news that made mothers weep;
> For the sons who had fought for a country so proud
> Were down there below with the sea as their shroud.
> They're sleeping in heavenly peace, sleeping in heavenly peace.

> Then came *George V*, the *Prince of Wales* too,
> They took in hand what the *Hood* had to do.
> The *Suffolk*, the *Norfolk*, the *Cossack* as well,
> Along with the *Rodney* shelled *Bismarck* to hell.
> They sank that ship, oh, we're glad; but for our lads we feel sad.

> So mothers and wives and sweethearts, be proud;
> Though your dear lads have the sea as their shroud,
> They were fighting for freedom, let's never forget.
> The freedom they fought for will be won yet.
> They're sleeping in heavenly peace, sleeping in heavenly peace.[16]

Other songs escape from their mould, and take on a life of their own.

[15] Noble, pp. 104–8 and 202–21.
[16] From memory.

One such is 'The *Jervis Bay*' (150), which is based on 'Suvla Bay', a song of the First World War, but can stand alone. Its author is again unknown, but it circulated widely in the navy during the 1940s, despite the active disapproval of officers who perhaps felt that it was bad for morale, but it is still remembered by many former sailors. To this day I have not seen more than a few lines of it in print.

The tradition of song-writing sailors persisted even after the Second World War. Some, like Don Goodbrand (152) and Harry Robertson (151) looked back afterwards on their experiences and put them into song. Others, like Cyril Tawney, wrote about the post-war navy. Tawney, who was born in 1930, wrote in the 1950s and '60s a series of minor classics such as 'The Grey Funnel Line', 'Sally Free and Easy', and 'Sammy's Bar', which dealt with sailors' life ashore and afloat, at home and abroad. His spell of several years in the submarine service, which is seldom celebrated in song, produced 'Diesel and Shale' (153).

Phil Colclough also writes (155) out of his own seagoing experience, this time as a merchant seaman, but several very successful songs have been written on the fishing industry in recent years by landsmen. John Conolly's 'Fiddler's Green' (157) on the fisherman's utopia has not only achieved world-wide recognition but has, it is claimed, been sung in every pub in Ireland. 'The Shoals of Herring' (154) by the doyen of British songwriters, Ewan MacColl, based on the life of a Norfolk fisherman, Sam Larner, has won similar fame. There is even a story that MacColl, unrecognized in the audience, heard an Irishman in a London pub prefacing a performance with the remark that this was a traditional song. In a sense, there could be no greater compliment to one who writes in the folk idiom. Perhaps MacColl's song will live for centuries in the mouths of singers, as some others have.

As well as composing songs, sailors often carefully preserved them in writing. Gale Huntington found a large body of songs noted between 1767 and 1905 in the journals and logbooks of American ships, chiefly from Massachusetts, and published a selection in his excellent book, *Songs the Whalemen Sang* (1964). Another American, a seaman called Timothy Connor, was taken prisoner by the British during the War of Independence. During his captivity from 1777 to 1779 at Forton, near Portsmouth, he carefully copied into a notebook the texts of sixty songs, many of them nautical. Some appear to have been copied from printed sheets, most taken down from oral tradition, which means Connor's own memory or that of his companions or guards. Connor was probably not exceptional, though the preservation of his songbook is.[17]

Other sailors preserved songs just as carefully, and Stan Hugill goes so far as to say that his father's 'ditty-box songbook' was 'the type of

[17] For Timothy Connor, see under Carey.

thing all seamen kept in the days of sail'.[18] Richard Cotten[19] served in the British navy a century after Connor was captured by it. He was on the *Comus* from 1879 to 1884 and on the *Bacchante* from 1885 to '86. It was on the first ship that he noted seven songs and poems in his diary in passing; then at Callao on 7 June 1883 he bought a fine notebook which he adorned with a drawing of his ship before copying down twenty-four more poems and songs, nearly all on subjects such as storm, shipwreck, shipboard life, privateering, slavery. They range from 'The Wreck of the *Hesperus*' to 'The *Flying Dutchman*' (106) and from 'The Fisherman's Glee' to 'The Dying Sailor Boy'. Some are clearly home-made, such as 'A Nautical Alphabet', which deals with the loss of the *Vanguard*, accidentally rammed by the *Iron Duke* in 1875 while on manoeuvres in the Irish Sea. It begins:

> A was the admiral never to blame,
> B was the blunder from which it all came;
> C was the court martial whose finding was vain,
> D was poor Dawkins* whose prospects were slain.

* Captain of the *Vanguard*.

Several other songs noted by Cotten are similarly critical in attitude, while others are examinations of seagoing life (129, 130).

George Boughton was a contemporary of Cotten's, but in the merchant service. He went to sea in 1882 at the age of twelve, sailing from Sunderland in the *Archos* on a voyage which lasted eight years. One of the things which struck him was the singing of shanties and he wrote many years later that he became so accustomed to singing when pulling on a rope that long after retiring from the sea 'I always fall a victim to it, quite unconsciously, when pulling up the clothes-line between the garden poles on washing day, or the overhead clothes-horse halliards in the kitchen, much to the amusement of my family and visitors'.[20]

Shanties (otherwise 'chanties' or 'chanteys') were sung to accompany certain specific tasks, and were very much sailor-made. 'They were used', wrote Captain Downie, 'to facilitate the heavy work of heaving up the anchor, pumping ship, and hoisting the heavy topsail yards of the period [the 1860s], besides the lighter labour of trimming sail . . . When chanteys were used, the men, singing in unison, were enabled at set intervals to throw their united weight on a rope or pump-brake all together, and thus avoided wasting their strength in ineffective pulls.'[21] Such songs are mentioned as early as the time of Henry VI (1422–61) in 'The Pilgrims', a ballad describing a sea voyage, and in 'The Complaint

[18] Hugill, p. 462.
[19] Cotten's manuscripts are in the National Maritime Museum.
[20] Boughton, p. 27.
[21] Downie, p. 26.

of Scotland' (1549) but almost all the shanties in English which have survived until the twentieth century are the product of the years between 1820 and 1860 when there was a huge expansion of trade, travel, and emigration, stimulated partly by the American and Australian gold rushes. Ironically enough, this was just at the time when the sailing ship was nearing its apogee and at the same time starting to be superseded by steam.

The shanties not only consolidated the effort of teams of men doing heavy work, but put heart into them and relieved the monotony of labour. 'The shanty was like a shot of grog to the men',[22] said one old sailor; and another: 'It was only just a few words we had, but it made the thing come lighter'.[23] Richard Dana and Joseph Conrad make interesting references to shantying, but none so fine as John Masefield's:

No shanties are sung with such gusto as those with which the crew get their anchors on leaving port for home. When all the hatches are on, and covered with tarpaulin; when the sails are all bent, and the house-flag slats at the truck, and the ensign, a stream of scarlet, flies astern; it is then that the sailors burst out a-singing in their best style ... If, at such a time, one is aloft, loosing the casting sails, one notices a strange thing. All the bass voices seem to get together upon a single capstan bar, and all the other voices group together in the same way; and the effect, as the men heave round, is very curious. I remember a barque sailing for home from one of the Western ports. I was aboard her, doing some work, I forget exactly what, just below the fore-rigging, and the effect of these differing voices, now drawing near and ringing out, then passing by, and changing, and fading, was one of strange beauty.... The song they were singing was the old, haunting pathetic shanty of the Rio Grande. As it was sung that sunny morning, under the hills, to the sound of the surf and the cheering sailors, its poor ballad took to itself the nobility of great poetry. One remembered it as a supremely lovely thing, in which one was fortunate to have taken a part.[24]

The words of shanties were subordinate to the task in hand; as soon as it was completed the song ceased, whatever point the singer had reached. It would never be sung after work was finished, either on ship or on shore, unless it were one of those songs which doubled as shanty and forebitter. Apart from the difference of function between work and recreation, the shanties were often obscene: 'the words which sailor John put to them when unrestrained were the veriest filth', says Whall.[25] Few such texts have been published, since either a sailor censored himself when singing for the record, or the collector bowdlerized or camouflaged his text before printing it. One of the few to record, though not to publish, undoctored words was Percy Grainger.[26]

[22] Barker, p. 144.
[23] Quoted in Sharp, *Folk Chanteys*, p. xiv.
[24] 'Sea Songs', pp. 62–4.
[25] Introduction.
[26] The obscene shanties collected by Grainger are discussed in M. Yates, 'The Best Bar

Shantymen treated texts with great freedom, adapting, improvising, moving lines and whole verses from one song to another, and they were similarly free with tunes. 'Blow the Man Down' (108), one of the best-known shanties, swallowed the words of a dozen other songs and took over several tunes. Despite this fluidity, perhaps because of it, shanties reflect all the preoccupations of the sailor, from sex to sentiment and from escapism to vitriolic complaint. Their mood is lyrical, ribald, uproarious, dignified. They provide some of the best portraits there are of life under sail (102, 103, and 105, for example).

They are now dead as functional songs, for even though sail is beginning to return to big ships it is now computer-controlled and mechanically adjusted. Yet there is intense interest in shanties, which is fostered by magnificent books such as Stan Hugill's *Shanties from the Seven Seas* (1961; 3rd impression, 1979). These sea songs *par excellence* are enjoying a vigorous afterlife on shore for many reasons, including nostalgia, conviviality, and the still-powerful social comment which they carry.

On warships and some East Indiamen work was carried out in silence. 'Merchant Jack laughs with contempt', wrote Symondson, 'as he watches their crew in uniform dress, walking round the windlass, weighing anchor like mechanical dummies. No hearty chanties there— no fine chorus ringing with feeling and sentiment, brought out with a sort of despairing wildness, which so often strikes neighbouring lands-folk with deepest emotion.'[27] However, a fifer or fiddler sometimes lightened the labour with his strains. In 1802 Lieutenant Dillon (later Admiral Sir William Dillon) was trying to motivate a 'malingering marine'. Having found out that he could play the fiddle, 'I ordered one to be brought aft, and desired him to mount the scuttle butt and play tunes to the men hoisting provisions. He was mounted on that cask . . . and struck up some lively and favourite airs to the amusement of all hands'.[28] Dillon does not say what the tunes were, but the tunebook of a ship's fiddler of precisely the same period has survived.[29] The man's name was William Litten, and he served with the British India Fleet from 1800 to 1802.

One form of music which navy men and merchant seamen shared was the forecastle song or forebitter. The forebitts was a construction of iron or timber near the foremast through which many of the principal ropes

of the Capstan: William Bolton, Sailor and Shantyman', pp. 10–11 in *Traditional Music*, No. 7, 1977, and V. Gammon, 'Song, Sex and Society in England, 1600–1850', pp. 208–45 in *Folk Music Journal*, 1982.

27 Symondson, p. 65.
28 Dillon, Vol. I, p. 363.
29 *William Litten's Fiddle Tunes*, ed. Gale Huntington, Vineyard Haven, Mass., 1977.

ran. Sailors would assemble there in good weather during dog-watches and other free times to talk and exchange songs. In bad weather the activity would take place in the quarters below, in the forecastle. Hence the two names for recreational songs.

As early as 1670 Dr John Covel wrote of officers exchanging visits in various ships off Land's End and observed: 'we seldome fail of some merry fellows in every ship's crew who will entertain us with several diversions, as divers sorts of odde Sports and Gambols; sometimes with their homely drolls and *Farses*, which in their corrupt language they nickname Interlutes; sometimes they dance about the mainmast instead of a may-pole, and they have variety of *forecastle songs*, ridiculous enough.'[30] Essentially the same thing was described by Private Wheeler when travelling aboard the *Impétueux* in 1811:

Through the week all is bustle, every hand is employed, the same cheerfulness prevailed, no cursing or ropes ends is brought into practice. The word of command or Boatswain's pipes is sufficient to set this mighty living machine in motion. Two evenings each week is devoted to amusement, then the Boatswain's mates with their pipes summons 'All hands to play'. In a moment the scene is truly animating. The crew instantly distribute themselves, some dancing to a fiddle, others to a fife. Those who are fond of the marvellous group together between two guns and listen to some frightful tale of Ghost and goblin, and another party listens to some weather beaten tar who 'spins a yarn' of past events until his hearers' sides are almost cracked with laughter. Again is to be found a party singing songs to the memory of Duncan, Howe, Vincent and the immortal Nelson, while others whose souls are more refined are singing praises to the God of Battles.[31]

There are frequent references to sailors' recreational songs. Downie says they were 'marvellous compositions of many verses, never complete without a chorus of some kind. They generally, if not always, told a tale "of moving incidents by flood", such as sea fights, encounters with pirates, etc., and were sung to droning, melancholy tunes, whereby they never found favour with shoregoing audiences, but were practically confined to ships' forecastles'. He concludes that 'there are very few men now living who can recollect the words of any of these old songs, for they have been supplanted by music-hall ditties and songs out of comic opera'.[32] Clements, too, laments the passing of such songs with the men who sang them and the ships they worked in:

Gone are the tall ships that gave them birth; gone the steady droning of the trade wind overhead, the sharp clang of the bell and the lookoutman's cheery; 'All's well, sir'; gone the jovial roar of many voices issuing from the open door of focsle

[30] Covel's diary was published by the Hakluyt Society in 1893. See p. 104.
[31] *The Letters of Private Wheeler*, ed. B. H. Liddell Hart, 1951, p. 47.
[32] Op. cit., p. 179.

or 'midship house, blending strangely well with the rustle of the sea, the wind's note and the murmurous fabric of the leaning ship.[33]

Fortunately, Downie and Clements were unduly pessimistic, and like the shanties, forebitters have enjoyed a new lease of life. They may mean something different to a twentieth-century town-dweller, but they still have meaning, and power, and beauty.

However, their primary purpose was perhaps never aesthetic; to borrow Wilfred Owen's phrase, 'the poetry is in the pity'. Of what he called 'the old and true sea songs' Christopher Stone remarked: 'Occasionally there was real poetry in them, but it was poetry of thought or idea, not of the phraseology'.[34] Yet there is a great deal of skill in such songs. Their art is public rather than private, and despite the role of print in dissemination, it is intended to be heard rather than read. Set openings grip the listener's attention: 'Come all you seamen bold', 'Good people all attend', 'Come people of England', 'Attend you and give hear awhile'. The narrative often begins abruptly, with the hearer immediately drawn in: 'On the fourteenth of February we sailed from the land', 'It's of a flash packet', 'When I was a youngster I sailed with the rest'.

The hearer is allowed moments when his attention may slacken by the use of stock phrases, epithets and verbs. Seas are salt, briny, raging, and the main is watery. Guineas are bright or good and red. Lofty winds blow; cannons, waves, and tempests roar. Seamen with hearts of gold plough the deep. There are passages of set questions and answers or even of series of questions and answers. On the other hand, the attention is quickened by rapid cross-cutting from one scene to another, from one protagonist to another, from third to first person in the narrative.

The language used is frequently memorable for its economy and vernacular vigour. The power of colloquial speech informs many songs in a way which did not come into more formal verse until perhaps the time of Browning. Enumeration of the names of ships and places is often used like an incantation: 'So the first land we made it is called the Deadman, Next Ram Head off Plymouth, Start, Portland and the Wight...' (54) Ships' names make a fine litany, as in 'There's the new-built *Terra Nova*, she's a model, with no doubt; There's the *Arctic* and the *Aurora* you've heard so much about...' (134). Nautical terminology can also be used extremely effectively, and its accuracy or otherwise was once keenly scrutinized by sailors. 'The Yankee Man-of-War' (62), otherwise known as 'The Stately Southerner', was popular on both sides of the Atlantic because of verses such as this:

[33] Op. cit., p. 30.
[34] Stone, p. iv.

'Out booms, out booms', our skipper cried; 'out booms, and give her sheet';
And the swiftest keel that ever was launched shot ahead of the British fleet,
And amidst a thundering shower of shot, with stunsails hoisting away,
Down the North Channel Paul Jones did steer just at break of day.

There is a great deal of variety in rhyme-scheme and length of line.
Half-rhymes and assonance are common, and internal rhyme is
frequent. Refrains, choruses, and repeated lines add to the diversity.
Lines may be as short as four syllables and as long as twenty-one, with
everything else in between. In a sense the metre is dictated by the music,
and the length or shortness of note gives greater or lesser stress. Certain
words, according to the exigencies of the situation, can be pronounced
as one syllable or two; 'poor', for example, or 'fire'. In some cases singers
insert supernumary syllables to help the flow of a song, and 'England'
becomes 'Engeland' or 'arms', 'arums'.

Where such spellings occur they have been left in the texts, but unless
the metre is adversely affected orthography has been modernized for the
sake of intelligibility. Punctuation has been lightened in general, but
inverted commas have been inserted to indicate direct speech, again for
the sake of clarity. Proper names, where they have variant forms, such as
'Cales' for 'Cadiz' have been left as in the original, and glossed where
necessary. In the case of a few particularly long songs, the stanzas have
been compressed by doubling up the lines, turning, for example, eight
short lines into four longer. (This is indicated in the list of sources.)
Words or letters added by the editor are placed in square brackets, and
this practice has also been followed in the (very few) places where an
additional verse has been inserted to fill a gap in the narrative. Unusual
terms and references are explained in the commentary after each song,
but nautical terms have been collected into a separate glossary at the
end.

Where they are known, tunes have been supplied, if possible from a
source close in date to that of the song. Many texts are united here with
their tunes for the first time. They have been drawn from printed,
manuscript and oral sources, and have been transposed if necessary into
keys which are both readable and singable. Rhythmic values normally
suit the first verse of the song, and it should be remembered that
adjustments are required as other verses are put to the tune. In some
cases, since the only version of a tune available is from an instrumental
score, it may well require adaptation before being used vocally.

The songs have been placed in rough chronological order. This is
often dictated by their subject matter, a specific battle or shipwreck, for
example, which took place on a particular date. In such cases a
contemporary or near-contemporary piece has been chosen, whenever
possible. There are times when several generations, or even longer,

elapse before a song surfaces into print or manuscript. One song on the loss of the *Ramillies* (47) circulated orally for 150 years, or so one must presume, before it was first noted.

Songs without a specific anchorage in dateable events are more difficult to pin down. They may appear in a dated or dateable manuscript or publication (book, broadside, garland, music sheet), but even then may have existed long before being fixed in this way. However, at least there is a point when they came to light. A few broadsides are dated; most are not, but the names and addresses of printers can sometimes provide a rough dating. Particular songs were often issued by successive printers, and I have tried to find (or at least mention) the earliest extant copy. It is always possible that earlier versions will be found. Many eighteenth-century garlands and slip-songs have no imprint, and even in the nineteenth century it is sometimes difficult to trace printers in the sporadic street and trade directories of the time. One is obliged at times to estimate dates from internal evidence, from typography, for instance, or even by making an educated guess.

In a few instances I have chosen a song as it existed at a particular time, even though it had circulated earlier. For example, 'The Banks of Newfoundland' (119), an account of the hardships experienced by seamen on the transatlantic run, was undoubtedly in existence by the 1840s, but I have included a version which was circulating twenty years later. The text mentions 1862. The singer was heard in 1915, but had not updated the song. He was a steward on a liner, and had probably decided that the matter of the song, if not the pleasure of singing it, was a thing of the past. While songs remained apposite to current conditions singers would not hesitate to update them, and one finds versions of 'The Greenland Whale Fishery' (72) in which the action is set in many different years, ranging from 1794 (which may not even be the earliest) until 1901 (which may not be the latest).

These songs have directness but also subtlety. They have depth, and also creative ambiguity, sometimes both within the same song. They reflect fierce patriotism and fearless protest. They face danger with unparalleled endurance, stoicism, courage. They explore relationships between the sexes with tenderness, love, affection, and also at times, ribaldry. They have a tremendous sense of humour, fun, exuberance. They are full of vigorous life, and are as uneven as life.

It is true that no epic poem celebrates the long life of our seafaring communities, yet these songs, taken as a body, have not only epic but tragic and also comic qualities, and endless fascination. One thinks of Paul Valéry's famous and evocative phrase, 'la mer toujours recommencée'. Let us hope that the epithet will apply both to our maritime history and to the songs of the sea.

John Dory

As it fell on a holy day,
And upon a holy tide, a,
John Dory bought him an ambling nag
To Paris for to ride, a.

And when John Dory to Paris was come
A little before the gate, a,
John Dory was fitted, the porter was witted
To let him in thereat, a.

The first man that John Dory did meet
Was good King John of France, a.
John Dory could well of his courtesy,
But fell down in a trance, a.

'A pardon, a pardon, my liege and my king,
For my merry men and for me, a,
And all the churls in merry England
I'll bring them all bound to thee, a.'

And Nicholl was then a Cornish [man],
A little beside Bohyde, a,
And he manned forth a good black bark
With fifty good oars on a side, a.

Bohyde] possibly a corruption of Polruan, a village across the river from Fowey.

'Run up, my boy, unto the maintop,
And look what thou canst spy, a.'
'Who ho, who ho, a goodly ship I do see;
I trow it be John Dory, a.'

They hoist their sails both top and top,
The mizen and all was tried, a;
And every man stood to his lot,
Whatever should betide, a.

The roaring cannons then were plied,
And dub a dub went the drum, a;
The braying trumpets loud they cried
To courage both all and some, a.

The grappling hooks were brought at length,
The brown bill and the sword, a;
John Dory at length, for all his strength,
Was clapped fast under board, a.

☞ In this story of the defeat of a French privateer by a Cornish captain there may be
confused echoes of the Hundred Years' War—King John the Good of France
died in English captivity in 1364—and of the seapower of the Doria dynasty of
Genoa. If Chappell is to be believed when he says that its tune was used for 'I
cannot eat but little meat' in *Gammer Gurton's Needle*, the song must have been
well known by 1562, for the play was first registered in that year. Richard Carew
in his *Survey of Cornwall* (1602) writes that 'John Dory' was 'an old three-man's
[three-part] song', and adds that Nicholas, as he calls him, was 'son to a widow
near Foy'. The earliest-known text is reprinted here from Ravenscroft's
Deuteromelia (1609). With its vigorous language and fierce patriotism the song
became widely known during the seventeenth century and was frequently
mentioned in literature. Another measure of its popularity was that the fish
known for centuries as a 'dory' acquired the name of 'John Dory'.

2   *Lustily, lustily*

Lustily, lustily, lustily, let us sail forth;
The wind trim doth serve us, it blows at the north.

All things we have ready and nothing we want
To furnish our ship that rideth hereby.
Victuals and weapons they be nothing scant;
Like worthy mariners ourselves we will try.

Her flags be new trimmèd, set slanting aloft.
Our ship for swift swimming, oh she doth excel.
We fear no enemies, we have escapèd them oft;
Of all things that swimmeth she beareth the bell.

And here is a master excelleth in skill,
And our master's mate he is not to seek;
And here is a boatswain will do his good will,
And here is a ship boy we never had his like.

If fortune then fail not, and our next voyage prove,
We will return merrily and make good cheer;
And hold all together as friends linked in love,
The cans shall be fillèd with wine, ale and beer.

☞ 'Here entreth the Mariners with a songe' is the stage direction which precedes
'Lustily, lustily' in an anonymous comedy of 1576 entitled *Common Conditions*.
The song has a good whiff of salt, and may have been heard by the playwright
during a sea journey.

3   *Upon Sir Francis Drake's Return from his Voyage about the World, and the Queen's meeting him*

Sir Francis, Sir Francis, Sir Francis is come,
Sir Robert and eke Sir William, his son;
And eke the good Earl of Huntingdon
Marched gallantly on the road.

Then came the Lord Chamberlain with his white staff,
And all the people began to laugh;
And then the Queen began to speak:
'You're welcome home, Sir Francis Drake.'

2 beareth the bell] a small bell was once given as a prize in horse races; by extension
the expression meant to win success of any kind.   not to seek] not lacking
prove] prove successful

3 eke] also

3

You gallants all o' the British blood,
Why don't you sail o' the ocean flood?
I protest you're not all worth a filbert
If once compared to Sir Humphrey Gilbert.

For he went out on a rainy day,
And to the new-found land found out his way,
With many a gallant fresh and green,
And he ne'er came home again. God bless the Queen.

☞ In 1580 Francis Drake returned from a three-year circumnavigation with
treasure worth half a million pounds, and was knighted aboard the *Golden Hind*
at Deptford by Queen Elizabeth. The first three verses of the song were
probably written in 1581 after Gilbert's departure, with the fourth added in
1584, after his death. The three 'Sir Francis' were Drake, Walsingham, and
Vere. The line, 'Sir Robert and eke Sir William, his son', if it refers to the
Burghleys, is corrupt, since Robert Cecil was William's son, rather than the
reverse, and was not knighted until 1591. Another reading of the first two lines
of the song runs: 'Sir Francis, Sir Francis, Sir Francis his son, Sir Robert and
eke Sir William is come'. The Earl of Huntingdon (l. 3) was Henry Hastings, but
another version has the Earl of Southampton, Henry Wriothesley, the patron of
Shakespeare. The appearance of the Lord Chamberlain (Sir Thomas Crofts) at
the ceremony aroused popular mirth because he was known to detest Drake and
to want peace with Spain. Sir Humphrey Gilbert, the half-brother of Sir Walter
Raleigh, took possession of Newfoundland for the Crown in 1583, but was lost
when his ship was wrecked afterwards.

4   *In Praise of Seafaring Men, in Hope of*
    Good Fortune

Who seeks the way to win renown,
Or flies with wings of his desire;
Who seeks to wear the laureate crown,
Or hath the mind that would aspire:
Let him his native soil eschew,
Let him go range and seek a new.

Each haughty heart is well content
With every chance that shall betide;
No hap can hinder his intent:
He steadfast stands, though fortune slide.
'The sun', quoth he, 'doth shine as well
Abroad as erst where I did dwell.'

4

In change of streams each fish can live,
Each fowl content with every air;
Each haughty heart remaineth still,
And not be drowned in deep despair:
Wherefore I judge all lands alike
To haughty hearts who fortune seek.

To pass the seas some think a toil,
Some think it strange abroad to roam;
Some think it a grief to leave their soil,
Their parents, kinfolks, and their home.
Think so who list, I like it not:
I must abroad to try my lot.

Who lists at home at cart to drudge,
And cark and care for worldly trash,
With buckled shoes let him go trudge,
Instead of lance or whip to slash:
A mind that base his kind will show
Of carrion sweet to feed a crow.

If Jason of that mind had been,
The Grecians when they came to Troy
Had never so the Trojans foiled,
Nor never put them to such annoy:
Wherefore who lust may live at home.
To purchase fame I will go roam.

☞ In 1585 Sir Richard Grenville commanded the fleet which carried a hundred English colonists to the island of Roanoke, off the coast of what is now called North Carolina. The entire community later vanished, and the mystery remains unexplained. Such happenings did not dampen the zeal of Grenville, who became very wealthy from his ventures, and personally provided three ships to join the English force which opposed the armada of 1583. The ballad, sometimes known as 'Sir Richard Grenville's Farewell', powerfully expresses the rawness and urgency of Elizabethan wanderlust.

Another of Seafarers, describing Evil Fortune

What pen can well report the plight
Of those that travel on the seas?
To pass the weary winter's night,
With stormy clouds, wishing for day;
With waves that toss them to and fro,
Their poor estate is hard to show.

When boistering winds begin to blow
On cruel coasts, from haven we;
The foggy mist so dims the shore
That rocks and sands we may not see;
Nor have no room on seas to try,
But pray to God and yield to die.

When shoals and sandy banks appear
What pilot can direct his course?
When foaming tides draw us so near,
Alas! what fortune can be worse?
Then anchors hold must be our stay,
Or else we fall into decay.

We wander still from luff to lee,
And find no steadfast wind to blow;
We still remain in jeopardy,
Each perilous point is hard to show;
In time we hope to find redress,
That long have lived in heaviness.

O pinching, weary, loathsome life,
That travel still in far exile.
The dangers great on seas be rife,
Whose recompense doth yield but toil.
O Fortune, grant me my desire:
A happy end I do require.

When frets and spates have had their fill
And gentle calm the coast will clear,
Then haughty hearts shall have their will,

luff to lee] windward to leeward; at the mercy of the winds; haphazardly   frets]
gusts of wind

That long have wept with morning cheer;
And leave the seas with their annoy,
At home at ease to live in joy.

☞ As the title indicates, this vivid counterblast to the seafaring philosophy is an answer to the previous ballad.

6   *A Joyful New Ballad*

Declaring the happy obtaining of the great galleazzo, wherein Don Pedro de Valdes was the chief, through the mighty power and providence of God, being a special token of his gracious and fatherly goodness towards us, to the great encouragement of all those that willingly fight in defence of the gospel and our good Queen of England

To the tune of 'Monsieur's Almaigne'

7

O noble England, fall down upon thy knee:
And praise thy God with thankful heart which still maintaineth thee.
The foreign forces, that seek thy utter spoil:
Shall then through his especial grace be brought to shameful foil.
With mighty power they come unto our coast:
To overrun our country quite, they make their brags and boast.
In strength of men they set their only stay:
But we, upon the Lord our God, will put our trust alway.

Great is their number of ships upon the sea:
And their provision wonderful, but Lord thou art our stay.
Their armèd soldiers are many by account:
Their aiders eke in this attempt do sundry ways surmount.
The Pope of Rome with many blessèd grains
To sanctify their bad pretence bestowed both cost and pains.
But little land is not dismayed at all:
The Lord no doubt is on our side, which soon will work their fall.

In happy hour our foes we did descry:
And under sail with gallant wind as they came passing by.
Which sudden tidings to Plymouth being brought,
Full soon our Lord High Admiral for to pursue them sought.
And to his train courageously he said:
'Now for the Lord and our good queen, to fight be not afraid.
Regard our cause, and play your parts like men.
The Lord no doubt will prosper us in all our actions then.'

This great galleazzo, which was so huge and high,
That like a bulwark on the sea did seem to each man's eye,
There was it taken, unto our great relief;
And divers nobles, in which train Don Pietro was the chief.
Strong was she stuffèd with cannons great and small,
And other instruments of war which we obtainèd all.
A certain sign of good success; we trust
That God will overthrow the rest as he hath done the first.

Then did our navy pursue the rest amain
With roaring noise of cannons great till they near Callice came.
With manly courage they followed them so fast,
Another mighty galleon did seem to yield at last.

---

galleazzo] galleas (galleon with oars as well as sails)   Valdez] one of the Spanish
admirals   High Admiral] Lord Howard of Effingham   Callice] Calais
quite] requite

And in distress for safeguard of their lives
A flag of truce they did hand out with many mournful cries;
Which when our men did perfectly espy
Some little barks they sent to her to board her quietly.

But these false Spaniards, esteeming them but weak,
When they within their danger came their malice forth did break.
With chargèd cannons they laid about them then,
For to destroy those proper barks and all their valiant men.
Which when our men perceivèd so to be,
Like lions fierce they forward went to quite this injury.
And boarding them with strong and mighty hand,
They killed the men until their ark did sink in Callice sand.

The chiefest captain of this galleon so high,
Don Hugo de Moncaldo he within this fight did die,
Who was the general of all the galleons great,
But through his brains with powder's force a bullet strong did beat.
And many more by sword did lose their breath;
And many more within the sea did swim and took their death.
There might you see the salt and foaming flood
Dyed and stained like scarlet red with store of Spanish blood.

This mighty vessel was threescore yards in length,
Most wonderful to each man's eye for making and for strength.
In her was placed an hundred cannons great,
And mightily provided eke with bread-corn, wine and meat.
There were of oars two hundred I ween,
Threescore foot and twelve in length, well measured to be seen.
And yet subdued, with many others more;
And not a ship of ours lost, the Lord be thanked therefore.

Our pleasant country, so fruitful and so fair,
They do intend by deadly war to make both poor and bare.
Our towns and cities to rack and sack likewise;
To kill and murder man and wife, as malice doth arise.
And to deflower our virgins in our sight,
And in the cradle cruelly the tender babe to smite.
God's holy truth they mean for to cast down,
And to deprive our noble queen both of her life and crown.

Moncaldo] Moncada, another Spanish admiral

9

Our wealth and riches which we enjoyèd long
They do appoint their prey and spoil, by cruelty and wrong.
To set our houses afire on our heads,
And cursedly cut our throats as we lie in our beds.
Our children's brains to dash upon the ground,
And from the earth our memory for ever to confound.
To change our joy to grief and mourning sad,
And never more to see the days of pleasure we have had.

But God almighty be blessed evermore,
Who doth encourage Englishmen to beat them from our shore.
With roaring cannons their hasty steps to stay,
And with force of thundering shot to make them fly away,
Who made account, before this time or day,
Against the walls of fair London their banners to display.
But their intent the Lord will bring to nought
If faithfully we call and cry for succour as we ought.

And you dear brethren which beareth arms this day,
For safeguard of your native soil mark well what I do say.
Regard your duties, think on your country's good,
And fear not in defence thereof to spend your dearest blood.
Our gracious queen doth greet you every one,
And saith she will among you be in every bitter storm.
Desiring you true English hearts to bear,
To God and her and to the land wherein you nursèd were.

Lord God almighty, which hath the hearts in hand
Of every person to dispose, defend this English land.
Bless thou our sovereign with long and happy life;
Indue her council with thy grace and end this mortal strife.
Give to the rest, of commons more and less,
Loving hearts, obedient minds and perfect faithfulness,
That they and we, and all with one accord,
On Sion hill may sing the praise of our most mighty Lord. [T.D.]

FINIS

London. Printed by John Wolfe, for Edward White, 1588

☞ Between June and November in 1588 twenty-four ballads dealing with the Spanish Armada were entered in the Stationers' Register, with titles such as 'The late wonderful distress which the Spanish Navy sustained in the late fight at sea and upon the west coast of Ireland'. Only four of these are still extant, three of them the work of Thomas Deloney, silk-weaver, writer, and ballad-journalist. He was known as 'the Balletting Silke Weaver of Norwich', though after 1596 he made a living entirely from his pen. Not very well, for he died 'poorly' in London in 1600. His 'Joyful New Ballad' was registered on 10 August 1588. The tune, 'Monsieur's Alemaine', was originally written in honour of François of Anjou, the younger brother of King Henri III of France. The fervent, hymn-like ballad rehearses some of the atrocities deemed likely in the event of a Spanish invasion, and relates certain incidents which happened at sea on 21 and 29 July 1588. These were also described by Camden in his *Annals of Elizabeth* (1625).

7 *Sir Francis Drake; or, Eighty-eight*

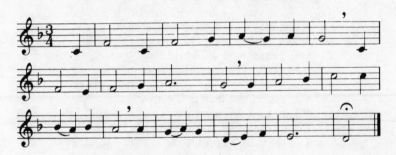

In eighty-eight, ere I was born,
As I can well remember,
In August was a fleet prepared,
The month before September.

Spain, with Biscayne, Portugal,
Toledo and Granado,
All these did meet and make a fleet,
And called it the Armado.

Where they had got provision,
As mustard, peas and bacon,
Some say two ships were full of whips,
But I think they were mistaken.

August] the main fighting was in fact over by the end of July.   Biscayne] Vizcaya, one of the Basque provinces   full of whips] a widely-held belief. Cf. Deloney's 'New Ballet of the straunge and most cruel Whippes which the Spanyards had prepared to whippe and torment English men and women'.

There was a little man of Spain
That shot well in a gun, a,
Don Pedro hight, as good a knight
As the Knight of the Sun, a.

King Philip made him admiral
And chargèd him to stay, a
But to destroy both man and boy
And then to run away, a.

The King of Spain did fret amain,
And to do yet more harm, a
He sent along, to make him strong,
The famous Prince of Parma.

When they had sailed along the seas
And anchored upon Dover,
Our Englishmen did board them then
And cast the Spaniards over.

Our queen was then at Tilbury,
What could you more desire, a?
For whose sweet sake Sir Francis Drake
Did set them all on fire, a.

But let them look about themselves,
For if they come again, a,
They shall be served with that same sauce
As they were, I know when, a.

☞ The ballad looks back at the armada, possibly from the time of James I. Some of the details have become blurred, though the picture of victory remains clear enough.

Don Pedro] the Spanish commander-in-chief was in fact Don Alonso Perez, Duke of Medina Sidonia.   hight] called   Knight of the Sun] hero of a Spanish romance, *The Mirrour of Princely Deedes and Knighthood*, which was widely known in England through translations.   amain] with all his might   Parma] the Duke of Parma's fleet was to have joined the armada from the Netherlands, but failed to do so. Tilbury] Queen Elizabeth delivered a rousing triumphal speech there in August 1588. She was mounted on a white horse, thus giving rise, it is said, to the nursery rhyme, 'Ride a cock horse'.

8

The Sailor's Only Delight

Showing the brave Fight between the George-Aloe, *the* Sweepstake, *and certain Frenchmen at Sea*

To the tune of 'The Sailor's Joy'

The *George-Aloe* and the *Sweepstake* too,
    With hey, with ho, for and a nony no,
O they were merchantmen and bound for Safee,
    And alongst the coast of Barbary.

The *George-Aloe* to anchor came,
    With hey, with ho, &c.
But the jolly *Sweepstake* kept along her way,
    And alongst, &c.

They had not sailed leagues two or three,
But they met with a French man of war upon the sea,

'All hail, all hail, you lusty gallants,
Of whence is your fair ship, whither are you bound?'

'We are Englishmen and bound for Safee,
Of whence is your fair ship, or whither are you bound?'

'Amain, amain, you gallant Englishmen.'
'Come, you French swads, and strike down your sails.'

They laid us aboard on the starboard side,
And they overthrew us into the sea so wide.

When tidings to the *George-Aloe* came,
That the jolly *Sweepstake* by a Frenchman was ta'en,

'To top, to top, thou little ship boy,
And see if this Frenchman thou canst descry,'

Safee] in fact, Salee, in what is now Morocco, a notorious base for pirates
Amain] lower the topsail, in token of surrender   swads] the *OED* defines the word in
the singular as: 'A country bumpkin; a clodhopper; a loutish or clownish fellow; a common
term of abuse.'

'A sail a sail, under our lee,
Yea, and another under her obey,'

'Weigh anchor, weigh anchor, O jolly boatswain,
We will take this Frenchman if we can,'

We had not sailèd leagues two or three,
But we met the French man of war upon the sea,

'All hail, all hail, you lusty gallants,
Of whence is your fair ship, and whither is it bound?'

'O we are merchantmen and bound for Salee.'
'Aye, and we are Frenchmen, and war upon the sea',

'Amain, amain, you English dogs.'
'Come aboard, you French rogues, and strike down your sails.'

The first good shot that the *George-Aloe* shot,
He made the Frenchmen's heart sore afraid,

The second shot the *George-Aloe* did afford,
He struck the mainmast over the board.

'Have mercy, have mercy, you brave Englishmen.'
        With hey, with ho, &c.
'O what have you done with our brethren on shore,
        As they sailed into Barbary?'

We laid them aboard on the starboard side,
        With hey, with ho, &c.
And we threw them into the sea so wide,
        And alongst, &c.

'Such mercy as you have showed unto them,
Then the like mercy shall you have again',

We laid them aboard on the larboard side,
And we threw them into the sea so wide,

Lord, how it grieved our hearts full sore,
To see the drownèd Frenchmen swim along the shore,

Come aboard] come alongside   swim] float

14

Now gallant seamen all, adieu,
With hey, with ho, for and a nony no.
This is the last news that I can write to you,
To England's coast from Barbary.

FINIS

London. Printed for F. Coles, T. Vere and J. [Wright]

☞ This laconic, incisive, and chilling account of sea conflict was 'probably the work of a ballad maker who had heard the men of returned crews give an account of their voyage'. The text given here was printed between 1663 and 1674, but the ballad has an earlier history. 'A Dittye of the fight uppon the seas the 4 of June last in the straytes of Jubraltare, betwene the George and the Thomas Bonaventure, and viij Gallies with three ffregates' was registered in 1590 but is now lost except for a fragment quoted in *The Two Noble Kinsmen* (1613), which begins: 'The George Alow came from the south, From the coast of Barbary a, And there he met with brave gallants of war, By one, by two, by three a'. The action was continued in a sequel, 'The second parte of the George Aloo and the Swiftestake', registered in 1611, now lost, but presumably substantially identical with 'The Sailor's Only Delight'. The tune of 'The Sailor's Joy', first mentioned in 1595, is also lost, but the ballad continued in oral circulation until the twentieth century in Britain and America under such titles as 'The Coast of Barbary' and 'High Barbary'. Many of the tunes sung are compatible with the earlier texts.

9   *The Winning of Cales*

Long the proud Spaniard advancèd to conquer us,
Threat'ning our country with fire and sword;
Often preparing their navy most sumptuous
With all the provision that Spain could afford.
    Dub a dub dub, this strikes their drums,
    Tan ta ra ra, tan ta ra ra, Englishmen comes.

To the seas presently went our Lord Admiral
With knights courageous and captains full good.
The Earl of Essex, a prosperous general,
With him preparèd to pass the salt flood.

At Plymouth speedily take they ships valiantly;
Braver ships never were seen under sails.
With their fair colours spread and streamers o'er their head,
Now bragging Spaniards take heed of your tail.

Unto Cales cunningly came we most happily
Where the king's navy securely did ride,
Being upon their backs piercing their butts of sack,
Ere that the Spaniard our coming descried.
>   *Tan ta ra ra, Englishmen comes,*
>   *Bounce abounce, bounce abounce, off went our guns.*

Great was the crying, running and riding,
Which at that season was made in that place;
Then beacons were firèd as need then requirèd.
To hide their great treasure they had little space.
And they crièd: 'Englishmen comes.'

There you might see the ships, how they were firèd fast,
And how the men drownèd themselves in the sea.
There you might hear them cry, wail and weep piteously,
When as they saw no shift to escape thence away.

The great *Saint Philip*, the pride of the Spaniards,
Was burnt to the bottom and sunk in the sea;
But the *Saint Andrew*, and eke the *Saint Matthew*,
We took in fight manly, and brought them away.

The Earl of Essex, most valiant and hardy,
With horsemen and footmen marched towards the town.
The enemies which saw them, full greatly affrighted,
Did fly for their safeguard, and durst not come down.

Now quoth the noble earl: 'Courage my soldiers all.
Fight and be valiant, and spoil you shall have;
And well rewarded all from the great to the small,
But look that women and children you save.'

The Spaniard at that sight saw 'twas in vain to fight,
Hung up their flags of truce, yielding the town.
We marchèd in presently, decking the walls on high
With our English colours which purchased renown.

Entering the houses then of the richest men,
For gold and treasure we searchèd each day.
In some places we did find pies baking in the ovens,
Meat at the fire roasting, and men run away.

eke] also

Full of rich merchandise every shop we did see,
Damask and satins and velvet full fair,
Which soldiers measured out by the length of their swords;
Of all commodities each one had a share.

Thus Cales was taken, and our brave general
Marched to the Market Place, there he did stand.
There many prisoners of good account were took;
Many craved mercy, and mercy they found.

When our brave general saw they delayèd time
And would not ransom the town as they said,
With their fair wainscots, their presses and bedsteads,
Their joint-stools and tables, a fire we made.
And when the town burnt in a flame,
With tan ta ra, tan ta ra ra, from thence we came.

☞ on 21 June 1596, Cadiz (of which Cales is an Anglicization) was attacked by an
English force led by the Earl of Essex as general and Lord Howard of Effingham
as admiral. Most of the shipping in the harbour was sunk or captured; the town
was sacked and burned. The ballad, which John Masefield describes as 'one of
the most vigorous in the language', was written by Thomas Deloney (for whom,
see p. 10). It is possible that he obtained his material at first hand, for there is a
tradition that he took part in the expedition himself. The wealth of striking detail
provides internal evidence to support the notion. The event also inspired
Deloney to write a quite different ballad with the self-explanatory title of 'The
Spanish Lady's Love for an English Sailor'. 'The Winning of Cales' was
probably first published in the edition of Deloney's *Garland of Goodwill*
mentioned by Thomas Nash in 1596. This is no longer extant, and the text given
here comes from the 1631 printing. No tune was specified. According to
Ebsworth, the ballad was sung to 'The Seaman's Tantara', but this has not
survived.

presses] cupboards   joint-stools] stools made by joiners

The Famous Sea Fight between Captain Ward and the Rainbow

To the tune of 'Captain Ward'

Strike up you lusty gallants
With music and sound of drum,
For we have descried a rover
Upon the sea is come.

His name is Captain Ward,
Right well it doth appear:
There has not been such a rover
Found out this thousand years.

For he has sent unto our king,
The sixth of January,
Desiring that he might come in
With all his company.

'And if your king will let me come,
Till I my tale have told,
I will bestow for my ransom
Full thirty ton of gold.'

'O nay, O nay,' then says our king,
'O nay this may not be.
To yield to such a rover
Myself will not agree.

'He has deceived the Frenchman,
Likewise the King of Spain;
And how can he be true to me
That hath been false to twain?'

With that our king provided
A ship of worthy fame.
Rainbow she is so called,
If you would know her name.

your king] James I, who reigned from 1603 until 1625.

18

Now the gallant *Rainbow*
She rows upon the sea;
Five hundred gallant seamen
Do bear her company.

The Dutchman and the Spaniard,
She made them for to fly,
Also the bonny Frenchman
As she met them on the sea.

When as this gallant *Rainbow*
Did come where Ward did lie,
'Where is the captain of this ship?'
This gallant *Rainbow* did cry.

'O that am I,' says Captain Ward,
'There's no man bids me lie,
And if thou art the king's fair ship
Thou art welcome unto me.'

'I'll tell thee what,' says *Rainbow*,
'Our king is in great grief
That thou shouldst lie upon the sea
And play the arrant thief.

'And will not let our merchant ships
Pass as they did before:
Such tidings to our king is come
Which grieves his heart full sore.'

With that this gallant *Rainbow*,
She shot out of her pride
Full fifty gallant brass pieces
Chargèd on every side.

Although these gallant shooters
Prevailèd not a pin;
Though they were brass on the outside
Yet Ward was steel within.

'Shoot on, shoot on,' says Captain Ward,
'Your sport well pleaseth me;
And he that first gives over
Shall yield unto the sea.

'I never wronged an English ship,
But the Turk and King of Spain,
For and the jovial Dutchman
As I met on the main.

'If I had known your king
But one-two years before,
I would have saved brave Essex life
Whose death did grieve me sore.

'Go tell the King of England,
Go tell him thus from me:
If he reign king of all the land,
I will reign king at sea.'

With that the royal *Rainbow* shot,
And shot and shot in vain,
And left the rover's company,
And returnèd home again.

'Our royal King of England,
Your ship's returned again,
For Ward's ship is so strong
She never will be ta'en.'

'O everlasting,' says our king,
'I have lost jewels three,
Which would a-gone to the seas
And brought proud Ward to me.

'The first was Lord Clifford,
Earl of Cumberland.
The second was the Lord Mountjoy,
As you shall understand.

'The third was brave Essex,
From field would never flee,
Who would have gone unto the sea
And brought proud Ward to me.'

London, printed for Fr[ancis] Coles at the sign of the Lamb in the Old Bailey

Essex] Robert Devereux (1566–1601), second Earl of Essex, courtier, soldier, administrator, was executed for treason by Queen Elizabeth.   Clifford] George Clifford
(1558–1605), third Earl of Cumberland, courtier, explorer and naval commander
Mountjoy] Charles Blount (1563–1606), eighth Lord Mountjoy, courtier, soldier, MP,
administrator

☞ John Ward was born at Faversham, Kent. After a spell as a fisherman he joined the navy, then turned pirate. With Tunis as his home port he made a fortune, of which £100,000 came from a single Venetian prize. He was famous (or infamous) enough to inspire several ballads, two pamphlets, and a play. At one stage he hankered for home, and made overtures to James I in the hope of paying for a pardon. The king not only refused but specifically named Ward in a proclamation of January 1609, for the apprehension of pirates. Ward stayed on in his palace at Tunis, and died there, of plague, in 1622. The ballad was issued between 1627 and 1680, though it might originally date from the time of the proclamation of 1609. There was a ship called the *Rainbow* in the British navy, but there is no record of its having encountered Ward. A Captain Rainsborough made a name for himself in a successful action against pirates off Malta in 1628, and a ballad-writer might, deliberately or accidentally, have confused the man and the ship. The tune, 'Captain Ward', has not survived, but some eighteenth-century editions of the ballad give ''Twas when the seas were roaring', a tune written in 1715, possibly by Handel, which was also used for 'John Barleycorn'. Other tunes continued to circulate orally, both in Britain and North America, until the twentieth century.

11   *The Praise of Sailors*

here set forth, with the hard fortunes which do befall them on the seas when the landmen sleep safe in their beds

To a pleasant new tune

As I lay musing in my bed,
Full warm and well at ease,
I thought upon the lodging hard
Poor sailors have at seas.

They bide it out with hunger and cold
And many a bitter blast,
And many a time constrained they are
For to cut down their mast.

Their victuals and their ordinance
And aught else that they have
They throw it overboard with speed,
And seek their lives to save.

11 ordinance] ordnance (piece of artillery)

When as the raging seas do foam,
And lofty winds do blow,
The sailors they go to the top
When landmen stay below.

Our master's mate takes helm in hand,
His course he steers full well
When as the lofty winds do blow,
And raging seas do swell.

Our master to his compass goes,
So well he plies his charge;
He sends a youth to the top amain
For to unsling the yards.

The boatswain he's under the deck,
A man of courage bold:
'To th' top, to th' top, my lively lads.
Hold fast, my hearts of gold.'

The pilot he stands on the chain,
With a lead and line to sound,
To see how far and near they are
From any dangerous ground.

It is a testimonial good
We are not far from land:
There sits a mermaid on the rocks,
With comb and glass in hand.

Our captain he is on the poop,
A man of might and power,
And looks where raging seas do gape
Our bodies to devour.

Our royal ship is run to rack
That was so stout and trim,
And some are put unto their shifts
Either to sink or swim.

---

amain] straightaway glass] mirror unto their shifts] are obliged to shift
for it

Second part, to the same tune

Our ship that was before so good,
And she likewise so trim,
Is now with raging seas grown leaked,
And water fast comes in.

The quartermaster is a man,
So well his charge plies he;
He calls them to the pumps amain
To keep their ship leak-free.

And many great dangers likewise
They do many times endure,
When as they meet their enemies
That come with might and power.

And seek likewise from them to take
Their lives and eke their goods:
Thus sailors they sometimes endure
Upon the surging floods.

But when as they do come to land,
And homewards safe return,
They are most kind good fellows all,
And scorn ever to mourn.

And likewise they will call for wine,
And score it on the post,
For sailors they are honest men,
And love to pay their host.

For sailors they are honest men,
And they do take great pains
When landed men and ruffling lads
Do rob them of their gains.

Our sailors they work day and night
Their manhood for to try
When landed men and ruffling jacks
Do in their cabins lie.

eke] also   mourn] complain   landed men] landsmen   ruffling] caus-
ing irritation or annoyance jacks] knaves

23

Therefore let all good-minded men
Give ear unto my song
And say also as well as I:
'Sailors deserve no wrong.'

Thus have I done for sailors' sakes
In token of goodwill;
If ever I can do them good
I will be ready still.

God bless them eke by sea and land,
And also other men;
And as my song beginning had
So must it have an end.

Printed for John Wright

☞ The ballad, which was printed between 1610 and 1646 (Ebsworth suggests *c.*
1605 and 1632), deals with some of the difficulties seamen encounter, together
with the skills and courage they deploy in response. The sighting of a mermaid is
taken as propitious, but the reverse is the case in a later ballad (50) which seems
partly to derive from this. The 'pleasant new tune' has not come to light, but the
later melody perfectly fits both texts.

12 *The Honour of Bristol*

showing how the Angel Gabriel *of Bristol fought with three Spanish ships,
who boarded us seven times, wherein we cleared our decks, and killed five
hundred of their men, and wounded many more, and made them fly into Cales,
where we lost but three men, to the honour of the* Angel Gabriel *of Bristol*

To the tune of 'Our Noble King in his Progress'

Attend you and give ear a while, and you shall understand
Of a battle fought upon the seas by a ship of brave command.
The fight it was so famous that all men's heart doth fill,
And makes them cry: 'To sea, with the *Angel Gabriel*.'

The lusty ship of Bristol sailed out adventurously
Against the foes of England, their strength with them to try:
Well victualled, rigged and manned, and good provision still,
Which makes men cry: 'To sea, with the *Angel Gabriel*.'

24

The captain, famous Netheway, so was he called by name;
The master's name, John Mines, a man of noted fame;
The gunner, Thomas Watson, a man of perfect skill;
With other valiant hearts in the *Angel Gabriel*.

They waving up and down the seas upon the ocean main:
'It is not long ago', quoth they, 'since England fought with Spain.
Would we with them might meet, our minds for to fulfil:
We would play a noble bout with our *Angel Gabriel*.'

They had no sooner spoken, but straight appeared in sight
Three lusty Spanish vessels, of warlike force and might.
With bloody resolution they sought our men to spill,
And vowed to make a prize of our *Angel Gabriel*.

Then first came up their admiral, themselves for to advance.
In her she bore full forty-eight pieces of ordinance.
The next that then came near us was their vice-admiral,
Which shot most furiously at our *Angel Gabriel*.

Our gallant ship had in her full forty fighting men;
With twenty pieces of ordinance we played about them then,
And with powder, shot and bullets we did employ them still;
And thus began the fight with our *Angel Gabriel*.

Our captain to our master said, 'Take courage, master bold.'
The master to the seamen said, 'Stand fast, my hearts of gold.'
The gunner unto all the rest, 'Brave hearts, be valiant still.
Let us fight in the defence of our *Angel Gabriel*.'

Then we gave them a broadside which shot their mast asunder,
And tore the bowsprit of their ship, which made the Spaniards
    wonder;
And caused them for to cry with voices loud and shrill:
'Help, help, or else we sink by the *Angel Gabriel*.'

Yet desperately they boarded us, for all our valiant shot;
Threescore of their best fighting men upon our decks were got.
And then at their first entrance full thirty we did kill,
And thus we cleared the decks of the *Angel Gabriel*.

With that their three ships boarded us again with might and main,
But still our noble Englishmen cried out: 'A fig for Spain.'
Though seven times they boarded us at last we showed them skill,
And made them feel the force of the *Angel Gabriel*.

Seven hours that fight continued, and many brave men lay dead;
With purple gore and Spanish blood the sea was coloured red.
Five hundred of their men we there outright did kill,
And many more were maimed by the *Angel Gabriel*.

They seeing of these bloody spoils the rest made haste away.
For why? They saw it was no boot longer for to stay.
Then they fled into Cales, and there they must lie still,
For they never more will serve to meet our *Gabriel*.

We had within our English ship but only three men slain
And five men hurt, the which, I hope, will soon be well again.
In Bristol we were landed, and let us praise God still,
That thus hath blest our men, and our *Angel Gabriel*.

Now let me not forget to speak of the gift given by the owner
Of the *Angel Gabriel*, that many years have known her.
Two hundred pounds in coin and plate he gave with free goodwill
Unto them that bravely fought in the *Angel Gabriel*.

London, printed for T. Vere, at the sign of the Angel without Newgate

☞ The *Angel Gabriel* was a privateer, that is, a private vessel licensed under letters of marque to prey on enemy shipping in time of war, for profit as much as for patriotism. (The system was not formally abandoned until 1856.) She sailed out of Bristol, one of the prime ports for privateering, between 1626 and 1630, when Britain was at war with France and Spain. Thomas Netheway was her captain in 1627, but the encounter described seems too extravagant to command credence. The ballad, with its concluding emphasis on the rewards involved, seems to have been designed as a recruiting advertisement. The text given here was printed between 1656 and 1682. It is said to have been written, to a tune now lost, by Laurence Price, the author, according to the DNB, of 'numberless ballads, pamphlets, and broadsides in verse on political or social subjects'. Many of his publications are now lost, though 68 remain. His earliest ballad was published in 1625, and his last in 1675. He frequently wrote on the same subjects as Martin Parker, in deliberate competition with him. For another example of his work, see 16.

Cales] Cadiz

Sailors for my Money

a new ditty composed in the praise of sailors and sea affairs, briefly showing the nature of so worthy a calling, and effects of their industry

To the tune of 'The Jovial Cobbler'

Countrymen of England who live at home at ease
And little think what dangers are incident o' th' seas,
Give ear unto the sailor who unto you will show
His case, his case, how e'er the wind doth blow.

He that is a sailor must have a valiant heart,
For when he is upon the sea he is not like to start,
But must with noble courage all dangers undergo,
Resolve, resolve, how e'er the wind doth blow.

Our calling is laborious and subject to much woe,
But we must still contented be with what falls to our share.
We must not be faint-hearted, come tempest, rain or snow,
Nor shrink, nor shrink, how e'er the wind doth blow.

Sometimes on Neptune's bosom our ship is tossed with waves,
And every minute we expect the sea must be our graves.
Sometimes on high she mounteth, then falls again as low,
With waves, with waves, when stormy winds do blow.

Then with unfeignèd prayers, as Christian duty binds,
We turn unto the Lord of Hosts with all our hearts and minds;

To Him we fly for succour, for He we surely know
Can save, can save, how e'er the wind doth blow.

Then He who breaks the rage, the rough and blusterous seas,
When His disciples are afraid will straight the storms appease;
And give us cause to thank, on bended knees fall low,
Who saves, who saves, how e'er the wind doth blow.

And when by God's assistance our foes are put to th' foil
To animate our courages we all have share o' th' spoil.
Our foes into the ocean we back to back do throw
To sink, or swim, how e'er the wind doth blow.

The second part, to the same tune

Thus we gallant seamen in midst of greatest dangers
Do always prove our valour, we never are no changers;
But whatsoe'er betide us we stoutly undergo,
Resolved, resolved, how e'er the wind doth blow.

If fortune do befriend us in what we take in hand
We prove ourselves still generous when e'er we come to land;
There's few that shall outbrave us, though ne'er so great in show,
We spend and lend, how e'er the wind doth blow.

We travel to the Indies, from them we bring some spice;
Here we buy rich merchandise at very little price.
And many wealthy prizes we conquer from the foe
In fight, in fight, how e'er the wind doth blow.

Into our native country with wealth we do return,
And cheer our wives and children who for our absence mourn.
Then do we bravely flourish, and wheresoe'er we go
We roar, we roar, how e'er the wind doth blow.

For when we have receivèd our wages for our pains
The vintners and the tapsters by us have golden gains.
We call for liquor roundly, and pay before we go,
And sing, and drink, how e'er the wind doth blow.

We bravely are respected when we walk up and down,
For if we meet good company we care not for a crown.
There's none more free than sailors, where'er he come or go,
Though th' hail roar on the shore, how e'er the wind doth blow.

Then who would live in England and nourish vice with ease
When he that is in poverty may riches get o' th' seas?
Let's sail unto the Indies where golden grass doth grow:
To sea, to sea, how e'er the wind doth blow. [M.P.]

FINIS

Printed at London for C. Wright

☞ Cuthbert Wright, the printer, died in 1638, so the ballad must have been issued
before then. Ebsworth suggests 1635, which was the year of the imposition of
Ship Money by Charles I. The author, Martin Parker, was a keen royalist (his
best-known work is 'When the King enjoys his own again'), and it is just possible
that 'Sailors for my Money' was intended to help Charles' cause. Whatever the
truth may be, the vigour and pugnacity of the ballad made it popular, albeit with
change and adaptation, over the next three hundred years. The text printed here
comes from a copy in the ballad collection of Samuel Pepys, which is preserved
at Magdalene College, Cambridge. The tune of 'The Jovial Cobbler' has, once
again, not survived, but a later version of the ballad prescribes 'When the stormy
winds do blow', which is given here. Other versions circulated orally, including
an adaptation in which shepherds rather than sailors cope with stormy winds.

14   *A Song of the Seamen and Land Soldiers*

'We seamen are the bonny boys
That fear no storms nor rocks, a,
Whose music is the cannon's noise,
Whose sporting is with knocks, a.'

'Mars has no children of his own,
But we that fight on land, a;
Land-soldiers kingdoms up have blown,
Yet they unshaken stand, a.'

' 'Tis brave to see a tall ship sail
With all her trim gear on, a;
As though the devil were in her tail
She 'fore the wind will run, a.'

'Our main battalion when it moves,
There's no such glorious thing, a,
Where leaders like so many Joves
Abroad their thunder fling, a.'

29

'Come let us reckon what ships are ours,
The *Gorgon* and the *Dragon*,
The *Lion* that in fight is bold,
The *Bull* with bloody flag on.'

'Come let us reckon what works are ours,
Forts, bulwarks, barricadoes,
Mounts, gabions, parapets, countermurs,
Casemates and palisadoes.'

'The bear, the dog, the fox, the kite,
That stood fast on the *Rover*,
They chased the Turk in a day and a night
From Scanderoon to Dover.'

'Field-pieces, muskets, groves of pikes,
Carbines and cannoneers, a,
Squadrons, half moons, with ranks and files
And fronts and vans and rears, a.'

'A health to brave land-soldiers all,
Let cans apiece go round, a;
Pell-mell let's to the battle fall,
And lofty music sound, a.'

☞ Under its 'generals-at-sea' the Commonwealth navy won a series of victories, interspersed with the occasional defeat, against the Dutch (1652–4), Barbary pirates (1654) and the Spanish (1656–7). This bellicose ballad, a dialogue between soldiers and sailors, is from a collection entitled *Wit and Drollery, Jovial Poems* which was edited by a Navy Board Comptroller, Sir John Mennes, and others, and published in 1656. No tune is specified, but 'Sir Francis Drake' (7) has the same metre.

15   *The Famous Fight at Malago,*
     or, The Englishmen's Victory over the Spaniards

Relating how five English frigates: viz. the Henry, the Ruby, the Antelope, the Greyhound, and the Bryan burnt all the Spanish ships in their harbour at

14 gabions] wicker containers filled with earth or stones   casemates] chambers with embrasures in the thickness of the wall of a fortress   bear, dog, fox, kite] ? nicknames of officers   Scandaroon] Iskanderun (now Alexandretta, in Turkey)

Malago, battered down their churches and their houses about their ears, killed
abundance of their men, and obtained an honourable victory

> Wherever English seamen goes,
> They are a terror to their foes.

To the tune of 'Five Sail of Frigates bound for Malago'. With Allowance

Come all you brave sailors that sails on the main,
I'll tell you of a fight that was lately in Spain;
And of five sail of frigates bound to Malago,
For to fight the proud Spaniard our orders was so.

There was the *Henry* and *Ruby* and the *Antelope* also,
The *Greyhound* and the *Bryan* for fireships must go;
But so bravely we weighèd and playèd our parts
That we made the proud Spaniards to quake in their hearts.

Then we came to an anchor so nigh to the mould:
'Methinks you proud English do grow very bold.'
But we came to an anchor so near to the town
That some of their churches we soon battered down.

They hung out their flag of truce for to know our intent,
And they sent out their longboat to know what we meant;
But our captain he answered them bravely; it was so:
'For to burn all your shipping before we do go.'

'For to burn all our shipping you must us excuse.
'Tis not five sail of frigates shall make us to muse.'

mould] mole

31

But we burnt all their shipping and their galleys also,
And we left in the city full many a widow.

'Come then,' says our captain, 'let's fire at the church';
And down came their belfry, which grievèd them much;
And down came the steeple which standeth so high,
Which made the proud Spaniards to the nunnery fly.

So great a confusion we made in the town
That their lofty buildings came tumbling down;
Their wives and their children for help they did cry,
But none could relieve them though danger was nigh.

The flames and the smoke so increasèd their woe
That they knew not whither to run nor to go;
Some to shun the fire leapt into the flood,
And there they did perish in water and mud.

Our guns we kept firing, still shooting amain,
Whilst many a proud Spaniard was on the place slain.
The rest being amazèd for succour did cry,
But all was in vain, they had nowhere to fly.

At length being forcèd they thought it most fit
Unto the brave Englishmen for to submit:
And so a conclusion at last we did make
Upon such conditions as was fit to take.

The Spanish Armado did England no harm,
'Twas but a braggado to give us alarm;
But with our five frigates we did them bumbaste,
And made them of Englishmen's valour to taste.

When this noble victory we did obtain,
Then home we returnèd to England again,
Where we were receivèd with welcomes of joy
Because with five frigates we did them destroy.

Printed for J. Clarke, W. Thackery and T. Passenger

☞ There was not much of a fight at Malaga, nor was it particularly famous, but
having been picked up by a ballad maker the story went through successive
editions over a period of half a century, and then circulated orally for another

fire at the church] a particular mark for the English because it had been built by the
hated Philip II.   bumbaste] thrash

two hundred years or so. General Mountagu (later Lord Sandwich, the patron
of Samuel Pepys) described the events rather more laconically and also more
accurately than the ballad in a letter to Secretary Thurloe of 31 July 1656: 'Wee
sent five or six shipps to Malaga to doe what mischiefe they could there. . . . The
shipps wee sent were the Lyme, the Newberrye, the Nantwich, and the Rubye;
captain Smith commanded them. They sett saile from Cales the same morninge,
as wee did, viz. July the 10th, and came suddenly upon them at Malaga, and with
the Fox fireshipp sett fire of two shipps under the moulde, and sett fire also of
one galley, and six or seven other small vessels there, and bestowed a greate
many shott (too many) upon the towne. In the encounter the Spaniards
forsakinge the moulde, where they had seven peeces of cannon, our men went
ashore, and spiked them up (6 of them). Captain Smith had nine men killed
outright in his ship, and I believe all the rest have not lost above as many more.'
The text given here from the Pepys Collection was printed between 1684 and
1686, but there must have been earlier editions. The air, 'Five Sail of Frigates',
is lost, but the words perfectly fit the tune of an oral version noted in 1911 by
Cecil Sharp from a Lincolnshire man, Joseph Jackson.

16   *The Seaman's Compass;*

or,
A dainty new ditty composed and penned,
The deeds of brave seamen to praise and commend.
'Twas made by a maid that to Gravesend did pass,
Now mark and you quickly shall know how it was.

To the tune of 'The tyrant hath stolen'

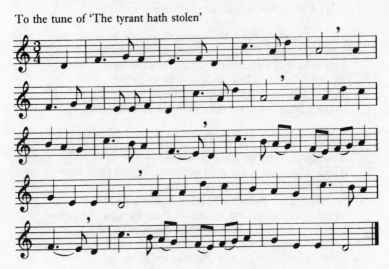

As lately I travellèd towards Gravesend
I heard a fair damosel a seaman commend;

33

And as in a tilt-boat we passèd along,
In praise of brave seamen she sung this new song:
'Come tradesman or merchant, who ever he be,
There's none but a seaman shall marry with me.

'A seaman in promise is faithful and just,
Honest in carriage and true to his trust;
Kind in behaviour and constant in love,
As firm in affection as the turtle dove.
Valiant in action in every degree,
There's none but a seaman shall marry with me.

'The seamen adventures their lives on the seas
Whilst landmen on shore takes pleasure and ease.
The seamen at all times their business must ply,
In winter and summer, in wet and in dry.
From toil and pains taking they seldom are free,
There's none but a seaman shall marry with me.

'Moreover I'd have you for to understand
That seamen brings treasure and profit to land.
Above and beneath ground for wealth they have sought,
And when they have found it to England 'tis brought
With hazard of lives; by experience we see
There's none but a seaman shall marry with me.

'Seamen from beyond seas bring silver and gold,
With pearls and rich jewels most rare to behold;
With silks and rich velvets their credits to save,
Or else you gay ladies could not go so brave.
This makes my heart merry, as merry may be:
There's none but a seaman shall marry with me.'

The second part, to the same tune
'The seamen brings spices and sugar so fine,
Which serve the brave gallants to drink with their wine;
With lemons and oranges all of the best
To relish their palates when they make a feast.
Sweet figs, prunes and raisins by them brought home be:
There's none but a seaman shall marry with me.

'To comfort poor people the seamen do strive,
And brings in maintainance to keep them alive,

tilt-boat] boat covered by an awning

34

As raw silk and cotton wool to card and to spin,
And so by their labours their livings come in.
Most men are beholding to seamen, we see:
With none but a seaman I married will be.

'The mercer's beholding, we know well enough,
For holland, lawn, cambric, and other gay stuff
That's brought from beyond seas by seamen so bold,
The rarest that ever men's eyes did behold.
God prosper the seamen wherever they be;
There's none but a seaman shall marry with me.

'The merchants themselves are beholding also
To honest seamen that on purpose do go
To bring them home profit from other strange lands,
Or else their fine daughters must work with their hands.
The nobles and gentry in every degree
Are also beholding to seamen, we see.

'Thus for rich and poor men the seamen does good,
And sometimes comes off with loss of much blood.
If they were not a guard and defence for our land
Our enemies soon would get the upper hand;
And then a woeful case straight we should be.
There's none but a seaman shall marry with me.

'To draw to conclusion and so make an end,
I hope that great Neptune my love will befriend,
And send him home safely with health and with life;
Then shall I with joyfulness soon be his wife.
You maids, wives and widows that seamen's loves be,
With hearts and with voices join prayers with me.

'God bless all brave seamen from quicksands and rocks,
From loss of their blood and from enemies' knocks;
From lightning and thunder and tempests so strong,
From shipwreck and drowning and all other wrong;
And they that to these words will not say "Amen",
'Tis pity that they should ever speak word again.' [L.P.]

FINIS

Printed for F.G. on Snow Hill. Entered according to order.

holland] linen fabric

35

☞ The ballad deals largely with the commercial role of sailors, and purports to give a feminine view. It was written by Laurence Price (for whom, see 12), and was first issued in 1657 by the London printer, Francis Grove. The tune-title named is an alternative for the well-known 'Bonny Sweet Robin'.

17

A Net for a Night Raven;
or, a Trap for a Scold

> *My honest friends, if you should know*
> *How to be quiet from a scolding shrew,*
> *And to get money now in these hard times,*
> *Then pray give ear and listen to these lines.*

The tune is 'Let us to Virginny go'

Here is a merry song; if that you please to buy it
'Twill show how you may money get, and lead your lives in quiet.
I'll teach you the receipt, shall cost you but a penny.
I think there's few that hath not heard of famous brave Virginny.

Where capons are so cheap and eggs are in such plenty;
Also such fowl and fish and other things most dainty,
As pigs, veal, lamb and venison, if travellers speak truly;
Which is the cause so many go and travels to Virginny.

Not far from hence there dwelled an honest man, a weaver,
Whose wife was witty, fair and proud, and yet her wit deceived her.
She was a grain too light, she called him fool and ninny;
Which made her husband oft to say he'd go unto Virginny.

Although he hard did work he ne'er could live at quiet.
She said her clothes they were too base, so was her homely diet.
Though nothing she did lack that could be bought for money,
'You rogue,' quoth she, 'when do you pack and go unto Virginny?'

She had a lusty lad, and vowed she'd leave him never.
At last her husband found a trick those loving mates to sever.
Quoth he, 'Your note I'll change, although now so sweetly sing ye.'
Unto a ship-master he went, that sailèd to Virginny.

17 receipt] recipe   penny] price of the ballad

Saying, 'Good sir, I know, of women you are lacking.
I now have one that I can spare, and her I can send packing.
The times are very hard; I'll sell my wife for money.
She is a proper handsome lass, and fitting for Virginny.'

'If she be young and fair, sir, I will entertain her;
Then tell me your lowest price, for I must be some gainer.'
'Ten pounds,' he answered. 'I cannot bate a penny.
She is good merchandise, you know, when you come to Virginny.'

'Bring her aboard my ship, and then you shall be paid,
For suddenly we must begone; time must not be delayed.'
He went home to his wife, saying, 'I am now ready.
Sweetheart, I must leave England now, and go unto Virginny.

'One thing of thee I beg, that you'll see me take shipping.'
This joyful news revived her mind, and set her heart a-leaping.
Unto herself she said, 'Now farewell, goodman ninny.
My love with me shall merry be when thou art at Virginny.

'To Gravesend I will go, whereas I now must leave thee.
A bottle of strong-water good I will bestow upon thee.
'Twill comfort thy poor heart, my dearest love and honey,
For I do fear you will be sea-sick in sailing to Virginny.'

They coming to the ship, the master bid them welcome.
Into his cabin they were brought, where his guest comes seldom.
He steps forth to her husband and paid him down his money,
Who straight took boat and rowed away, and sent her to Virginny.

She seeing him go thence, and that she there was stayed,
Then she did cry most bitterly, and said she was betrayed.
'Dear husband, take me with you; I'll never more offend thee.'
'Send you good shipping,' he did say, 'and well unto Virginny.'

Then straight they set up sail, and had good wind and weather;
Full seven long weeks they were at sea before that they came thither.
He for a maiden sold her, for fifty pounds in money,
And she another husband got when she came to Virginny.

Her lover ne'er could tell what became of his sweeting,
Which divers times both night and day had many a merry meeting.

bate] reduce   goodman] husband

37

The goodman now lives quiet, and with his friends is merry.
Now divers do entitle him a merchant of Virginny.

Thus I conclude my song, hoping there's none offended;
And where that things are done amiss, I wish they may be mended.
Beware, you scolding wives, if no fair means will win ye,
Lest that your husbands you entrap, and send you to Virginny.

Printed for F. Coles, T. Vere and J. Wright

☞ England's colonies were populated by various pioneers and volunteers. There were also unwilling settlers such as transported criminals and kidnapped people sold into service or slavery. The kidnappers were otherwise known as 'spirits', and the expression 'to spirit away' came into the language to describe their activity. The trade was lucrative, and in addition a useful way of removing the importunate or the unwanted. In 1670 kidnappers became liable to the death penalty, but after a time the act seems to have been no longer invoked. Luttrell mentions a case of 1682 concerning a thirteen-year-old boy taken to Jamaica in which a witness claimed that over 500 children had been 'sent away' in similar fashion during the two previous years. A royal proclamation of 1684 castigated 'the frequent Abuses of a lewd sort of people, called *Spirits*, in seducing many of His Majesties subjects to go on shipboard, where they have been seized, and carried by force to His Majesties Plantations in *America*'. Only two years later a further Order in Council proved necessary on the same subject. A number of publications, both fictional and otherwise, appeared in the late seventeenth and early eighteenth centuries on abductions to Virginia. The name was used to mean not only Virginia itself but the American or even the West Indian colonies in general. The ballad was issued between 1663 and 1674, and reprinted between 1705 and 1709 as 'The Woman Outwitted; or, the Weaver's Wife cunningly catched in a Trap by her Husband'. The tune, 'Let us to Virginny go', is lost, but the ballad turned up in Scots oral tradition in the early twentieth century as 'The Scolding Wife'.

18   *The Seamen and Soldiers' Last Farewell*
              to their Dearest Jewels

> *He must begone, the fates have so decreed,*
> *To serve his king and country in their need:*
> *In fight against the Dutch upon the main,*
> *Yet he's in hopes to see his love again:*
> *He cheers her up, and bids she should not mourn,*
> *But wait with patience for his safe return.*

17 entitle him] give him the title of

The tune is 'I am so deep in love', or, 'Cupid's Courtesy'

Farewell, my dearest dear, now I must leave thee;
Thy sight I must forbear although it grieves me.
From thy embraces, love, I shall be parted,
Yet I will constant prove and be true-hearted.

My fortune I will try upon the ocean,
And fight most valiantly to gain promotion;
My dearest blood I'll spend for this our nation,
My country to defend from foes' invasion.

Princes of high renown are now engagèd
To pull the courage down of foes enragèd;
Dukes, lords and gentry high, all are preparing
Their valour for to try, no cost is sparing.

Why should I grudge to fight under the banners
Of such approvèd knights and brave commanders?
My chance I mean to try, I scorn to hide me;
I'll face the enemy whate'er betide me.

When I am on the seas in hail and thunder
Where storms do raise the waves to all men's wonder;
When billows brush the sky and tempests threat me,
Still on thy name I'll cry: I'll not forget thee.

Though Hogan Mogan states do brag and bluster,
And call upon their mates forces to muster,
We'll make them for to know we can disturb them:
Once again they must bow, England will curb them.

Hogan Mogan] slighting nickname for the Dutch

In midst of skirmish hot, when blows are dealing,
Fiery balls fly about and ships are reeling;
When cannons are roaring and bullets are flying,
He that will honour win must not fear dying.

My dearest, do not mourn, let not grief move thee.
When I am from thee gone still I will love thee.
If fortune me befriend thou may'st be certain
I'll often to thee send after our parting.

Thy love I'll think upon in greatest danger.
When I am from thee gone I'll love no stranger.
No flesh alive shall make me prove unconstant;
I will wait for thy sake till the last instant.

This piece of gold we'll break, love, for a token;
Which as a pledge we'll keep of faith unbroken.
When thou the same dost see in my long absence,
Then, love, remember me though at a distance.

Hark how the drums do beat with trumpets sounding.
Soldiers in furious heat foes would be wounding.
From thy sweet company, although it grieves me,
I must divided be and forced to leave thee.

My captain calls away; in haste they hurry.
To march without delay I may not tarry.
Patiently thou must bear. Love, leave thy weeping.
Farewell, my dearest dear, till our next meeting.

FINIS

With allowance Printed for F. Coles, T. Vere, R. Gilbertson and J. Wright

☞ The separation of lovers by war is one of the classic themes, not only of ballads, but of literature in general. The Second Dutch War began in February 1665, and this ballad came out soon afterwards, certainly within the year. It seems to have been the starting point for a song which persisted in oral tradition until recent years, usually under the title of 'Our Captain cried all hands'. The best-known version was collected by Vaughan Williams, who applied its tune to Bunyan's poem, 'To be a Pilgrim'. The air originally intended for the ballad was first mentioned in 1664, but the version given here was published early in the eighteenth century.

Captain Mansfield's Fight with the Turks at Sea

Our goodly ship was loaded deep,
With anchors three beneath her bow;
'Twas east-north-east we steered our course,
And as near the wind as we could stow.
We had not sailèd glasses three,
Nor yet ten leagues from loaden port,
Before we spied ten Turkish men-of-war,
And after us they did resort.

'O hail, O hail, you English dogs.
O hail, and strike your sails quickly,
For you shall go with us this night,
And ever after into slavery.'
O then bespoke the captain bold,
And a well-bespoken man was he:
'If you must have my topsails down,
Come on board and strike them for me.

'To the top, to the top, my merry boatswain,
To the main topmast-head so high,
And see your business you supply.
To the top, to the top, my boatswain's mate,
To the fore topmast-head with speed,
And sling me here the fore topsail yard,
For we never had any more need.

'To the top, to the top, my little cabin boy,
To the mizen topmast-head so high,
And spread abroad St George's flag,
For by that we live or die.'
O then bespoke our gunner bold,
And a well-bespoken man was he:
'Swab your guns, brave boys, while they're hot,
For powder and ball you shall have free.'

'Keep aluff, keep aluff,' says the master's mate,
'Keep aluff whilst that you may;
We'll fight it out like English boys;
It never shall be said we run away.'

So to it we went like lions bold,
As enemies do when they meet;
From twelve o'clock to sun rising
We spied but one sail of their fleet.

O three we burnt and three we sunk,
And the other three run away;
And one we brought to old England
To show we had won the day.
All you that know our gallant ship
And want to know our captain's name,
It is Captain Mansfield of Bristol town,
And the *Marigold* a ship of fame.

☞ In December 1669, Captain John Kempthorne in the warship, *Mary Rose*, was attacked by seven Algerian vessels, but managed to repulse them, after a fierce action lasting four hours, and make his way to Cadiz. On returning to England, Kempthorne was knighted for his efforts, a signal honour for a 'tarpaulin', an officer who had first risen to command in the merchant navy. He took his son, Morgan, to the ceremony, and Charles II said: 'Bring him up to the sea. We desire more of the breed.' Morgan duly went to sea, and was killed in 1681 when commanding the *Kingfisher* in a battle with five Algerian ships off Leghorn. Wenceslas Hollar engraved the father's battle, and Van de Velde the son's. It seems likely that the ballad was inspired by the father's battle, and updated for the son's, though no contemporary printing of either has survived. The version given here dates from the eighteenth century, which perhaps explains why the names have been changed. Oral versions from landsmen and sailors of recent times show further variations, but the essential theme of British grit remains.

20   *A Song on the Duke's Late Glorious*
Success over the Dutch

One day as I was sitting still
Upon the side of Dunwich Hill,
And looking on the ocean,
By chance I saw de Ruyter's fleet
With royal James's squadron meet;
In sooth it was a noble treat
To see that brave commotion.

20 the Duke] James, Duke of York (1633–1701), brother and successor of Charles II; Lord High Admiral, 1660–73 and 1684–8   Ruyter] Michiel Adrienszoon de (1607–76), Dutch admiral in the three wars against England

I cannot stay to name the names
Of all the ships that fought with James,
Their number or their tonnage;
But this I say, the noble host
Right gallantly did take its post,
And covered all the hollow coast
From Walberswick to Dunwich.

The French, who should have joined the duke,
Full far astern did lag and look,
Although their hulls were lighter;
But nobly faced the Duke of York:
Though some may wink and some may talk,
Right stoutly did his vessel stalk,
To buffet with de Ruyter.

Well might you hear their guns, I guess,
From Sizewell Gap to Easton Ness;
The show was rare and sightly:
They battered without let or stay
Until the evening of that day.
'Twas then the Dutchmen run away,
The duke had beat them tightly.

Of all the battles gained at sea
This was the rarest victory
Since Philip's grand armado.
I will not name the rebel Blake;
He fought for whoreson Cromwell's sake,
And yet was forced three days to take
To quell the Dutch bravado.

But now we've seen them take to flight,
This way and that where'er they might,
To windward or to leeward.
Here's to King Charles and here's to James,
And here's to all the captains' names,
And here's to the House of Stuart.

☞ The first battle of the Third Dutch War (1672–4) took place off the Suffolk
coast at Sole Bay (now called Southwold Bay) on 28 May 1672. The Duke of

all the ships] there were in fact 98   Walberswick, Dunwich] small towns on
Suffolk coast   Sizewell Gap to Easton Ness] stretch of coastline   Blake] Robert
(1599–1657), successful Commonwealth general-at-sea during the First Dutch War

York personally commanded a large fleet of English and French ships (the latter taking very little part) against a Dutch attack. In the end the Dutch broke off the action, after considerable losses on both sides. Final honours were fairly even, but both sides claimed victory. The broadside ballad makes no mention of the loss of men and ships.

21 *The Benjamins' Lamentation for their sad loss at Sea, by Storms and Tempests*

Being a brief Narrative of one of His Majesty's Ships called the Benjamin, *that was drove into Harbour at Plymouth, and received no small harm by this Tempest*

To the tune of 'The Poor Benjamin'

Captain Chilver's gone to sea,
    Hey, boys, O, boys,
With all his company, *hey*.
Captain Chilver's gone to sea
With all his company
    In the brave 'Benjamin', O.

Thirty guns this ship did bear,
    Hey, boys, O, boys,
They were bound for Venice fair, *hey*.
Thirty guns this ship did bear
And a hundred men so clear,
    In the brave 'Benjamin', O.

But by ill storms at sea,
    Hey, boys, O, boys,
Which bred our misery, *hey*.
But by ill storms at sea
Were drove out o' th' way
    In the brave 'Benjamin', O.

We had more wind than we could bear,
    Hey, boys, O, boys,
Our ship it would not steer, *hey*.

21 Benjamins] the men of a ship were collectively known by its name
His Majesty] James II

44

We had more wind than we could bear:
Our masts and sails did tear
    In the poor 'Benjamin', O.

The first harm that we had,
    Hey, boys, O, boys,
It makes my heart so sad, *hey.*
The first harm that we had
We lost our fore-mast head.
    O the poor 'Benjamin', O.

The seas aloud did roar,
    Hey, boys, O, boys,
We being far from shore.
The seas no favour shows
Unto friends nor foes.
    O the poor 'Benjamin', O.

The next harm that we spied,
    Hey, boys, O, boys,
Then we to heaven cried, *hey.*
Down fell our main-mast head
Which struck our senses dead
    In the poor 'Benjamin', O.

Then we with seas were crossed,
    Hey, boys, O, boys,
And on the ocean tossed, *hey.*
Then we with seas was tossed,
Many a brave man was lost
    In the poor 'Benjamin', O.

The next harm that we had,
    Hey, boys, O, boys,
We had cause to be sad, *hey.*
The next harm that we had
We lost four men from the yard
    In the poor 'Benjamin', O.

Disabled as I name,
    Hey, boys, O, boys,
We were drove on the main, *hey.*
So the next harm we had
We lost our rudder's head
    In the poor 'Benjamin', O.

Then we all fell to prayer,
   Hey, boys, O, boys,
The Lord our lives would spare, *hey.*
Then we all fell to prayer
And at last he did hear
   Us in the 'Benjamin', O.

Although we sailed in fear,
   Hey, boys, O, boys,
The Lord our ship did steer, *hey.*
Our prayers so fervent were
That we had passage clear
   Into brave Plymouth Sound, O.

We came in Plymouth Sound,
   Hey, boys, O, boys,
Our hearts did then resound, *hey.*
When we came to Plymouth Sound
Our grief with joy was crowned
   In the poor 'Benjamin', O.

When we came all on shore,
   Hey, boys, O, boys,
Every man at his door, *hey;*
When we came all on shore
Our grief we did deplore
   In the poor 'Benjamin', O.

You gallant young men all,
   Hey, boys, O, boys,
'Tis unto you I call, *hey.*
Likewise brave seamen all,
Lament the loss and fall
   Of the poor 'Benjamin', O.

Printed for J. Wright, J. Clarke, W. Thackeray and T. Passenger

☞ In 1680 was written a soldiers' ballad, 'The Granadeers' Rant', which begins with the words, 'Captain Hume's gone to sea, *Hey, boys, ho, boys*'. It seems that a naval adaptation followed soon afterwards, for this copy of 'The Benjamins' Lamentation' was printed between 1681 and 1684. No vessel called *Benjamin* appears in the navy lists of the time, but perhaps a fictional ship was launched into a real storm. No contemporary record of the air exists, but the words survived in or   tradition to a very fine tune at least until 1907, when H. E. D.

Hammond noted a version from a singer in Dorset. The distinctive metre seems to have been popular, and several disparate texts were set to it, including a miners' song, 'The Dudley Boys'.

22   *Sir Walter Raleigh Sailing in the*
Lowlands

Showing how the famous ship called the Sweet Trinity *was taken by a false Galley, and how it was again restored by the craft of a little Sea-boy, who sunk the Galley, as the following Song will declare*

To the tune of 'The Sailing in the Lowlands'

Sir Walter Raleigh has built a ship
 In the Netherlands,
Sir Walter Raleigh has built a ship
 In the Netherlands;
And it is called the *Sweet Trinity*,
And was taken by the false galley,
 Sailing in the Lowlands.

Is there never a seaman bold
 In the Netherlands,
Is there never a seaman bold
 In the Netherlands
That will go take this false galley,
And to redeem the *Sweet Trinity*,
 Sailing in the Lowlands?'

Then spoke the little ship-boy
 In the Netherlands,
Then spoke the little ship-boy
 In the Netherlands:
'Master, master, what will you give me,
And I will take this false galley,
And release the *Sweet Trinity*,
 Sailing in the Lowlands?'

22 Sir Walter Raleigh] adventurer and explorer (*c.* 1552–1618) galley] in the original the word is printed 'gallaly'. Lowlands] synonymous with Holland

'I'll give thee gold and I'll give thee fee
  In the Netherlands,
I'll give thee gold and I'll give thee fee
  In the Netherlands;
And my eldest daughter thy wife shall be,
  Sailing in the Lowlands.'

He set his breast, and away he did swim
  In the Netherlands,
He set his breast, and away did swim
  In the Netherlands,
Until he came to the false galley,
  Sailing in the Lowlands.

He had an auger fit for the once,
  In the Netherlands,
He had an auger fit for the once,
  In the Netherlands,
The which will bore
Fifteen good holes at once,
  Sailing in the Lowlands.

Some were at cards and some at dice
  In the Netherlands,
Some were at cards and some at dice
  In the Netherlands,
Until the salt water flashed in their eyes,
  Sailing in the Lowlands.

Some cut their hats and some cut their caps
  In the Netherlands,
Some cut their hats and some cut their caps
  In the Netherlands,
For to stop the salt water gaps,
  Sailing in the Lowlands.

He set his breast and away did swim
  In the Netherlands,
He set his breast and away did swim
  In the Netherlands,
Until he came to his own ship again,
  Sailing in the Lowlands.

'I have done the work I promised to do
  In the Netherlands,
I have done the work I promised to do
  In the Netherlands,
For I have sunk the false galley
And released the *Sweet Trinity*,
  Sailing in the Lowlands.

'You promised me gold and you promised me fee,
  In the Netherlands,
You promised me gold and you promised me fee,
  In the Netherlands;
Your eldest daughter my wife she must be,
  Sailing in the Lowlands.'

'You shall have gold and you shall have fee,
  In the Netherlands,
You shall have gold and you shall have fee,
  In the Netherlands;
But my eldest daughter your wife shall never be
  For sailing in the Lowlands.'

'Then fare you well, you cozening lord,
  In the Netherlands,
Then fare you well, you cozening lord,
  In the Netherlands,
Seeing you are not so good as your word,
  For sailing in the Lowlands.'

And thus I shall conclude my song
  Of the sailing in the Lowlands,
And thus I shall conclude my song
  Of the sailing in the Lowlands,
Wishing all happiness to all seamen both old and young
  In their sailing in the Lowlands.

This may be printed. R.L.S. Printed for J. Conyers at the Black Raven, the first
shop in Fetter Lane next Holborn

☞ Raleigh, who was somewhat disliked by the people when he was Queen
Elizabeth's favourite, became the focus for popular sympathy when he was
imprisoned, persecuted, and executed by James I. His name was probably put

R.L.S.] Sir Robert L'Estrange, licenser of ballads from 1663 to 1685

into the title and first verse of the ballad merely as a device for catching the potential listener's attention. Without adducing any evidence, John Ashton suggests that it dates from about 1635, but the earliest edition appeared between 1682 and 1685. (The printer, Conyers, finished his apprenticeship in the former year, and the licenser, L'Estrange, ended his tenure in the latter.) Once again, there is no contemporary record of a tune, but the ballad, having almost certainly circulated orally before being printed, continued to do so afterwards. It was popular with sailors. F. T. Bullen first heard it in these circumstances: 'In the early part of 1870, being then a boy of twelve, I was shipwrecked upon the Alacranes Reef in the Bay of Campeche, Gulf of Mexico. We all got safe to land, where on a little patch of sand and rock only a few acres in extent we stayed for several days. We had no hardships and plenty of excellent food, but the chief joy to me was the long delightful evenings when lolling beneath a great tent we had rigged over our upturned longboat and facing an enormous fire of driftwood, songs and stories were contributed by all. It was there that I learned the song.' In his version, as in many others, the *Sweet Trinity* has become the *Golden Vanity* and 'the false galley' a 'Turkish roveree'.

23   *The* Caesar's *Victory*

It being an Account of a Ship so called, in her Voyage to the East Indies, richly laden, was beset with five Sail of Pirates; but the Caesar *so rarely behaved herself that she came off with Conquest, and put her Foes to flight, losing no more than one Man, and but seven wounded, one of which was Francis Stevens, a Waterman, who formerly plied at Puddle Dock, who lost his Arm*

Tune of 'Cannons roar'. This may be printed, R.P.

23   Puddle Dock] on the River Thames in London   R.P.] Richard Pocock, licenser of ballads from 1685–88

As we was sailing on the main,
Well laded with great store of gain,
We was in danger to be ta'en;
Five pirates' ships appearèd,
Who sailèd up with courage bold
As if they would not be controlled;
But we brave noble hearts of gold
Their courage never fearèd.

We soon did understand their will,
And therefore used our chiefest skill,
Resolving there our blood to spill
Rather than lose our *Caesar*.
We vowed she should not be their prey,
And therefore, boys, we showed them play;
It was upon the sabbath day,
No pirates could appease her.

The master, flourishing his sword,
Did comfort to us all afford,
Both seamen, soldiers then on board,
True courage to awaken.
Then with one voice we all did cry,
'We are resolved to make them fly,
Or in the *Caesar* we will die,
Rather than be taken.'

Before the fight we this did do,
Our bread into the sea we threw
To make room for the whole ship's crew
To fight and keep foes under.
This truth can never be denied,
We soon did quell their haughty pride
By giving them a full broadside;
Our cannons roared like thunder.

Full five long hours there we fought
In the brave *Caesar* fierce and stout;
At length we put them to the rout,
Who aimèd at our treasure.

bread into the sea] provisions were frequently thrown overboard when going into battle,
to make more room for the business of fighting, or to lighten the ship.

We poured them in whole showers of lead
So that they tumbled down for dead,
And in the ocean made their bed
Where they may lie at leisure.

Their admiral did want to be
Aboard of *Caesar*, this we see,
That they might have rich plunder free,
The thing which they delight in;
But yet there was not one that dare
To come on board of *Caesar* there;
They knew their lives we would not spare,
So fierce we was for fighting.

Good fortune she our courage crowned
Or else aboard on us they'd found
The sum of fourscore thousand pound,
Besides all other lading.
Could they but once have seen us fall
Their booty then had not been small:
Two hundred thousand pound in all,
This would have spoiled our trading.

I hope we gave them all their due
Yet saved our coin and cargo too.
Believe me, this is perfect true,
It is no feignèd story;
For though our foes were five to one,
Yet we at last did make them run;
And when we see our work was done
To God we gave the glory.

Who did indeed our rights maintain,
For in this skirmish on the main
Of us there was but one man slain,
And seven others wounded;
But those that sought our overthrow
They lost a many more we know.
Thus providence did kindness show
When we was so surrounded.

Printed for J. Deacon at the Angel in Giltspur Street

☞ The *Caesar*, a ship of the East India Company, was attacked by five pirate vessels
off the island of St Jago on 31 October 1686. After a five-hour battle the pirates,

having failed in their attempts to board or disable the *Caesar*, broke off the engagement, in which they sustained considerable damage themselves. Of the two hundred soldiers and sailors aboard the East Indiaman, one man was killed and eight wounded. Unusually, the ballad reduces the number of wounded by one, but as if to compensate, considerably exaggerates the sums of money involved. In fact there was no treasure on board, but the cargo was valued at £100,000, enough to make the East India Company grateful to the extent of rewarding every man on the ship. The lower ranks received a month's pay apiece, and the officers a medal. The ballad appeared in 1687, when the news reached England. It was set to a highly popular tune, written by Christopher Fishburn in 1683.

24 *The Golden Voyage;*
or, the prosperous Arrival of the James and Mary

Who having searched the Ocean for Treasure, finding the value of two hundred thousand pounds in Gold and Silver, was joyfully received at the City of London

Tune of 'Ladies of London'. This may be printed, R.P.

24 R.P.] Richard Pocock, ballad licenser from 1685–88

Listen awhile and I here will unfold
What seemeth to promise promotion;
There is great plenty of silver and gold
Now newly took out of the ocean.
Forty-three years this treasure has lain,
Since the galleon was staved asunder
Among the shoals and the rocks in the main,
Yet this may be now the world's wonder.

It being seventeen leagues from the shore,
'Tis wonderful if you do mind it;
Many has searched for this treasure before
But none had the fortune to find it,
Till the brave *James and Mary* of fame,
Whom fortune hath highly befriended,
She most successfully sailed on the main,
And was from all dangers defended.

She was informed where this treasure did lie
By some that had gi'en information.
Therefore some nobles did freely comply
Without any more disputation
To fit her forth; this favour they show,
It being their free will and pleasure.
With a fair gale to the ocean they go
Where they find great plenty of treasure.

'Twas in the midst of September they went
Forth in the brave *James and Mary*.
All the ship's crew with a loyal consent,
They being both cheerful and airy,
And in a short time they there did arrive
Where they was with rocks so surrounded
That they did hardly know how to contrive
To keep themselves from being drownded.

There they was forced some time for to lose,
And lie at an anchor together;
As for their engine they then could not use
Because of the turbulent weather.

engine] diving bell

54

Yet at the last to diving they went,
Where silver and gold they receivèd;
When in the water their breath was near spent
They were by their engine relievèd.

Six weeks together they worked in the cold,
Still diving in nine fathom water,
Loading their *Mary* with silver and gold,
Then up to fair London they brought her;
Where they receivèd her with delight
As you may observe by the ditty,
And they unloaded her cargo in sight
Of many brave men of the city.

Carts heavy loaden came thorough the town
On which the whole multitude gazèd;
This to the seamen hath purchased renown,
No question but they may be praisèd.
Still far and near their fame let it ring,
And let them be highly commended,
Since they did venture so hard in this thing,
And was with a blessing attended.

But here is one thing we must not forget:
While they were the treasure possessing
On the great rocks they might soon have been split,
Had not heaven yielded a blessing;
Or while they searched the depth of the main
To hazards they could be no strangers,
Yet men and boys came all safe home again,
Though they had gone through such dangers.

Printed for J. Blare at the Looking Glass on London Bridge

☞ 'There was about this time brought into the Downes', wrote John Evelyn on 12 June 1687, 'a Vast treasure which after 45 yeares being sunk in a Spanish Galioon, which perish'd somewhere neere Hispaniola or Bahama Ilands coming home; was now weighed up, by certaine Gentlemen and others, who were at the Charge of Divers etc: to the suddaine enriching of them, beyond all expectation: The Duke of Albemarles share came (tis believed) to 50000, and some private Gent: who adventured but 100 pounds and little more, to ten, 18000 pounds, and proportionably; his Majesties tenth to 10000 pounds'. The commander of the salvage ship, Captain Phipps, was knighted by James II, and four years later (he was a native of Maine), appointed governor of Massachusetts. The ballad was apparently based entirely on a prose broadsheet giving full details of the expedition. The tune, from a d'Urfey song, was currently in vogue.

25

The Boatswain's Call;

or, the courageous Mariner's Invitation to all his brother Sailors to forsake Friends and Relations for to fight in the Defence of their King and Country

To the tune of 'The Ring of Gold'. Licensed according to Order

Stout seamen, come away, never be daunted;
For if at home you stay, then it is granted
The fleet can never be manned for the ocean,
To fight the enemy and gain promotion.

Lewis, that Christian Turk, makes preparation;
His engines are at work in consultation:
Thinking to ruin quite all Christian princes;
But we their wrongs will right, at life's expenses.

The mighty force of France we never value,
For when we once advance we will not dally;
But on the ocean wide, through blest permission,
We'll soon subdue their pride and grand ambition.

Therefore with courage bold, boys, let us venture;
Like noble hearts of gold now freely enter
Your names on board the fleet, all friends forsaking,
That we may soon complete this undertaking.

Is it not that the land might be defended
By a victorious hand? Though France intended
To lay a heavy yoke on a free nation,
Boys, let a fatal stroke prove their vexation.

But yet methinks I hear some cowards crying;
The press they dread and fear as much as dying,
And skulk like frighted slaves here in distraction,
To hide in dens and caves from warlike action.

Yet some declare they'd fight, but a dear mother
Who counts him her delight above all other,
She loves him as her life: parting would grieve her;
Another has a wife, he's loath to leave her.

Lewis] Louis XIV   value] pronounced 'vally'   venture] pronounced
'venter'   press] pressgang

Thus cowards they can find excuses many
To tarry here behind. Yet there's not any
Right valiant, noble soul heeds a relation;
He'll fight against control for this his nation.

Has not men wished and cried, 'A war with France, boys,
That on the ocean wide we may advance, boys?'
To storm and shake their throne, no danger fearing:
This has been still their tone oft in my hearing.

Where are those heroes now, those sons of thunder,
That would make Lewis bow, and bring him under?
Your wishes now you have, France is the centre;
Like seamen stout and brave, boys, freely venture.

In a fight fierce and hot once I was wounded;
We received showers of shot, being surrounded.
Yet I again will go, and scorn to hide me;
I'll face the daring foe, whate'er betide me.

He that has been in fight fears not another.
He leaves with much delight father and mother
To embrace those true joys which men admire.
We can be merry, boys, in smoke and fire.

If we the conquest gain, that brings promotion;
If we by chance are slain, then the wide ocean
Shall be our watery tomb, near Neptune's palace.
This, boys, shall be our doom, in spite of malice.

Printed for P. Brooksby, J. Deacon, J. Blare and J. Back

☞ Having led an invasion of England in 1688, the Prince of Orange was invited by Parliament in 1689 to become king. War with Louis XIV started soon afterwards, thus beginning a long struggle against France which lasted until 1815. The ballad, which Chappell called 'the production of a genuine seaman', mentions the French preparations for war, and therefore probably dates from 1689. 'The Ring of Gold' is an alternative title for the tune, 'Cupid's Courtesy', for which, see 18 above.

26

The Sea Martyrs;

or, the Seamen's sad Lamentation for their faithful Service, bad Pay and cruel Usage; being a woeful Relation how some of them were unmercifully put to Death for pressing for their Pay, when their Families were like to starve

> *Thus our new government does subjects serve,*
> *And leaves them this sad choice: to hang or starve.*

To the tune of 'Banstead Downs'

Good people do but lend an ear
And a sad story you shall hear.
A sadder you never heard,
Of due desert and base reward,
Which will our English subjects fright
For our new government to fight.

Our seamen are the only men
That o'er the French did victory gain:
They kept the foe from landing here,
Which would have cost the court full dear;
And when for their pay did hope
They were rewarded with a rope.

The roaring cannons they ne'er feared,
Their lives and blood they never spared;

new government] the reign of William and Mary, formally dating from 1689

Through fire and flame their courage flew,
No bullets could their hearts subdue.
Had they in fight but flinched at all,
King James had now been in Whitehall.

Thus England and our new king too
Their safety to their valour owe;
Nay, some did 'gainst their conscience fight
To do some great ones too much right;
And now, oh barbarous tyranny,
Like men they fought, like dogs they die.

Thousands of them their lives did lose
In fighting stoutly with their foes,
And thousands were so maimed in fight
That 'twas a sad and piteous sight;
And when they hoped their pay to gain
They have their labour for their pain.

Their starving families at home
Expected their slow pay would come;
But our proud court meant no such thing:
Not one groat must they have till spring.
To starve all summer would not do,
They must still starve all winter too.

It might a little ease their grief
And give their misery some relief,
Might they in trade ships outward go,
But that poor boon's denied them too;
Which is as much as plain as say:
'You shall earn nothing, nor have pay.'

Their poor wives with care languishèd,
Their children cried for want of bread;
Their debts increased, and none would more
Lend them or let them run o' th' score.
In such a case what could they do
But ask those who did money owe?

Therefore some, bolder than the rest,
The officers for their own request,

groat] fourpenny coin

59

They called them rogues, and said nothing
Was due to them until the spring;
The king had none for them, they said:
Their betters they must first be paid.

The honest seamen then replied
They could no longer want abide,
And that nine hundred thousand pound
Was given last year to pay them round;
Their money they had earnt full dear,
And could not stay another half year.

A council then they straight did call
Of pickthanks made to please Whitehall,
And there they were adjudged to die;
But no man knows wherefore, nor why.
What times are these. Was't ever known
'Twas death for men to ask their own?

Yet some seemed milder than the rest,
And told them that, their fault confessed,
And pardon asked and humbly craved,
Their lives perhaps might then be saved;
But they their cause scorned to betray
Or own't a crime to ask their pay.

Thus they the seamen's martyrs died,
And would not yield to unjust pride;
Their lives they rather would lay down
Than yield it sin to ask their own.
Thus they for justice spent their blood
To do all future seamen good.

Wherefore let seamen all and some
Keep the days of their martyrdom,
And bear in mind these dismal times
When true men suffer for false crimes.
England ne'er knew their like till now,
Nor e'er again the like will know.

But now suppose they had done ill
In asking pay too roughly; still

council] ? court-martial   pickthanks] sycophants

When 'twas their due and need so pressed
They might have pardon found at least.
The king and queen some merciful call,
But seamen find it not at all.

To robbers, thieves and felons they
Freely grant pardons every day;
Only poor seamen who alone
Do keep them on their father's throne
Must have at all no mercy shown;
Nay, though there wants fault, they'll find one.

Where is the subjects' liberty?
And eke where is their property?
We're forced to fight for nought, like slaves,
And though we do we're hanged like knaves.
This is not like old England's ways:
'New lords, new laws', the proverb says.

Besides the seamen's pay that's spent
The king for stores, ships and what's lent
Does owe seven millions at the least,
And every year his debt's increased,
So that we may despair that we
One quarter of our pay we'll see.

Foreigners and confederates
Get poor men's pay, rich men's estates;
Brave England does to ruin run,
And Englishmen must be undone.
If this trade last but one half year,
Our wealth and strength is spent, I fear.

God bless our noble Parliament,
And give them the whole government,
That they may see we're worse than ever,
And us from lawless rule deliver;
For England's sinking unless they
Do take the helm, and better sway.

FINIS

eke] also

☞ On 18 December 1690, Luttrell noted in his diary: 'some seamen belonging to the Suffolk man of war, having mutinied for want of their pay, are secured and sent to the Marshalsea in order to their triall'. On 7 February 1691, he added: 'The seamen which formerly belonged to the Suffolk and had deserted the same, had been tried and condemned, but the queen [Mary, in the absence of William in Holland] had been pleased to pardon them; and so they were sent on board again.' Delays in the payment of wages and prize money could last years; Samuel Pepys thought that it could 'never be well with the navy till poor seamen can be paid once in a year at furthest'. The ballad, which is preserved in his collection, was probably penned by a seaman or sympathiser between the sentence and the reprieve in February 1691. The tune-title, 'Banstead Downs', seems to be an alternative for 'Come live with me', which in turn is otherwise known as 'Jane Shore's Lamentation'.

27 *An Excellent New Song,*

entitled

A hot Engagement between a French Privateer and an English Fireship

I'm a prize for a captain to fall on,
My name it is seafaring Kate;
My sails they are top and top-gallant.
A frigate that's of the first rate.

With a fa la la, [la la la la].

A Frenchman came lately to press me,
Which was not a very hard thing,
And swore that he first would embrace me,
And loaden me then for the king.

27 frigate that's of the first rate] a frigate was not only not a first rate vessel but was most unlikely to be used as a fireship.

Last summer he sailed from the Shannon,
And long at an anchor had rid;
On his midship he had a good cannon,
Which was all the great guns he had.

His mainyard he hoisted, and steerèd
His course; and gave me a broadside:
My poop and my stern-port sheerèd
Betwixt the wind, water and tide.

Still under his lee I did hover
With all the force I could afford,
But as he had been a rank rover
He briskly did lay me on board.

He lookèd for some hidden treasure,
And fell to his doing of feats,
But found me a fireship of pleasure
When he entered the mouth of the straits.

It was a high tide, and the weather
With an easterly gale did blow;
Our frigates were foul of each other,
And could not get off, or ride so.

My bottom was strongly well plankèd,
My deck could a tempest endure;
But ne'er was poor dog in a blanket
So tossèd as was the Monsieur.

No near than his course he still steerèd,
And clapped his hand down to his sword;
But as his love tackle he clearèd
I brought down his maintop by the board.

Then he fearèd to burn a sea martyr,
For my gunroom was all in a fire;
And I blew up my second deck quarter
Just as he began to retire.

I peppered him off from the centre;
Monsieur was ne'er served so before.
I burnt his mainyard at a venture
So that he will press me no more.

rid] ridden   venture] rhymes with centre, and is spelled 'venter' in the original

Then Monsieur got off and was grievèd,
And cursèd the English first rates;
But till then he could never believe it
That Strumbolo lay in the straits.

Printed by T. Moore for S. Green 1691

☞ Fireships, small vessels filled with combustible materials and sent blazing into
enemy fleets to cause damage and confusion, were an essential part of naval
tactics throughout the era of wooden sailing ships. The vessel in this 'hot
engagement' quickly turns out to consist of more than wood and canvas. Such
ambiguities delighted seamen for centuries (see also 101), and there is the
added pleasure here that the victim of the encounter is French. Very unusually,
the tune for the ballad was printed on the same sheet. No title is given, but it is
called 'The Rant'. No music is supplied for the chorus, but the last line would be
repeated to accommodate it.

28   *England's Great Loss by a Storm of Wind*

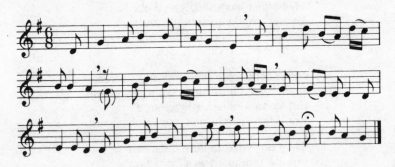

You gentlemen of England fair
Who live at home free from all care,
Little do you think or know
What we poor sailors undergo.
We whine and toil upon the waves,
We work like Turks or galley slaves.

27 Strumbolo] Stromboli, a volcanic island in the Straits of Messina

'Twas on November the second day
When first our admiral bore away,
Intending for his native shore;
The wind at west south-west did roar,
Attended by a dismal sky,
And the seas did run full mountains high.

The very first land that we did make,
It chanced to be the old Ram's Head,
Which made us all rejoice around
To see our flag-stem in Plymouth Sound,
Stretching well over for Fish's Nose,
Thinking to fetch up in Hamose.

The tide of ebb not being done
She set strong to the westward run,
Which put us all in dread and fear
To see our ships they would not wear.
The wind and weather increasèd sore,
And drove nine sail of ships on shore.

When we came to Northumberland Rock
The *Lion*, *Lynx* and *Antelope*,
The *Loyalty* and *Eagle* too,
The *Elizabeth* made all to rue:
She ran astern and the line broke,
And sunk the *Hardwick* at a stroke.

Now you shall hear the worst of all:
The largest ships had the greatest fall.
The great *Coronation* and all her men
Were all drowned except nineteen;
The master's mate and eighteen more
Got in their long boat safe on shore.

As to our ships, we value not,
Had it not fallen to our sailors' lot.

admiral] Edward Russell (1653–1727), supporter of William of Orange, appointed admiral in 1689   Ram's Head] headland to the west of Plymouth, now called Rame Head   Fish's Nose] Fisher's Nose: name for part of the foreshore at the entrance to Sutton Harbour, Plymouth   Hamose] Hamoaze: name for the mouth of the River Tamar   Northumberland Rock] this line in one version reads: 'Ashore went the Northumberland'.

The greatest loss is to their wives
In losing of their husbands' lives;
And to old England it may be more
Than nine sail of ships on shore.

☞ The outcome of the storm of September (not November) 1691, was less disastrous than the ballad indicates: two ships, the *Coronation* and the *Harwich*, were lost, and two more, the *Royal Oak* and the *Northumberland*, went aground but were later refloated. The text is slightly garbled, having probably been taken down from oral tradition some time after the events it described. Captain Marryat called it 'a regular forecastle song' in the early nineteenth century, and Helen Creighton took down another version a hundred years later from Ben Henneberry, of Devil's Island, Nova Scotia, whose tune is given here. His last verse runs: 'As I was a-walking Plymouth one day I heard two loving sisters say, "May God reward all jolly tars And keep them from a man-of-war. May God reward them for their deed Flogging poor sailors when there is no need".'

29   *The Sea Fight in '92*

Thursday in the morn, the Ides of May,
Recorded for ever the famous ninety-two;
Brave Russell did discern by dawn of day
The lofty sails of France advancing now:
'All hands aloft, aloft, let English valour shine;
Let fly a culverin, the signal for the line.
Let every hand supply his gun.
Follow me and you'll see
That the battle will be soon begun.'

Tourville on the main triumphant rolled
To meet the gallant Russell to combat on the deep;
He led the noble train of heroes bold
To sink the English admiral at his feet.
Now every valiant mind to victory doth aspire.
The bloody fight's begun, the sea itself on fire,
And mighty fate stood looking on
Whilst a flood all of blood
Filled the scupper-holes of the *Royal Sun*.

Sulphur, smoke and fire disturbed the air,
With thunder and wonder affright the Gallic shore;
Their regulated bands stood trembling near,
To see the lofty streamers now no more.
At six o'clock the Red the smiling victors led
To give a second blow, the fatal overthrow.
Now death and horror equal reign;
Now they cry, 'Run or die.
British colours ride the vanquished main.'

See they fly amazed through rocks and sands;
One danger they grasp at to shun the greater fate.
In vain they cry for aid to weeping lands.
The nymphs and sea-gods mourn their lost estate:

Ides of May . . . ninety-two] in fact the battle began on 19 May 1692   Russell] Edward (1653–1727), commanded the Anglo-Dutch fleet in 1692. Dismissed after the battle (on the ground that he did not do enough to ensure the complete destruction of the French fleet), but reinstated later.   culverin] large cannon   line] line of battle   Tourville] Anne-Hilarion de Cottentin, Comte de (1642–1701), commanded the French fleet   blood Filled the scupper-holes] literally true, according to Macaulay. Tourville's flagship, called *Soleil Royal* after Louis XIV's device, was first badly damaged by gunfire, then later destroyed by fire.   regulated bands] French militia   the Red] English Red Squadron, led by Vice-Admiral Sir Ralph Delaval

'For evermore adieu, thou royal dazzling *Sun*,
From thy untimely end thy master's fate begun.
Enough thou mighty god of war.
Now we sing: "Bless the king."
Let us drink to every English tar.'

[*The last two lines of each verse are repeated*]

☞ The sea battle of May 1692 was affected by changes of wind and weather, and spread over five days and a wide expanse of sea from the Isle of Wight to the Channel Islands. The small town of St Vaast-la-Hougue in the Cotentin Peninsula, off which the final episode took place, provided the name for the Battle of La Hogue. Admiral Russell commanded a force of 82 English and Dutch ships against the 45 French led by Tourville. Only one English fireship was lost, to sixteen French men-of-war sunk or burned down to the keel. As a result the loyalty of the navy to William III was established and the possibility of a Jacobite invasion of England vanished. 'The public joy was therefore all but universal,' wrote Macaulay. 'During several days the bells of London pealed without ceasing. Flags were flying on all the steeples. Rows of candles were in all the windows. Bonfires were at all the corners of the streets.' The celebrations included a crop of ballads, with titles like 'The Glorious Victory', 'The Triumph of the Seas' and 'Admiral Russell's Scouring the French Fleet', the last of which is an alternative heading for the text given here, which comes with its tune from the 1707 edition of *Pills to Purge Melancholy*.

30   *The Seamen's Wives' Vindication;*
*or, an Answer to the pretended Frolic which was said to be by
them over a Bowl of Punch*

*You writ that we drank liquor free, but for your writing so
You are to blame—nay, blush for shame—since it was nothing so.*

To the tune of 'O so ungrateful a creature'

Why does the poets abuse us, we that are seamen's poor wives?
Have they not cause to excuse us, knowing our sorrowful lives?
We are, alas, broken-hearted, as we can very well prove,
When from our joys we are parted, those loyal husbands we love.

You that declare we are jolly do but abuse us, we find,
For we are most melancholy, always tormented in mind.
While that our husbands are sailing on the tempestuous seas
Here we are sighing, bewailing; nothing affordeth us ease.

68

Here you have newly reported that we are girls of the game,
Who do delight to be courted. Are you not highly to blame,
Saying we often are merry, punch is the liquor we praise,
Though we are known to be weary of these our sorrowful days?

How could you say that there was many wives that did drink, rant
   and sing,
When I protest there's not any of us that practise this thing?
Are we not forcèd to borrow, being left here without chink?
'Tis in a cup of cold sorrow if we so often do drink.

Though we have little to nourish us while our husbands are there,
Merchants in London they flourish through their industrious care.
They are the stay of the nation, men of undaunted renown.
Why should a false accusation run the poor seamen's wives down?

Saying we swallowed our liquor with a great gossipping crew,
Making our tongues to run quicker than they had reason to do?
Thus they would blast all our glory by the soft wits of their brains.
He that invented that story was but a fool for his pains.

We are so far from such pleasure, making of jolly punch bowls,
That we lament out of measure, every woman condoles;
When she in bed should lie sleeping, if the high winds they do roar
There she in sorrow is weeping, fearing to see him no more.

They are to dangers exposèd, as we may very well guess.
How can our eye-lids be closèd in such a time of distress?
You that are free from that [terror], having your husbands secure,
Little consider the horror that we do daily endure.

Though there is joy in our meeting when they come safe home
   from the main,
Yet 'tis a sorrowful greeting when we are parted again.
Landmen in a full fruition feeds on the fat of the land;
This is a happy condition, having all things at command.

Though we have not such a plenty, yet I can very well prove
That there is not one in twenty but who her husband doth love.
You that have caused those distractions, writing a story not true,
May be ashamed of your actions, and thus I bid you adieu.

Printed for J. Deacon at the Angel in Giltspur Street
  chink] money

69

☞ This attack on journalists for sensational and inaccurate writing has a thoroughly modern ring, though it was probably published between 1693 and 1695. The tune has not survived.

31   *The Sailor's Complaint;*
or, the true Character of a Purser of a Ship

To the tune of 'Iantha', &c. Licensed and entered

Of all the curst plagues that e'er fate did decree
To vex, plague and punish poor sailors at sea,
There's none to compare with the purser, that evil,
Who's worse than a jailer, a bum or a devil.
Sure, when he was framed Dame Nature lay dying;
Hell then took a purge, hell then took a purge,
And Pluto sh--t him flying.

As his name foully stinks, so his butter rank doth smell;
Both hateful to sailors, scarce good enough for hell.
The nation allows men what's fitting to eat,
But he, curse attend him, gives to us musty meat,

31 bum] bailiff   Pluto] god of the underworld

With biscuit that's mouldy, hard stinking Suffolk cheese,
And pork cut in pounds, and pork cut in pounds
For to eat with our peas.

Because it is cut off the best fatted hogs
He thinks it too good for eternal lousy dogs.
Then our urine to purge, that the men may piss clear,
Instead of what's better his petty-warrant beer
Is by him allowèd, which makes us complain;
Which he ne'er regards, which he ne'er regards,
So he gets but the gain.

His oatmeal or grout, known by the name burgoo,
Is fitting for nothing but make a sailor spew.
His bruis, no better than a common kitchen grease,
The sailors are forcèd to eat with their peas.
Such beef fat, so nasty, we constantly use
That's but fit for the mast, that's but fit for the mast,
Or the greasing our shoes.

When a sailor's obliged to make use of his store
He then must expect to be miserable poor,
For consider what price for their goods we do pay:
He has treble worth of each man, I dare say.
Such dealings as these are not just, I am sure,
Yet such hardships as these, yet such hardships as these
We do daily endure.

Now since he's so friendly I'd give as 'tis due
By way of requital a kind wish or two.
And first, may his brandy run all over the deck,
And he end his days in a rope with aching neck;
Or may he still eat and be never satisfied,
Still craving of more, still craving of more,
But never be cloyed.

And may he have nothing to drink all the year
When droughth shall attend him, but petty-warrant beer;

---

so] provided that   bruis] the *OED* gives, under 'brewis': 'broth, liquor in which
beef and vegetables have been boiled' or 'bread soaked in boiling fat pottage, made of
salted meat'.   for the mast] for greasing the part of the mast up and down which the
yards moved   droughth] thirst   petty-warrant] reduced rations to crews who looked
after ships laid up in port

May fate ne'er allow him a candle to his cabin,
And be in the dark by Old Nick taken napping;
And by him or his agents be bore swift away,
To plague, vex and punish, to plague, vex and punish
For ever and aye.

May Charon be careful and ferry him o'er
To Pluto's grand court on the Stygian shore;
May ten thousand furies still on him attend
To plague and torment him unto the world's end,
While each jolly sailor to make themselves merry
Shall take a full glass, shall take a full glass
To his passage o'er the ferry.

Printed for W.O., and to be sold by the booksellers of Pie Corner and London
Bridge

☞ Food was the subject of perennial complaint by seamen. Rotten meat, sour beer, smelly water, cheese hard as wood, biscuits full of weevils: the litany was long, and usually justified. Bad was made worse by the unscrupulous cheating of victuallers and pursers. The purser (pronounced 'pusser') was the ship's warrant officer responsible for provisioning, and his name was synonymous with greed and peculation. The ballad was probably printed between 1693 and 1695, but its grievances would have been familiar to generations of seamen, both before then and afterwards. The song which gives the tune its name was first printed in 1705, but the version of the music used here appeared in about 1710.

32   *A Copy of Verses composed by Captain*
Henry Every

lately gone to Sea to seek his Fortune

To the tune of 'The two English Travellers'. Licensed according to Order

31 Charon] ferryman who conveyed the dead across the River Styx   W. O.]
William Onley

Come all you brave boys whose courage is bold,
Will you venture with me? I'll glut you with gold.
Make haste unto Corona; a ship you will find
That's callèd the *Fancy*, will pleasure your mind.

Captain Every is in her and calls her his own;
He will box her about, boys, before he has done.
French, Spaniard and Portuguese, the heathen likewise,
He has made a war with them until that he dies.

Her model's like wax and she sails like the wind;
She is riggèd and fitted and curiously trimmed,
And all things convenient has for his design.
God bless his poor *Fancy*, she's bound for the mine.

Farewell, fair Plymouth, and Cat-down be damned;
I once was part-owner of most of that land,
But as I am disownèd so I'll abdicate
My person from England to attend on my fate.

Then away from this climate and temperate zone
To one that's more torrid you'll hear I am gone,
With an hundred and fifty brave sparks of this age
Who are fully resolvèd their foes to engage.

These northern parts are not thrifty for me.
I'll rise the Anterhise, that some men shall see;
I am not afraid to let the world know
That to the South Seas and to Persia I'll go.

Our names shall be blazèd and spread in the sky,
And many brave places I hope to descry,

Corona] Corunna   box] sail   model's like wax] ?moulded like waxwork
trimmed] decorated   mine] ?main   Cat-down] Cattedown: land near the
junction of the River Plym with Plymouth Sound   thrifty] ?fitting   rise the
Anterhise] ?cruise the Antarctic

73

Where never a Frenchman e'er yet has been,
Nor any proud Dutchman can say he has seen.

My commission is large, and I made it myself,
And the capstan shall stretch it full larger by half;
It was dated in Corona, believe it, my friend,
From the year ninety-three unto the world's end.

I honour St George, and his colours I wear;
Good quarters I give but no nation I spare.
The world must assist me with what I do want:
I'll give them my bill when my money is scant.

Now this I do say and solemnly swear,
He that strikes to St George the better shall fare;
But he that refuses shall suddenly spy
Strange colours abroad of my *Fancy* to fly.

Four chiviliges of gold in a bloody field
Environed with green, now this is my shield;
Yet call out for quarters before you do see
A bloody flag out, which is our decree.

No quarters to give, no quarters to take.
We save nothing living, alas 'tis too late;
For we are now sworn by the bread and the wine,
More serious we are than any divine.

Now this is the course I intend for to steer.
My false-hearted nation, to you I declare
I have done thee no wrong; thou must me forgive.
The sword shall maintain me as long as I live.

London   Printed for Theophilus Lewis

☞ John Avery, otherwise known as Henry Every, was born at Plymouth in 1653, the
oldest son of a sea-captain. He served in the navy and on family-owned ships,
then shipped as mate on the *Charles II*, an English vessel being leased to Spain to
guard the coast of Peru. At Corunna Avery took advantage of a dispute over pay
to seize the ship. After renaming her *Fancy* he set off south and took up station

the capstan shall stretch it] by raising the anchor for further voyages   quarters]
mercy   strange colours] battle ensign in the form of a black flag (the 'Jolly Roger'),
under which quarter might be given   chiviliges] ?chevrons   shield] coat of
arms   bloody flag] battle ensign in the form of a red flag, under which no quarter was
given

off the mouth of the Red Sea, where he soon captured two ships, the second of which was perhaps the richest ever taken by a pirate. This was the *Gunsway* (in fact, *Gunj Suwai*, meaning 'exceeding treasure'). Her contents were worth between a third and half a million pounds, and her passengers included high-ranking ladies who had been making the pilgrimage to Mecca. In reaction to their treatment some of these preferred to jump overboard. Avery sailed in 1696 to New Providence (now Nassau) in the Bahamas and presented his ship to the governor in return for being allowed ashore with his booty. He then left for England, and disappeared. There are stories that he was buried a pauper in 1727 or '28 at Bideford in his native Devon under the name of Henry Bridgman, having been cheated of all his wealth by Bristol merchants. Another tradition is that he married the Great Mogul's daughter, whom he captured on the *Gunj Suwai*, and became King of Madagascar. Defoe made him the subject of a long pamphlet, *The King of the Pirates* (1720), and made the fictional Captain Singleton his comrade-in-arms. In fact, a reward of £500 was offered in London for Avery's capture, and £50 for that of each of his men. Avery escaped justice, but between 1696 and 1700 some twenty or thirty of his men were tried and executed for piracy.

The ballad given here appears to date from soon after Avery's takeover of the *Charles II*, in May 1693. Some of its obscurities are clarified in an eighteenth-century reissue, where the ship is called the *Fanny*. The tune prescribed is lost, but the ballad lived in oral tradition at least until 1907, when it was noted from a Hampshire singer, John Hatch, whose melody fits the text of 1693.

33   *Captain Kid's Farewell to the Seas;*
or, the Famous Pirate's Lament

To the tune of 'Coming down'

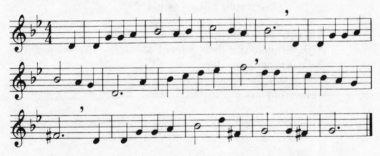

My name is Captain Kid, who has sailed, [who has sailed],
My name is Captain Kid, who has sailed.
My name is Captain Kid;
What the laws did still forbid,
Unluckily I did while I sailed, [while I sailed].

Upon the ocean wide, when I sailed, &c.,
Upon the ocean wide, when I sailed,
Upon the ocean wide
I robbed on every side
With most ambitious pride, when I sailed, &c.

My faults I will display, while I sailed, &c.,
My faults I will display, while I sailed.
My faults I will display,
Committed day by day.
[Damnation is my lot, as I sailed,] &c.

Many long leagues from shore, when I sailed, &c.,
Many long leagues from shore, when I sailed;
Many long leagues from shore
I murdered William Moore,
And laid him in his gore, when I sailed, &c.

Because a word he spoke, when I sailed, &c.,
Because a word I spoke, when I sailed;
Because a word he spoke
I with a bucket broke
His skull at one sad stroke, while I sailed, &c.

I struck with a good will, when I sailed, &c.,
I struck with a good will, when I sailed;
I struck with a good will,
And did a gunner kill,
As being cruel still, when I sailed, &c.

A *Quida* merchant then while I sailed, &c.,
A *Quida* merchant then, while I sailed;
A *Quida* merchant then
I robbed of hundreds ten,
Assisted by my men, while I sailed, &c.

A banker's ship of France, while I sailed, &c.,
A banker's ship of France, while I sailed;
A banker's ship of France
Before us did advance.
I seizèd her by chance, while I sailed, &c.

Quida merchant] the merchant ship, *Quedah*, captured in February 1698
banker's ship] French fishing boat on the way to the Newfoundland Banks, captured in
June 1696

Full fourteen ships I see, when I sailed, &c.,
Full fourteen ships I see, when I sailed;
Full fourteen ships I see,
Merchants of high degree.
They were too hard for me, when I sailed, &c.

We steered from sound to sound, while we sailed, &c.,
We steered from sound to sound, while we sailed;
We steered from sound to sound,
A Moorish ship we found.
Her men we stripped and bound, while we sailed, &c.

Upon the ocean seas while we sailed, &c.,
Upon the ocean seas while we sailed,
Upon the ocean seas
A warlike Portuguese
In sport did us displease, while we sailed, &c.

At famous Malabar when we sailed, &c.,
At famous Malabar when we sailed,
At famous Malabar
We went ashore, each tar,
And robbed the natives there, when we sailed, &c.

Then after this we chased, while we sailed, &c.,
Then after this we chased, while we sailed,
Then after this we chased
A rich Armenian, graced
With wealth, which we embraced, while we sailed, &c.

Many Moorish ships we took while we sailed, &c.,
Many Moorish ships we took while we sailed,
Many Moorish ships we took;
We did still for plunder look.
All conscience we forsook while we sailed, &c.

I, Captain Cullifoord, while I sailed, &c.,
I, Captain Cullifoord, while I sailed,

fourteen ships] Kidd attacked a merchant fleet off Mocha in the Red Sea in August
1697, but quickly disengaged in the face of spirited resistance.   Malabar] part of the
coast of the Deccan in India   rich Armenian] the *Quedah* flew the Armenian flag,
and the merchants on board offered Kidd 20,000 rupees if he would allow them to go on
their way.   Captain Cullifoord] an enemy of Kidd's, rather than an associate, Robert
Culliford was found guilty of piracy on the same day as Kidd but was reprieved since he

77

I, Captain Cullifoord,
Did many merchants board,
Which did much wealth afford, while we sailed, &c.

Two hundred bars of gold, while we sailed, &c.,
Two hundred bars of gold, while we sailed,
Two hundred bars of gold
And rich dollars manifold
We seizèd uncontrolled, while we sailed, &c.

St John, a ship of fame, when we sailed, &c.,
St John, a ship of fame, when we sailed,
St John, a ship of fame,
We plundered when she came,
With more that I could name, when we sailed, &c.

We taken was at last, and must die, &c.,
We taken was at last, and must die,
We taken were at last
And into prison cast.
Now, sentence being passed, we must die, &c.

Though we have reigned awhile, we must die, &c.,
Though we have reigned awhile, we must die,
Though we have reigned awhile,
While fortune seemed to smile,
Now on the British Isle we must die, &c.

Farewell the ocean main, we must die, &c.,
Farewell the ocean main, we must die,
Farewell the ocean main;
The coast of France or Spain
We ne'er shall see again. We must die, &c.

From Newgate now in carts we must go, &c.,
[From Newgate now in carts we must go],
From Newgate now in carts
With sad and heavy hearts
To have our due deserts we must go, &c.

had surrendered himself under an offer of mercy from William III. He was released by
Queen Anne in April 1702.

Some thousands they will flock when we die, &c.,
Some thousands they will flock when we die,
Some thousands they will flock
To Execution Dock,
Where we must stand the shock and must die, &c.

☞ Captain William Kid (or Kidd) was born in Scotland in about 1645. Little is known of him before 1688, by which time he was living in New York. In the following year he saw action against the French in the West Indies as captain of his own sloop. In 1691 he married, and acquired a comfortable estate in Manhattan. Four years later he travelled to London in search of a command in the navy. Kidd was persuaded instead to accept a privateering commission against pirates and the French. The venture was funded partly by Kidd himself, but mainly by Lord Bellomont (Governor of New England), various Whig grandees in London, and even William III himself (though his share of the capital was not in fact paid). Kidd fitted out a small ship, the *Adventure* galley, and left Deptford in February 1696, for the Red Sea. However, after calling at Plymouth he made for New York, where he hoped to strengthen his crew. On the passage he captured a French 'banker', a fishing vessel bound for New-foundland, and sold her as a prize in New York. After a delay of several months he sailed for the Indian Ocean, where, after an argument, he fatally injured the gunner, Thomas Moore, by hitting him over the head with a bucket. After various incidents the *Adventure* galley took two ships, both considered legitimate prizes because they bore French passes. The second of these, the *Quedah*, had a valuable cargo. In 1698 Kidd abandoned his own ship, which had become unseaworthy, and set off for America in the *Quedah*. He arrived at Anguilla (Leeward Islands) in April 1699, to discover that he had been declared a pirate in London. He took the *Quedah* to Hispaniola, transferred the more valuable of her contents to a small vessel which he purchased, and sailed to New York, then Boston, to enlist the aid of Lord Bellomont. Kidd's defence was that although Moore was mutinous, he had not intended to kill him; and that the prizes had been lawfully taken. He handed the French passes to Bellomont. Nevertheless Kidd was taken to London, where he lay for a year in Newgate Gaol awaiting trial. A political storm was raging over the Tories' accusation that the Whigs were implicated in piracy. Kidd was called to the bar of the House of Commons to answer questions, and later put on trial. The passes and other documents vital to his defence were not produced—indeed, were probably deliberately suppres-sed— and Kidd was found guilty of both murder and piracy. His effects, worth six and a half thousand pounds, were confiscated and given to Greenwich Hospital. Some of the money went towards building what is now the National Maritime Museum.

Kidd did not see New York again, nor his wife and daughter, and on 23 May 1701, as Luttrell noted the next day: 'captain Kidd and 3 others ... were executed at execution dock in Wapping, the halter of the 1st broke, but he was tied up again.' Perhaps Kidd was more fool than knave, but he was remembered as an atrocious villain. The ballad, in time-honoured manner, purports to give his goodnight or farewell to the world. John Masefield said in 1906 that it could still be heard at sea, and Joanna Colcord observed that 'many a forecastle has resounded to the endless and lugubrious verses'. It was certainly sung on land until recent times, though more widely in America than in Britain. The tune, 'Coming down', exists in several traditional versions. The variant given here appeared in 1719–20 under the title of 'A Young Man and a Maid'. Kidd's ghostly ship used to be seen gliding in the mist off the coast of New England, and his spectre terrified with upraised cutlass some of the many who dug for his buried treasure. As recently as 1984 an Englishman was released from imprisonment in Vietnam after being arrested near the Gulf of Thailand, where he had been digging for some of Kidd's booty.

34   *Cordial Advice*

to all rash young Men who think to advance their decaying Fortunes by Navigation; showing the many Dangers and Hardships that Sailors endure

> *All you whose rambling thoughts are bent to please*
> *Themselves by sailing on the briny seas,*
> *How much you are mistaken; here you'll see*
> *What dangers there, and what their hardships be,*
> *When thundering storms with testy Neptune rage,*
> *Seas, winds and fire at once with ships engage.*
> *Besides the small allowance that they share,*
> *What stripes and labour they are forced to bear.*
> *These weighed together and considered well,*
> *You need no more, although I worse could tell.*

To the tune of 'I'll no more to Greenland sail', &c.

You merchant men of Billingsgate, I wonder how you can thrive;
You bargain with men for six months and pay them but for five;
But so long as the water runs under the bridge and the tide doth
    ebb and flow,
> *I'll no more to Greenland sail, no, no, no.*

Our drink it is fair water that floweth from the rocks,
And as for other dainties, we eat both bear and fox,
Then boil our biscuits in whale oil all to increase our woe,
> *But I'll no more, &c.*

34 Billingsgate] fishmarket district in London   bargain . . . for six months and pay . . . for five] the men worked for six lunar months but were paid for five calendar months.

Our captains and commanders are valiant men and stout;
They've fought in France and Flanders and never would give out.
They beat our men like stock-fish all to increase our woe,
    Then I'll no more, &c.

In storms we must stand to it when thundering tempests rage,
When cables snap and mainmasts split and the briny seas engage;
Whilst sable blackness spreads its veil all to increase our woe,
    But I'll no more, &c.

Testy Neptune's mounting waves still o'er our hatches tower;
Each minute threatens silent graves for fishes to devour,
Or be entombed by some vast whale, and there to end our woe,
    But I'll no more, &c.

To face the cold north-eastern winds whilst shrouds and tackle roar,
And man our racking pinnace which mountain high is bore;
To larboard, starboard tack we trail, our joints benumbed with
   snow,
    But I'll no more, &c.

'Abaft, before, helm a-lee, all hands aloft', they cry,
When straight there comes a rolling sea and mounts us to the sky.
Like drownèd rats we cordage haul while scarce we've strength to
   go,
    But I'll no more, &c.

For if we faint or falter to ply our cruel work
The bosun with a halter does beat us like a Turk;
Whilst we in vain our case bewail he does increase our woe,
    But I'll no more, &c.

Then to take our lading in we moil like Argier slaves,
And if we to complain begin the capstal lash we have;
A cursèd cat with thrice three tails does much increase our woe,
    But I'll no more, &c.

And when we faint, to bring us back they give us bruis strong,
The which does not creepers lack to usher it along,
With element which smells so stale, all to increase our woe,
    Then I'll no more, &c.

stock-fish] cod split open and dried   racking] straining   moil] work
Argier] Algiers   capstal lash] ?capstan lash, for which see under 'nipper' in Glossary
bruis] see note to 31   creepers] ? weevils

Therefore young men I all advise before it be too late,
And then you'll say that you are wise, by dashing of your fate,
The which your rashness did entail for to insist your woe,
Then I'll no more to Greenland sail, no, no, no.

London: Printed by W[illiam] O[nley], and for E. Brooksby, at the Golden Ball
in Pie Corner

☞ Seventeenth-century whalers favoured the waters off Spitzbergen (popularly
called Greenland), but as these began to fail they turned to Greenland itself. A
series of companies came and went, but it was not until the middle of the
eighteenth century that government bounties helped to make a success of the
trade. The practice of hunting whales from double-ended six-man rowing boats
persisted until the First World War. The animal was harpooned by hand, played
like a fish for anything from four to forty hours, and eventually killed with long
lances. It was then towed back by the whaling ship and winched on to a beach for
flensing. This ballad, printed between 1696 and 1703, and reissued a few years
later, says far more about the harsh treatment of whalers than of whales. The
tune is now lost.

35 ## The Death of Admiral Benbow

O we sailed to Virginia and thence to New York,
Where we watered our shipping and so weighed then all.
Full in view on the seas seven sail we did spy;
O we mannèd our capstan and weighed speedily.

The first two we came up with were brigantine sloops;
We asked if the other five were as big as they looked,

35 Virginia . . . New York] in fact, to Barbados, then Port Royal (Jamaica)

But turning to windward as near as we could lie
We found they were French men-of-war cruising hard by.

We took our leave of them and made quick dispatch,
And then steered our course to the island of Vache,
But turning to windward as near as we could lie,
On the fourteenth of August ten sail we did espy.

They hoisted their pendants and their colours they spread,
And they hoisted their bloody flag on the main topmast head;
Then we hoisted our jack-flag at the mizen peak,
So brought up our squadron in a line most complete.

O we drew up our squadron in a very nice line
And fought them courageous for four hours' time,
But the day being spent, boys, and night coming on,
We let them alone till the very next morn.

The very next morning the engagement proved hot,
And brave Admiral Benbow received a chain-shot.
O when he was wounded to his men he did say:
'Take me up in your arms, boys, and carry me away.'

O the guns they did rattle and the bullets did fly,
While brave Admiral Benbow aloud for help did cry:
'Carry me to the cockpit and soon ease my smart;
If my men they should see me 'twill sure break their heart.'

And there Captain Kirby proved a coward at last,
And with Wade played at bopeep behind the main-mast;
And there they did stand, boys, and quiver and shake,
For fear that those French dogs their lives they should take.

The very next morning at break of the day
We hoisted our topsails and so bore away;
We bore to Port Royal where the people flocked much
To see Admiral Benbow carried to Kingston Town church.

Come all you brave fellows wherever you have been,
Let us drink a health to great George our king;
And another good health to the girls that we know,
And a third in remembrance of Admiral Benbow.

Fowler, printer, Salisbury

George our king] originally, Anne our queen

☞ John Benbow (1653–1702) was born at Shrewsbury. He ran away to sea and rose to be a master's mate in the Royal Navy, but left after being court-martialled for making disparaging remarks about his captain, and bought a trading vessel of his own. In 1685 his ship was boarded off Cadiz by Moorish pirates, who were fiercely repulsed. The thirteen dead left behind were decapitated and the heads preserved in brine so that Benbow could claim the head-money. He rejoined the navy in 1689 as captain of the *Britannia*, and two years later William III sent him to the West Indies as Admiral of the Blue, with a fleet of ten ships. In 1702 he sailed from Jamaica in search of the French fleet, sighted it off Santa Marta (now in Colombia) on 19 August, and chased it for five days across the Caribbean. In his flagship, *Breda*, Benbow finally brought the French to action on the fifth day, but was enraged and cruelly disappointed when his captains refused to support him. During the battle his 'right Leg', wrote Campbell, 'was shattered to Pieces by a Chain-shot, and he was carried down; but he presently ordered his Cradle on the Quarter-deck and continued the Fight till Day'. Although he was 'ill of a Fever', on returning to Kingston Benbow ordered that seven of his captains be tried on charges which included cowardice in the face of the enemy. One died a few days before the trial, one was vindicated, two suspended, and the worst offenders, Kirby and Wade, were found guilty, and ordered to be shot. The sentence was carried out on board the ship which took them home, when it docked at Plymouth in April 1703. Meanwhile, in November 1702, Benbow had died, of fever, of wounds, and perhaps of chagrin. He was an able commander, popular with his men but less so with his officers. He was remembered in two ballads, both sung for two hundred years after his death, and both indifferently called either 'Admiral Benbow' or 'The Death of Admiral Benbow'. Nevertheless, they are separate songs. One, beginning 'Come all ye seamen bold', has the same metre as 'Captain Kid's Farewell' (33); the same tune could as well serve a hero as a villain. The other is given here, from a broadside printed between 1778 and 1787, which is why 'Anne our queen' (Anne succeeded William a few months before Benbow's battle) has been changed in defiance of the rhyme to 'George our king'. The tune appeared with a shortened form of the words in *The Vocal Enchantress*, a songbook published in 1783.

36   *The Greenland Voyage;*
    or, the Whale Fisher's Delight

being a full description of the manner of the taking of Whales on the Coast of Greenland

To the tune of 'Hey to the Temple', &c.

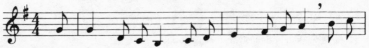

Why stay we at home now the season is come?
Jolly lads, let us liquor our throats;
Our interest we wrong if we tarry too long.
Then all hands, let us fit out our boats.
Let each man prepare of the tackling his share;
By neglect a good voyage may be lost.
Come, I say, let's away; make no stay or delay,
For the winter brings whales on the coast.

Harry, Will, Robin, Ned, with bold Tom in the head,
And Sam in the stern bravely stands,
As rugged a crew if we give them their due
As ever did take oars in their hands.
Such heroes as these will with blood stain the seas
When they join with their resolute mates,
Who with might void of fright with delight boldly fight
Mighty whales as if they were but sprats.

Come coil in the warp, see the hatchets be sharp,
And make ready the irons and lance;
Each man ship his oar and leave nothing on shore
That is needful the voyage to advance.
See the buoy be made right and the drug fitted right
So that nothing be wanting anon.
Never doubt, but look out round about. There's a spout.
Come away, boys, let's launch if we can.

drug] rope

The suff runs too high, 'twill be down by and by.
Take a slatch to go off, now 'twill do.
Huzza, launch amain, for the sea grows again;
Pull up briskly a stroke, boys, or two.
Ha, well rowed. 'Tis enough. We are clear of the suff.
A yare hand heave out water apace.
There's the whale. That's her back; that looks black. There's her
    wake.
Pull away, boys, let's give her a chase.

Ha, well rowed, jolly trouts. Pull away: there she spouts,
And we gain of her briskly, I find.
We're much about her ground, let's take a dram round,
And her rising be sure let us mind.
She's here, just ahead. Stand up, Tom. Pull up, Ned.
We are fast; back astern what ye may.
Hold on, lad. I'm afraid she's a jade. She's so mad,
She's a scrag. For your lives, cut away.

Though we have met with misfortune already,
'Tis courage must do, for the proverb you know:
A faint heart never won a fair lady.
Come, this is no disgrace. Pull up, lads, another chase.
Our mates will be fast without doubt.
So, what cheer? We are near. She is there. No, she's here,
Just astern. Jolly hearts, pull about.

Pull briskly there, she's risen very fair.
Back astern, it is up to the strap.
Well done, Tom. Bravely throwed. Cheerly, lads, bravely rowed.
'Tis not always we meet with mishap.
Veer out warp; let her run. She will quickly have done.
Well done, mates. 'Twas a brave second stroke.
Now she jerks. Who can work? Veer our warp. She tows sharp.
Hang the blacksmith; our lance is broke.

Pull ahead, haul in warp, for she tows not so sharp,
But's beginning to flounce and to strike.
Fit a lance, let us try if we can by and by,
Give her one gently touch to the quick.

suff] rush of sea   slatch] slack   amain] at once   yare] ready
trouts] friends   jade] vicious   scrag] fin whale   cheerly] cheerily,
willingly

Bravely throwed, jolly lad. She's nothing nigh so mad
As she was. T'other lance may do good.
Well done, Tom. That was home to her womb; makes her foam.
She's sick at the heart; she spouts blood.

The business is done. Lance no more, let's alone.
'Tis her flurry, she is dead as a herring.
Let's take her in tow and all hands stoutly row;
And, mate Sam, prithee mind well thy steering.
The wind begins to blow and the seas bigger grow.
Every man put his strength to his oar.
Leave to prate now 'tis late. Well rowed, mate. Hey for Kate.
She's aground. Cut away. Let's ashore.

Come turn up the boats, let's put on our coats,
And to Ben's: there's a chirruping cup.
Let's comfort our hearts, every man his two quarts,
And tomorrow, all hands to cut up.
Betimes leave your wives, bring your hooks and your knives,
And let none lie abed like a lubber;
But begin with the sun to have done before noon,
That the carts may come down for the blubber.

☞ This exceptionally graphic song, described as old in a collection published in the
1720s, shows a close acquaintance with whaling, and has the immediacy of a
running commentary. The tune, alternatively known as 'Basse's (or Hunter's)
Career' is from *Pills to Purge Melancholy*.

37   *The Sailor's Lamentation*

36 chirruping] cheering

Come all you valiant sailors of courage stout and bold,
That value more your honour than misers do their gold,
When we receive our orders we are obliged to go
O'er the main to proud Spain, let the wind blow high or low.

'Tis of the valiant *Canterbury*, as I to you shall tell,
Since providence has spared my life, the truth to [you] I'll tell;
And all our whole ship's company as well as I do know,
When we were in despair in the Bay of Biscay, oh.

The fourteenth of September from Spithead we set sail
With the *Romney* in our company, blest with a pleasant gale;
And so we kept together to the Bay of Biscay, oh,
Till anon the storm came on and the wind began to blow.

The sign of the storm came on, the *Romney* bore away,
And left the *Canterbury* all alone, for she could no longer stay;
But when they came to Gibraltar they told the people so
That they thought we were lost in the Bay of Biscay, oh.

But as providence would have it, [it] was not quite so bad;
The first we lost our mizenmast and along with it our flag.
The next we lost our mainmast, two of our guns also,
And nine men [were] drowned then in the Bay of Biscay, oh.

When our foremast went away at nine o'clock at night
Our men [were] in our fore-top, did put us in a fright;
Ourselves we could not save them, but overboard did go:
They [were] lost with that mast in the Bay of Biscay, oh.

We stove our barge and long-boat, and flung them overboard,
Because we had no tackle or else we might them board;

Spithead] anchorage off Portsmouth   The sign of the storm came on] Then,
seeing that the storm came on   Gibraltar] invariably with four syllables in the
original: 'Giberalter'   might them board] might have lowered and boarded them

88

With which the waters coming in, which made [our] chests to flow,
And we rolled and we trolled in the Bay of Biscay, oh.

We lay in that condition full seven or eight long days,
Till our furnace coming down which put us in amaze;
For we could get no victuals dressed, as I am very sure,
We did eat all raw meat till we came to Gibraltar.

It being dark and dismal, besides a dreadful night,
Two men in our forecastle was killed there outright.
With their rings upon their fingers in pieces broke also,
There they lay till next day we overboard them throw.

As for our admiral and captain they are stout hearts of gold,
Besides our three lieutenants of courage hard and bold;
And all our old ship's company we made a gallant show,
Though we were in despair in the Bay of Biscay, oh.

The storm it blew over, we got up jury-mast
And steered away to Gibraltar, to which we came at last;
And when we came to Gibraltar ashore our yawl did go
For to tell what befell in the Bay of Biscay, oh.

Within two or three days after we all came into the mole,
The people all came flocking down our ship to behold.
They said it was as strange a thing as ever they did know,
But we ne'er repine, but drink wine and drownèd all our woe.

As for our oatmeal and our peas we ne'er got none of that,
The purser put it in his pocket to make him fat;
But if e'er we live to come home, boys, we'll tell him on shore,
Though he know 'twas our due, 'twould help to increase his store.

☞ The *Canterbury* sailed from Spithead on 18 September 1728, and arrived at
Gibraltar on 14 October. A description of the storm is given in the ship's log,
which survives: 'Monday, September 23.—About 11 this forenoon we were
taken with a violent squall out of the N.-W., which carried away our mizen mast
and split the main topsail. In this squall we lost sight of the Romney. 24.—For
the most part strong gales of wind with violent squalls. Yesterday in the
afternoon we lowered down our fore and main yards and got the sails reefed and
furled and cut away the main topsail yard, sail and all, as it was split. About nine
last night we lost our mainmast, and soon after the foremast, which fell to

chests] sea chests   we rolled and we trolled] both verbs have the same meaning
furnace] galley fire

windward, and took away our best bower anchor stock. In the fall of the mast it stave both barge and pinnace (which we hove overboard) and fell on the outer part of one of our quarterdeck guns, which it carried overboard with it. Also we likewise lost seven of our men, and had one man's thigh broke, and another very much bruised.' The ballad, with its concluding jibe at the hated purser, seems very much the work of a lower-deck seaman. It appears to have circulated orally before being printed: the original text has *Rumbley* for *Romney*, 'Biskey' for 'Biscay', and 'Giberalter' for Gibraltar. The word, 'tackle', is spelled 'taickle', which indicates the normal nautical pronunciation. Two other copies, one of which is entitled 'Admiral Cavendish's Distress on Board the *Canterbury*', also have numerous idiosyncracies. The tune intended was probably 'When the stormy winds do blow', a descendant of Martin Parker's 'Sailors for my Money' (13). An oral version from Aberdeenshire took over the tune of 'The Plains of Waterloo'.

38   *English Courage Displayed;*
or, Brave News from Admiral Vernon

being a copy of verses giving an account of the taking of Porto Bello, the 22nd November last, written by a seaman on board the Burford, *the admiral's ship, and sent here from Jamaica*

Tune of 'Glorious Charles of Sweden'

Come loyal Britons all rejoice with joyful acclamations,
And join with one united voice upon this just occasion;
To Admiral Vernon drink a health, likewise to each brave fellow
Who with that noble admiral was at the taking of Porto Bello.

From Jamaica he did sail with Commodore Brown to attend him,
Against the Spaniards to prevail, for which we must commend him.
At Porto Bello he arrived where each brave gallant fellow
With Admiral Vernon bravely fought at the taking of Porto Bello.

Two men-of-war of twenty guns, likewise five guarda-costas,
They in the harbour quickly took—to surrender they were forced,
    sir.
Then the town he summonsed straight to surrender at his will, O,
Which they refusing he did bombard the town of Porto Bello.

He did bombard it above two days, and they again returned it.
The bombs and mortars loud did play; he vowed that he would
    burn it,
Which when they came to understand, and that he was so brave a
    fellow,
They did surrender out of hand the town of Porto Bello.

Then with his men he went on shore, who straight began to
    plunder;
'Tis as they served our ships before, and therefore is no wonder.
With plenty of rum and good strong wines our men did soon get
    mellow,
Then swore that never a house should stand in the town of Porto
    Bello.

The governor to the admiral sent, and to him made an offer
Of thirty thousand pieces of eight the houses to save did proffer,
Which the admiral did accept with a right and free goodwill, O,
And therefore let the houses stand in the town of Porto Bello.

Their Iron Castle he destroyed, and all their guns he seizèd.
The Spaniards ne'er was more annoyed; he did just what he
    pleasèd.
The South Sea snow he did release and many a stout English fellow
Whom they had robbed upon the seas, and carried into Porto Bello.

snow] type of ship

All their brass guns he took away, the iron ones he nailèd,
And then threw them into the sea before from thence he sailèd.
Many a jolly sailor's pouch was crammed with white and yellow,
For they from plunder could not be kept in the town of Porto Bello.

Besides, brave Vernon freely gave amongst his men as follows,
Who bravely did behave themselves, full thirty thousand dollars.
This must their courage animate; each tar is a rich fellow;
And this is good encouragement for the taking of Porto Bello.

When he had stayed there nineteen days, with just resentment firèd,
Their forts demolishèd and castles razed he from them retirèd,
But first he to Panama sent for many a gallant fellow,
Who in prison lay confined, to be brought to Porto Bello.

While trumpets they did loudly sound and colours were displaying
The prizes he with him brought away while sailors were huzza-ing;
And when they to Jamaica come, a glorious tale to tell, O,
Of the noble action they had done in taking of Porto Bello.

To Admiral Vernon toss off a glass, may heaven protect and defend
   him;
And when he has the Spaniard thumped, may a safe return attend
   him.
To Commodore Brown toss another down, and to each gallant
   fellow
Who did so bravely play their parts at the taking of Porto Bello.

☞ Edward Vernon (1684–1757) served in the navy from 1700 until 1713, rising to
post-captain. He entered Parliament in 1722, and when war broke out with
Spain in 1739 he was sent as vice-admiral with a squadron of six ships to harry
Spanish settlements in the West Indies. In November 1740 he captured the
stronghold of Porto Bello, on the Panama isthmus, with total British casualties
of only six killed and thirteen wounded. The news was received with rapture in
England. Public houses were renamed after Vernon, and many towns have to
this day a Portobello Road. A pressed man in the squadron wrote home to his
wife: 'When I left you hevens noes it was with an akin hart to be hauld from you
by a gang of rufins but hover i soon overcome that when I found that we were
about to go in ernest to rite my natif contry and against a parcel of impodent
Spaniards by whom I have often been ill treted and god nows my heartt I have
longed this fore years to cut of some of their Ears, and was in hopes I should haf
sent you one for a sample now, but our good Admiral God bless him was to
merciful we have taken Port Belo with such coridge and bravery that i never saw

white and yellow] silver and gold

92

before, for my own Part my heart was raised to the clouds and would ha scaled the Moon had a Spaniard been there to come at him, as We did the Batry'.

The ballad, with its gallant attempts at finding English rhymes for 'bello', echoes these sentiments, and may well be, as it claims, by a lower-deck sailor. The tune was widely known under titles as diverse as 'Frisky Jenny', 'The Tenth of June', 'The First of August', 'The Constant Lover' and 'The Weavers' March', as well as 'Charles of Sweden'.

39   *The Disappointed Sailor*

Early one morning in the spring
I went on board to serve the king,
Leaving my dearest dear behind,
Who swore to me her heart inclined.

Oft did I fold her in my arms;
I doted on her thousand charms.
Our troth we plight 'mid kisses sweet,
And vow we'll wed when next we meet.

While I was sailing on the sea
I found an opportunity
To forward letters to my dear,
But, oh, from her I ne'er did hear.

When before Carthagena town,
Where cannon balls flew up and down,
While in the midst of dangers there
My thoughts dwelt always on my dear.

39 Carthagena] Cartagena, in what is now Colombia

And when arrived on Britain's shore
I hastened where I did adore,
Her father said: 'What do you mean?
D'ye really love my daughter, Jean?'

Surprised, he made me this reply:
'My daughter does your love deny.
She's married now, sir, for her life,
So, young man, seek another wife.'

I cursed the gold and silver too,
And all false women that prove untrue,
Who first make vows then such vows break,
And all for cursèd riches' sake.

I would rather be on yonder shore
Where thundering cannons loudly roar;
I would rather be where bullets fly
Than in false woman's company.

So I'll bid adieu to all womankind.
I'll sail the ocean round and round;
I'll sail the sea until I die,
Although the waves run mountains high.

Now from a window lattice high
The lady she made this reply:
'I pray, let reason take its place
Before you do our sex disgrace.

'Do hold your tongue, you cruel man,
For of your letters I ne'er got one.
If the fault be great, love, 'tis none of mine,
So don't speak so harshly of womankind.'

☞ Vernon's attack on Cartagena in 1741 was a failure, and afterwards the sailors of
the fleet and the soldiers of the expeditionary force were decimated by yellow-
jack fever. Tobias Smollett, who was present, described the action and its
aftermath in his novel, *Roderick Random* (1751). The song, put into the mouth of
a survivor, is concerned with making love, not war. It is an updating of the late
seventeenth-century 'Seaman's Complaint for his Unkind Mistress, of Wapping', in which the place besieged is unspecified ('When we were booming of a
town Where cannon balls flew up and down'). The tune prescribed, 'I love you
dearly', fits 'The Disappointed Sailor', and is akin to versions later found in oral
tradition in Britain and America.

The Valiant Sailor

Come all you wild young men
And a warning take by me,
And see you go no more, my brave boys,
Into any strange foreign country.
Into any strange foreign country,
And see you go no more, my brave boys,
Into any strange foreign country.

As I myself have done
The very last day of May;
It was then that I parted from all of my friends,
For I could no longer stay, &c.

From Portsmouth Town I went,
To London was my intent;
But by the press masters I was pressed
And to the sea I was sent, &c.

We sailed all that long night
And part of the very next day.
The first ship we spied was a French man-of-war,
And at length we were forced to draw nigh, &c.

We bore her head upright
And our bloody flag we let fly;
And then every man he was prepared,
But the Lord knows who should die, &c.

Our captain being wounded full sore
And seventy more of our men;
Our yards and masts and rigging they were all shot away
And at length we were forced to give in, &c.

Our decks were all covered with blood
And so loudly the great guns did roar,
And many's the thousand times I wished myself at home
All along with my Polly on the shore, &c.

She's a tall and slender girl
With a black and a rolling eye,
And here I lie a-bleeding on the deck
And it's all for her safety I shall die, &c.

☞ There is a wide range of incident and emotion in this short song. It was first
published in 1744, and circulated orally for over a hundred and fifty years
afterwards.

41 *Disconsolate Judy's Lamentation*

for the Absence of her True Love, Johnny on board the Victory *with Admiral
Balchen, now missing*

Tune of 'Down by a crystal river side'

Come pity me, young maidens all,
Who am brought into wretched thrall.
My love was pressed away to sea,
And is on board the *Victory*.

When of him I did take my leave
He said, 'Dear Judy, do not grieve;
Although I absent from you be,
Stout is our ship, the *Victory*.

'Brave Balchen is a gallant man,
And will conduct us safe to land;
Then my dear Judy I shall see
When safe returns the *Victory*.'

Ah, John, indeed my heart did fail
When you to Lisbon was to sail,
For dangers they are great at sea.
Oh, now where is the *Victory*?

O John, my lovely sailor dear,
My heart is sore oppressed with fear.
A letter, true love, send to me
From on board the *Victory*.

No cruel balls has hurt my dear,
No fatal rocks you have come near;
Nor taken by an enemy,
You nor the gallant *Victory*.

Nine hundred men on board you have,
A jolly crew both stout and brave
As ever did go out to sea.
God send safe home the *Victory*.

Dear Johnny, I at Portsmouth wait
And watch for you early and late,
Wishing each moment for to see
Come sailing in the *Victory*.

☞ The fourth of the Royal Navy's ships to bear the name, *Victory*, was held to be the finest ship afloat. She encountered a violent storm in the Channel on 3 October 1744. On the following day distress flares were seen and warning guns heard, but no trace of the ship was found after the storm had subsided. Over the next few weeks wreckage including sea chests was found on the French coast, and the maintop was washed ashore on Guernsey. The *Victory* was assumed to have been lost with all hands on a reef called the Caskets, near the island of Alderney. There were 1,100 men aboard, including Admiral Sir John Balchen. The ballad (to a tune which sounds traditional but has not been positively identified) must have been written and printed while the fate of the ship and crew was still uncertain.

A New Song on the Blandford *Privateer*

Ye seamen who's a mind to go
In pursuit of new adventures,
Repair on board the *Blandford*,
With Captain Stonehouse enter;
Who cruising goes to meet his foes,
Such passions sure must please us.
We'll prizes make of all we take,
This will to fortune raise us.

Here is one chief encouragement,
Our ship belongs to Bristol.
Poor Londoners when coming home
They surely will be pressed all.
We've no such fear when home we steer
With prizes under convoy;
We'll frolic round all Bristol Town,
Sweet liberty we enjoy.

Why should we hear our time delay
In London void of pleasure?
Let's haste away to Biscay Bay
And ransack there for treasure.
Here we must creep and play bo-peep
To shun the damned press-masters;
We live in strife, even die in life,
Confined by catchpole bastards.

A health to Captain Stonehouse;
Success attend the *Blandford*.
Five guineas is advancèd us,
Come then let us enter on board.
With the *Blandford* guns we'll smoke the Dons,
Their ragged staff we'll humble.
Jack Frenchman too shall cry 'Morblew',
We'll give 'em cause to grumble.

Come fill your flowing glasses,
Let us drink and be merry.

liberty] shore leave   catchpole] bum-bailiff   morblew] morbleu, euphemism
for mordieu, 'God's death'   Dons] Spaniards   ragged staff] emblem

Take leave of all your lasses,
We can no longer tarry.
Girls, never fear; you soon shall hear
Of the *Blandford's* late arrival.
To Bristol Town then haste ye down,
Your sweethearts to revive all.

☞ The *Blandford* was launched at Bristol in 1745. Captain George Stonehouse was very successful, and in 1746 took at least nine prizes. (England was at war with France and Spain.) In January 1747 the *Blandford* brought back the *St Philip*, valued at £30,000, but Captain Stonehouse, whose leg had been shattered in the fight, died after an amputation. Later in the same year the *Blandford* was captured by a French ship. The ballad is a typical plea for recruits, emphasizing the qualities of the ship and captain, and the likelihood of success. The value of prizes was divided between the government (10 per cent) and owners (90 per cent). A captain would receive twelve shares in the spoils, an 'able sailer', one, and a boy, half. Other songs celebrated other captains and other ships, such as the *Resolution, Polly*, or *Amazon* of Liverpool and the *Antigallican* of Shields. See also 45 (below) for the *Terrible*, privateer.

43   *The Lucky Sailor*
or, The Sailor's Invitation to go with Admiral Anson

Come jolly sailors join with me,
Come jolly sailors join with me,
To fight with Anson for renown,
That we the French pride may pull down.
We'll take 'em all upon the seas,
We'll take 'em all upon the seas;
We'll make 'em strike where'er we meet,
Or serve 'em all as we've done these.

My boys, you heard what we have done,
My boys, you heard what we have done,
Ten sail of men-of-war we took,
And made the merchantmen to run.
Our admiral he ordered then,
Our admiral he ordered then
Three men-of-war to chase 'em all,
To sink and take whate'er they can.

The *Centurion* first led the van,
The *Centurion* first led the van,
And held 'em till we came up;
Then we their hides did sorely bang,
Our broadsides we on them did pour,
Our broadsides we on them did pour.
We gave the French a sour drench,
And soon their topsails made them lower.

And when they saw our fleet come up,
And when they saw our fleet come up,
They for quarters called without delay,
And their colours they that moment struck.
O, how we did rejoice and sing,
O, how we did rejoice and sing
To see such prizes we had took
For ourselves and for George our king.

O now, my boys, I'm come on shore,
O now, my boys, I'm come on shore,
I'll make you drink before we part;
Such luck I never had before.
Here is a health to those brave men,
Here is a health to those brave men
That did command this noble fleet,
Bold Anson and brave Warren.

My boys, our prizes is arrived,
My boys, our prizes is arrived,
Which when the people they did see
It did their very hearts revive.
With joy and mirth we spent the night,
With joy and mirth we spent the night
In drinking loyal healths all round,
It was such a welcome sight.

Our ships are all a-fitting up,
Our ships are all a-fitting up;
Again with Anson we will go,
I wish we may have but good luck.
My boy, I'd have you to go too,
My boy, I'd have you to go too,

drench] draught, dose

For Anson is a lucky man;
Where'er he comes he makes 'em rue.

This is the second time you've seen,
This is the second time you've seen
The waggon loads of money come,
And all taken by brave Anson.
Come now, my boys, drink off a glass,
Come now, my boys, drink off a glass.
Let's not forget now we're come home
Each bold sailor's pretty lass.

☞ George Anson (1697–1762) was a fearless and also a fortunate man. In 1740, at
the beginning of the war with France and Spain, he set off for the Pacific in
command of six ships. He returned four years later with only one, the *Centurion*,
but with treasure worth £800,000 which was paraded through London on
wagons. 'The crew of the *Centurion*', wrote the *Gentleman's Magazine*, 'receiv'd
300l. 1s. each, as part of their prize money; after which about forty of them,
attended by fiddlers, bag pipers, &c., with cockade in their hats, went to
Stratford [in the East End of London] to regale themselves'. In May 1747,
Anson, by now a vice-admiral, was cruising with a fleet off Cape Finisterre when
he encountered a force of French men-of-war with a convoy of outward-bound
merchantmen. The French scattered and, as Clowes puts it, 'after a running
fight lasting from 4 to 7 p.m., in which several French captains behaved with
great courage and others conducted themselves with equal cowardice, all the
ships which had remained in the French line struck'. Thirteen ships were taken
and £300,000 in money was found aboard the prizes. Anson was made a peer,
and his deputy, rear-admiral Peter Warren, a Knight of the Bath. A medal was
struck to commemorate the victory and also Anson's circumnavigation. The
ballad reflects the euphoria of success but fails to mention the price in lives.
Over a thousand seamen died on the voyage and the same number again, French
and English, in the battle.

44   *New Sea Song*

Our boatswain calls out for his bold British heroes,
Come listen awhile to what I do sing.
Let every man toss off his full bumper,
And drink a good health unto George our king.
And drink a good health to Suke, Moll and Kitty;
With mirth and good liquor we'll lead merry lives.
We will not be afraid to kiss or to venture
On Saturday night to our sweethearts and wives.

Our ship she is in harbour, brought safe to an anchor;
The boats are alongside, they begin for to throng.
The girls that are in them they are crying for husbands;
The one sings out 'Jemmy', the other [calls] 'John',
While the other bawls out, 'Where is my dear Harry?
If I do not see him, may I never thrive.'
Alongside of those girls you may lie but not marry
On Saturday night to our sweethearts and wives.

Our ship she is unriggèd, all ready for docking;
Straightway on board of those hulks we repair,
Where we work hard all day and at night go a-kissing:
Jack Tar is safe moored in the arms of his dear.
Straightway to the town of Venus we will venture
Our spirits to freshen, our bodies to thrive.
We will not be afraid to kiss nor yet to venture
On Saturday night to our sweethearts and wives.

Our ship she is all rigged and ready for sea, boys;
The girls that's on board they begin to look blue.
The boats are alongside to take them on shore, boys;
Says one to the other, 'Girls, what shall we do?'
Then we put to sea with a fresh-blowing breeze, boys,
And through the foaming white billows do [roar].
We paid off all debts with the flying fore-topsail,
Bid adieu to these girls and the rogues on the shore.

Now we are on the seas, like bold hearts of thunder,
Now we are on the seas we will rant and roar.
We will make all the French and the Spaniards knock under
When our two-and-thirties begin for to roar.
For to handle their dollars my fingers are itching;
If I don't be at them may I never thrive.
We will not be like misers to hoard our riches,
But we will spend them on shore with our sweethearts and wives.

☞ The war with France and Spain ended in 1748, and the ballad probably dates
from shortly before that time.

two-and-thirties] guns firing 32 pounder shot

You Britons all of courage bold,
Listen awhile and I'll unfold;
How we behaved you soon shall hear
On board the *Terrible* privateer.

Death it was our commander's name;
From London with good heart we came,
And put to sea with a pleasant gale
Over our enemies to prevail.

We touch at Plymouth for to get men,
And then to sea, boys, put again,
Once more our fortunes for to try,
When we a French ship did espy.

A letter of marque she proved to be,
And fought with us so gallantly;
But we like bold Britons did her so maul
Till down the French flag she did haul.

The *Great Alexander* was her name,
And she from Sandamingo came.
If we had but lived to bring her in
A noble prize to us she'd been.

We took her as you understand,
And boarded her with sixteen hands,
And straight for Plymouth we did steer,
But we meet with another bold privateer.

Well manned and fitted out of France,
And by them called the *Vengeance*,
She crowded sails and down on us bore
While thundering cannons aloud did roar.

When many gallant Britons fell
On board our ship, the *Terrible*,
But we boldly gave them gun for gun,
Till the blood out of our scuppers did run.

letter of marque] privateer   Sandamingo] ? Saint Domingue (Haiti)

But when down 'longside of us they came
Our shot we so smartly did exchange,
Till our anchor fluke in their forechains got
Or else 'longside of us they'd knocked.

Fain they would have got away,
When our best bower caused them to stay;
For four long ells did our anchor fluke:
This is the reason we were took.

Our third lieutenant and twelve men,
Besides three boys made the whole sixteen,
Was all was left I do declare
Before the French could board us there.

Sure, decks like ours was ne'er spread
With legs and arms; and bodies dead
Lay scattered, much to our great grief,
And our wounded men could get no relief.

But forcèd to lay in their bloody gore
Until the battle was all o'er.
So they took us and our prize that day,
And for St Maloes bore away.

But when we on board of the *Vengeance* came,
And there like captives for to remain
Until our prize could be brought in,
And our sorrows shall in fresh begin.

They stowed us down in our hold below,
Both sick and well and wounded too;
And [we] was obliged for to stay there
Till seven and twenty smothered were.

For want of air for to give them breath
Was the occasion of their death.
This was the usage we did receive
From them, as you may believe.

But when we into St Maloes got
In their town gaols, boys, was our lot;
And there on cold stones and straw to lay
All the while that we did stay.

ells] an ell was a measurement of 45 inches

But of our valiant captain's death,
To our great loss resigned his breath;
And the *Vengeance* was our overthrow,
But with vengeance we'll revenge the blow.

But still in this resolution, we
Are still resolved to let them see
That from Monsieur we'll never run:
Kill or be killed. God's will be done.

But for to conclude and make an end
Of these few lines that I have penned;
But since, thank God, we have got free,
Revenged the *Terrible*'s cause shall be.

☞ The *Terrible* privateer was fitted out at Execution Dock in London. Her captain was called Death, her first lieutenant, Devil, and her surgeon, Ghost. In December, 1756, the *Terrible* encountered the *Grand Alexandre*, homeward bound for St Malo, presumably from Saint Domingue (which is now called Haiti). The French ship was made a prize, after a sharp action in which sixteen seamen and Death's brother were killed. The *Terrible* and the *Alexandre* set a course for England, but were intercepted by another French vessel, the *Vengeance*. First the prize was retaken, then both ships attacked the *Terrible*. In the withering exchange of fire which followed, the French commander and two-thirds of his crew were killed, but so were Captain Death and most of his people. The news caused grief in England, but also pride. Some of the survivors reached England nine months later, and published accounts of the fight and their imprisonment. Several ballads also appeared. The text given here was noted in 1778 by an American sailor called Timothy Connor in a collection of songs which he wrote down during his imprisonment at Forton, near Portsmouth.

46   *Admiral Byng*

Come all ye British tars, lend an ear, lend an ear,
Come all ye British tars, lend an ear;
Come all ye British tars fro' aboard a man-o'-war,
And of bribery have a care on the seas.

I of late was admiral on the seas, on the seas,
I of late was admiral on the seas;
I of late was admiral of a squadron stout and tall,
But for gold I sold them all on the seas.

I receivèd an express from London, from London,
I receivèd an express from London;
I receivèd an express to sail up to the west,
The French to disperse from New Home.

Up the Mediterranean coast we sailed on, we sailed on,
Up the Mediterranean coast we sailed on;
Up the Mediterranean coast where the French did brag and boast,
With their whole fleet almost, near New Home.

When the French fleet did appear, and drew near and drew near,
When the French fleet did appear, and drew near;
When the French fleet did appear it puts us in a steer,
And our valour turned to fear at New Home.

I said unto brave West, 'Take the van, take the van,'
I said unto brave West, 'Take the van';
I said unto brave West, for he loved the fight the best,
'I on the rear will rest, take the van'.

When brave West did warmly act on the seas, on the seas,
When brave West did warmly act on the seas;
When brave West did warmly act I kept my mainsail back,
Lest they had been ca'd to wrack on the seas.

To further my design on the seas, on the seas,
To further my design on the seas;
To further my design I shot across the line,
Lest victory had been mine on the seas.

So now my honour's lost and is gone, and is gone,
So now my honour's lost and is gone;

express] message by express bearer   New Home] Port Mahon   steer] stir
wrack] ruin, downfall

106

So now my honour's lost, no more of Benwell boast,
Up the Mediterranean coast near New Home.

It's decreed me by the king, as I hear, as I hear,
It's decreed me by the king, as I hear;
It's decreed me by the king to be shot by my marines
For the misdeeds I have done on the seas.

All traitors gets their doom, so maun I, so maun I,
All traitors gets their doom, so maun I;
All traitors gets their doom, wears the sackcloth in their bloom,
Because it is their doom, so maun I.

☞ The Hon. John Byng (1704–57) was the fourth son of Viscount Torrington, Admiral of the Fleet. By 1745 he was an admiral himself, and at the beginning of the Seven Years' War in 1756 he commanded a fleet sent to Minorca to assist the British forces there which were under siege from the French. By the time he arrived the island was in French hands except for Port Mahon, where the British garrison was holding out. In an action against the French fleet Admiral West fought well, but Byng was indecisive, and four days later he left Port Mahon to its fate and returned to Gibraltar. When the news reached England there was a tremendous outcry, including assertions that Byng had been bribed by the French. He was court-martialled, and on 14 March 1757, shot on the quarter-deck of the *Monarch*, in Portsmouth harbour. Voltaire wrote in *Candide* that the British seemed to need to shoot an admiral from time to time '*pour encourager les autres*'. A clutch of ballads celebrated the scandal in England, with titles like 'A Rueful Story, Admiral B---g's Glory; or, Who run away first?' and 'An Address from the Regions below to A---l B---g'. The text given here surfaced in Aberdeenshire only in 1908. It shares the metre of 'Captain Kid's Farewell' (33) and was presumably sung to the 'Coming down' tune, a variant of which is given.

47   *The Wreck of the* Rambler

46 Benwell] near Newcastle upon Tyne. The connection with the Byng family is not clear.   maun] must

It happenèd to be on one certain day,
A ship, the *Rambeler*, at anchor did lay;
The very night the gale came down
She broke from her anchor and away she did go.

Oh, the rain pouring down was a dismal sight,
The sea running high over our foretop;
We had some canvas that was neatly spread,
Thinking we could weather the old Ram Head.

'A boat, a boat, my good fellows all,
And ready to answer when I on you call.
Come launch your boats your lives for to save,
I'm afraid this night the sea will be your grave'.

The boats they were launchèd, and in the seas were tossed;
Some got in, but soon were lost.
There were some in one place and some in another,
And the watch down below they were all smothered.

Now when this sad news reached Plymouth town,
The loss of the *Rambeler* and most of her men,
There was only three that could tell the tale,
How our ship did behave in that dreadful gale.

So come all you pretty maids wheresoever that you be,
The loss of your true loves in the *Rambelee*;
For Plymouth Town it flowed with tears
When they heard of the sad and dread affair.

[The last two lines of each verse are repeated]

☞ In February 1760 the *Gentleman's Magazine* reported: 'Friday 15. It blew a
hurricane, by which much damage was done both at land and in the river. . . . At

Rambler, Rambeler, Rambelee] Ramillies   was a dismal sight] one version has: 'in
terrible drops'

108

sea it did incredible damage to the shipping; in almost every harbour some persons perished in boats and in ships; but the loss most to be regretted is that of the unfortunate *Ramillies*, capt. *Taylor*, with 734 men. Being embay'd within the Bolt-head (which they had mistaken for the Ram-head, and imagined they were going into *Plymouth Sound*) and close up on the rocks, they let go their anchors, and cut away all their masts, and rode safe till five in the evening, when the gale increased so much 'tis impossible to describe; they parted, and only one midshipman and twenty-five men out of the whole, jumped off the stern on the rocks, and were saved.' A song about the wreck survived, apparently without benefit of print, for almost two hundred years. This version was sung to the composer, E. J. Moeran, in a Suffolk pub in 1947.

48   *Captain Barton's Distress on Board the*
              Lichfield

being under Slavery seventeen Months and fourteen Days

Come all you brave seamen that ploughs on the main,
Give ear to my story [so] true to maintain,
Concerning the *Lichfield* that was cast away
On the Barbary shore by the dawn of the day.

The tenth of November, the weather being fine,
We sailed from Kinsale, five ships of the line,
With two bombs and two frigates, with transports also,
We was bound unto Goree to fight our proud foe.

The twenty-ninth of November by dawn of the light
We spièd land that put us in a fright;
We strove for to weather but we run quite aground;
The seas mountain high made our sorrow abound.

Our mast we cut away our wreck for to ease;
And being exposed to the mercy of the seas,
Where one hundred and thirty poor seamen did die,
Whilst we all for mercy most loudly did cry.

Two hundred and twenty of us got on shore;
No sooner we landed but [were] stripped by the Moors,
Without any subsistence but dead hogs and sheep
That was drove on shore by the sea from the ship.

48 Kinsale] in Ireland   Goree] in West Africa

For seven days together with us did remain,
Our bodies quite naked for to increase our pain
Till some Christian merchant that lives in the land,
Sent us relief by his bountiful hand.

Unto our fleet the same fate did share,
Then unto Morocco we all marchèd there,
Where they are captives in slavery to be
Till old England thought proper for to set them free.

When the black king we all came before
He stroked his long beard; by Mahomet he swore,
'They are all stout and able, and fit for the hoe.
Pray, to my gardens, pray let them go.'

We had cruel Moors our drivers to be.
By the dawn of the day at the hoe we must be
Until four o'clock in the afternoon,
Without any submission, boys. Work was our doom.

If that you offer for to strike a Moor,
Straightway to the king they will have you before,
Where they will bastinade you till you have your fill.
If that will not do you, blood they will spill.

So now in Morocco we shall remain
Until our ambassador cross the main,
Where our ransom he'll bring, and soon set us free,
And then to Gibraltar we will go speedily.

So now, my brave boys, to old England we're bound,
We will have store of liquors our sorrow [to] drown.
We will drink a good health. Success never fail.
Success to the bawd and the whores of Kinsale.

☞ In December 1758 Goree was seized from the French. Commodore Keppel's
fleet encountered a gale while outward bound on 28 November. The loss of the
Lichfield is mentioned in a ballad celebrating the victory at Goree:

> So, steering on the lee shore until the break of day,
> We spied a lofty sail on the Barbary shore to lay.
> In great distress she seemed to be;

black king] the Emperor of Morocco   submission] remission   bastinade]
beat on the soles of the feet

Her guns all overboard threw she,
Which proved the *Lichfield* for to be,
With all her British boys.

Captain Matthew Barton (?1715–95) and some 220 survivors of his crew of 350 were ransomed by the British Government, and arrived at Gibraltar in June 1760. The ballad given here probably appeared soon afterwards.

49   *The Jolly Sailor's True Description of a*
Man-of-War

When first on board of a man-of-war
We go, whether by press or enter,
And alongside of our ship we come,
We boldly in her venture.
Such twigging then at we fresh men:
'They're clever fellows', some say;
While the buffers stand with their rattans,
Crying, 'Keep down out of the gangway'.

Then aft upon the quarter-deck
We go, it being common;
Our officers examine us, to know
Who and who are seamen.
There's some are seamen, some are freemen;
Some one thing, some another.
Then we down below on the maindeck go,
Boys, after one another.

Next to old Trinculo we go
For an order to get our hammocks,
Then aft again and down amain,
Not forgetting our stomachs.
The steward pens, he takes our names,
And tells us to our messes;
But nipping there they can't forbear,
For the devil them possesses.

49 by press or enter] as a pressed man or a volunteer   venture] rhymes
with 'enter'   twigging] beating   rattans] canes   amain] straightaway
tell us] allocates us   nipping] sarcasm

Then up again upon the deck
So briskly, boys, we bundle;
Since we have well secured our peck
We have no cause to grumble.
Then we clap on what we heave upon,
Some piping, others singing.
There's 'Hoist away', likewise 'Belay';
Thus we make a beginning.

When once our ship has got all in,
And nothing now neglected,
To think of sea we do begin,
Our orders soon expected.
Then with a career we get all clear,
In readiness for unmooring;
Boats alongside with wind and tide
To carry the women ashore in.

'All hands unmoor', the boatswain calls,
And he pipes at every hatchway.
If you Tom Cockswain's traverse tip him,
Take care he don't catch you;
For without doubt if he finds you out
You may be sure within you,
Over face and eyes to your surprise
He'll arm you without mercy.

The capstan is already manned.
Shall we hear the boatswain holloa?
Sometimes he's listening at a stand
To hear what answers follow.
We have not brought to, there's such ado,
While some are calling the swabbers;
Now heave away without delay.
Boys, hold on the nippers.

The boatswain and his mates are piping,
Crying, 'Men, heave a rally';
And often forward they are piking
To have a rout in the galley.

peck] food   clap on] hold on to   career] rush   Tom Cockswain's
traverse tip him] avoid work   arm you] strike you; possibly a misprint for 'warm you'
at a stand] at a standstill   piking] going; 'skiving off', in modern slang   have a
rout] roust people out

'What are you about? Away with us out.'
To leave our victuals we abhor it;
With cuffs and knocks leave kettles and pots,
And the devil cuff them for it.

'Heave and in sight, men, heave away,'
From forward the boatswain is calling;
'Heave a turn or two without delay,
Stand by the capstan for pealing.'
Then one and all to the cat do fall;
We haul both strong and able
Till presently from forward they cry,
'Below, stick out the cable.'

We cat our anchors then with speed,
And nimbly pass the stoppers;
Then next to fish it we proceed,
Our shank-painter so proper,
Which we do pass securely fast,
And clap well on a seizing.
Our anchors be sure can't be too secure,
It stands to sense and reason.

When once our ship she is unmoored,
Our swelling sails so neatly,
With foretack and maintack also,
Our sheets hauled aft completely;
Then away we sail with a fresh gale
On a voyage or a station;
Like English hearts we'll play our parts
In defence of the British nation.

The best cry we like to hear
On board, as I'm a sinner,
Is when from the quarterdeck they call
To the boatswain to pipe to dinner.
Such crowding then amongst the men;
Some grumble, others jangle.
You're nobody there without you swear,
And boldly stand the wrangle.

There's greenhorn fellows; some on board
Before ne'er saw salt water;
When come to sea, upon my word,
The case with them does alter.

They better know how to follow the plough,
With good fat bacon and cabbage;
When seasick took like death they look,
Ready to bring up guts and garbage.

When stormy winds begin to blow
Our ship is in great motion;
To carry our victuals safe down below
It requires a good notion.
We often fall down the hatchway with all,
From the top to the bottom; lie sprawling.
Such laughing then among the men,
And loudly the butcher calling.

There are snotty boys of midshipmen,
Ha'n't yet done shitting yellow;
As to their age, some hardly ten
Strike many a brave fellow,
Who dare not prate at any rate,
Nor seem in the least to mumble.
They'll frap you still, do what you will;
It is but a folly to grumble.

Now to conclude and make an end
In a full flowing brimmer,
Let every one drink to his friend:
The bowl it seems to look thinner.
We'll fill it again like sons of men,
And drink bad luck to the purser.
He cheats us with ease of oatmeal and peas,
Such rogues there can't be worser.

Printed and sold in Aldermary Church Yard, Bow Lane, London

☞ The ballad must have been written by a seaman or an ex-seaman, for it shows an intimate knowledge of life on a man-of-war. It was probably published between 1762 and about 1795, though it has the same woodcut of a ship in full sail as 31. A shortened version appeared some time in the 1790s.

frap] strike

The Seamen's Distress

As we lay musing in our beds,
So well and so warm at ease,
I thought upon those lodging beds
Poor seamen have at seas.

Last Easter Day in the morning fair
We was not far from land,
Where we spied a mermaid on a rock,
With comb and glass in hand.

The first came up the mate of our ship,
With lead and line in hand,
To sound and see how deep we was
From any rock or sand.

The next came up the boatswain of our ship,
With courage stout and bold:
'Stand fast, stand fast, my brave, lively lads.
Stand fast, my brave hearts of gold.'

Our gallant ship has gone to wreck,
Which was so lately trimmed;
The raging seas have sprung a leak,
And the salt water does run in.

Our gold and silver, and all our clothes,
And all that ever we had,
We forcèd was to heave them overboard,
Thinking our lives to save.

115

In all the number that was on board
Was five hundred and sixty-four,
And all that ever came alive on shore
There was but poor ninety-five.

The first bespoke the captain of our ship,
And a well-spoke man was he:
'I have a wife in fair Plymouth town,
And a widow I fear she must be.'

The next bespoke the mate of our ship,
And a well-bespoke man was he:
'I have a wife in fair Portsmouth town,
And a widow I fear she must be.'

The next bespoke the boatswain of our ship,
And a well-bespoke man was he:
'I have a wife in fair Exeter,
And a widow I fear she must be.'

The next bespoke the little cabin boy,
And a well-bespoke boy was he:
'I am as sorry for my mother dear
As you are for your wives all three.

'Last night when the moon shined bright
My mother had sons five,
But now she may look in the salt seas
And find but one alive.'

'Call a boat, call a boat, you little Plymouth boys,
Don't you hear how the trumpet sound?
For the want of a boat our gallant ship is lost,
And the most of our merry men drowned.'

Whilst the raging seas do roar,
And the lofty winds do blow,
And we poor seamen do lie on the top,
Whilst the landmen lies below.

☞ In a seventeenth-century ballad, 'The Praise of Sailors' (11), the appearance of
a mermaid (perhaps in line with Robert Graves' identification of her with
Aphrodite) is taken as a good omen. Here, in a text from a garland printed in
about 1765 and deriving from the earlier ballad, the reverse is true. Disaster is

not only presaged, but it occurs. The title given to many versions is simply 'The Mermaid', and the usual tone is light-hearted, and at variance with the meaning of the words. The fine Aeolian tune given here from the singing of a Hampshire man befits a serious text.

51 *The* Dolphin's *Return*

Tune, 'The Lilies of France' 1768

Ye bold British tars, who to glory are free,
Who dare venture your lives for your fortunes at sea,
Yourself for a while of your pleasures disrobe,
And attend to a tale of a voyage round the globe;
For the *Dolphin*'s returned, and such tidings does bring
As may welcome us home to our country and king.

The twentieth of August, the year sixty-six,
By command of our captain the signal we fix;
In the Sound of old Plymouth our ship we unmoored,
With our consort, the *Swallow*, and consort well stored;
But now we're returned, and such tidings we bring
[As may welcome us home to our country and king].

The wind being fair the next day we set sail,
Blest at once with a fresh and prosperous gale,

And straightway our course for Madeira we steered.
No danger we saw and no hardship we feared,
For we sailed round the world such tidings to bring
As might welcome us home to our country and king.

We touched at Madeira, St Jago likewise,
For the sake of fresh water and other supplies;
But at neither of these could we make any stay,
For the course of our voyage would admit no delay.
We were bound round the world such tidings to bring
As might welcome us home to our country and king.

When Magellan's Straits we first entered we found
Such giants of men that in all the world round
None with them could compare or for size or for height,
For the smallest of these were from six feet to eight.
Yet these are but trifles of tidings to bring;
We've a present more worthy our country and king.

In Port Famine we anchored and took in our store
Of both water and wood, for it yielded no more.
Discharging our store ship, our anchors we weighed,
And we worked through the straits; no time we delayed;
But now are returned, and such tidings we bring
As may welcome us home to our country and king.

A tedious long passage it was for to go
With our consort so dull that we took her in tow;
But on April the twelfth we got clear of the straits,
Though the *Swallow*, we fear, a longer time waits.
Yet we are returned, and such tidings we bring
As may welcome us home to our country and king.

Then we ploughed the South Ocean, such land to discover
As amongst other nations has made such a pother.
We found it, my boys, and with joy be it told:
For beauty such islands you ne'er did behold.
We've the pleasure ourselves the tidings to bring
As may welcome us home to our country and king.

St Jago] Sao Tiago (Cape Verde Islands)   giants] this notion originated in an estimate given by Captain John Byron (the poet's grandfather), who commanded the *Dolphin* on its record twenty-two month circumnavigation starting in June 1764. Wallis stopped to measure a number of Patagonians. Their height varied between six feet five and six feet seven inches, which made them very tall, but not giant.   Port Famine] ? nickname for Punta Arenas   pother] fuss, commotion

For wood, water, fruit and provision well stored
Such an isle as King George's the world can't afford,
For to each of these islands great Wallis gave name,
Which will e'er be recorded in annals of fame.
We'd the fortune to find them, and homeward to bring
The tidings, a tribute to country and king.

☞ After the Seven Years' War the European powers bent their energies to a frantic
rush to discover, and if possible annex, new territories. In August 1766 the
frigate, *Dolphin* (Captain Samuel Wallis), and the tiny sloop, *Swallow* (Commander Philip Carteret), set off round the world. In the Straits of Magellan
Wallis left behind the sluggish *Swallow* and went on to find Tahiti, which he
named George III Island. Carteret in his turn discovered Pitcairn Island, which
he called after the midshipman who first sighted it. After many hardships Wallis
returned to Plymouth in May 1768, and Carteret in the following March. The
ballad was written between the two dates, to a dance tune.

52   *Captain James*

who was hung and gibbeted in England for starving to death his cabin boy

Come all you noble, bold commanders
That the raging ocean use,
By my sad fate now take a warning,
Your poor sailors don't abuse.

Richard Pavy was my servant,
And a sprightly boy was he;
His parents did apprentice bind him
For to cross the raging sea.

'Twas in a voyage to Carolina,
And as we were returning home
Cruelly this boy I murdered
In a manner never known.

'Twas some little offence he gave me,
Did my bloody heart enrage,
Then straightaway to the mast I tied him,
Where I kept him many days.

With his legs and arms extended,
Him no succour would I give,
Saying if my men relieved him
Not one moment should they live.

When three days thus I had kept him
He for hunger loud did cry:
'Oh for Christ's sake now relieve me
Or with hunger I shall die.'

Eighteen bitter stripes I gave him,
Made the purple gore to run;
There was none that dared to save him,
Such a thing was never known.

When seven days I thus had kept him
He now to languish did begin,
Begging for a little water.
I some urine gave to him.

He, poor soul, refused to drink it;
What I prepared, when I'd done,
I made him drink the purple gore
That from his bleeding wounds did run.

Oh the cries he sent unto me,
'Twould have pierced a Christian's heart.
Oftentimes he cried: 'Dear mother,
Did you know the cruel smart

'That your little son doth suffer?
Sure your tender heart would break.
My bitter grief no tongue can utter,
O Lord relieve me from this fate.

'Oh that I had but one small morsel
That the dogs they would despise.
I pray God send me down some water
From the blessed lofty skies.'

When nine days I thus had kept him,
Up to him I then did go.
He cried: 'Dear and loving master,
One good favour to me show.

'Do not leave me here to perish;
Kill me—send me to my grave,
Or one bit of bread afford me.'
His excrements I then him gave.

Excrements which he had voided,
Forcing him the same to eat;
And because he did refuse it,
Eighteen stripes I gave him straight.

With that the distressèd creature
To his saviour loud did cry.
In this wretched situation
This poor creature now did die.

Often did my men upbraid me;
I like fury cursed and swore,
Saying, 'I'll have you hanged for pirates
If I live to get on shore.'

Sailors, seeing my intention,
Little unto me did say;
But they had me apprehended
When we returnèd from the sea.

I thought my money would have saved me,
Knowing the boys' friends were poor.
Oh the cries of his dear mother
Would have grieved your heart full sore.

She resolved to prosecute me;
She no gold nor bribe would take.
Captain James, for cruel murder,
Now the gibbet is my fate.

How now can a glance of pity
Be cast on me for this great crime?
It doth appear to every Christian
A foul blot upon mankind.

How now can I call for mercy,
Who no mercy would afford
To an innocent poor creature;
Yet some mercy show me, Lord.

I do lay upon thy mercy
For my death approaches nigh.
Captain James for cruel murder
Now must on a gibbet die.

Nathaniel Coverly, Jun. Printer, Milk Street, Boston [Massachusetts]

☞ This text was originally printed between 1810 and 1814, but the ballad was
circulating orally as early as 1768, when a version was copied into the back of the
logbook of the American brig, *Two Brothers*. 'Captain Jones' turns up again in
further logbooks in 1840 and 1847, and from Nova Scotia and New Brunswick
singers over a century later. 'A copy of verse made as Capt. Elder's cruelty to his
Boy' seems to be a British adaptation of 'Captain Jones'. A parallel, and possibly
related, song in Britain, 'The Captain's Apprentice', may derive from a
broadside of about 1800, entitled 'A New Copy of Verses made on Captain
Mills, now under Confinement in Newgate, at Bristol, for the murder of
Thomas Brown, his Apprentice Boy'. Both may well deal with actual incidents,
but if not they reflect real events such as the murder of a foremast hand and a
cabin boy, for which a Liverpool captain was tried and acquitted in 1764, the
death of a marine at Portsmouth severely beaten on the orders of his commanding officer and left all night 'fastened to the mizen shrouds with his arms
extended' in 1766, and the killing of a cabin boy by a blow from a handspike, for
which his captain stood trial in 1798. The murder of a seaman by his captain in
1857 has an uncanny resemblance, down to the revolting details, to the case of
Captain James (see 115).

53   *William Taylor*

William was a bashful lover,
William loved a lady fair.
Bells a-ringing, birds a-singing,
To the church they did repair.

Four-and-twenty brisk young sailors
Dressed themselves in rich array;
Instead of William being married,
Pressed they were and sent to sea.

She followed after her true lover,
Went by the name of William Carr;
Her soft hands and milk-white fingers
All besmeared with pitch and tar.

She dressed herself in man's array,
And boldly fought among the rest.
At last the wind blew open her waistcoast,
And exposed her milk-white breast.

Then the news went to the captain.
He says: 'Pray, what wind has blown you here?'
'Kind sir', says she, 'I'm in search of my lover
Whom you have pressed I love so dear.'

'If you are in search of your true lover
Tell to me his name, I pray.'
'Kind sir', says she, ''twas William Taylor
Whom you pressed the other day.'

'If William Taylor is your true lover
He has proved cruel and severe.
If you rise early in the morning
You will see him walking with his lady fair.'

Then she called for her sword and pistol,
Sword and pistol at her command,
And she shot sweet William Taylor
With his bride at his right hand.

Then the news went to the captain;
He heartily laughed at all the fun.
Then he called her his best lieutenant
Over a ship of five hundred ton.

☞ The themes of pressed man and female sailor combine here. The first is real enough to historians, but the second might be seen as fanciful. However, there are plenty of documented examples, including Hannah Snell, who appeared on the stage in the mid-1750s and sang about her nautical adventures as James Gray, and the nameless woman described in an account of 1757: 'A young person, five feet high, aged about nineteen, who entered in January last on board the *Resolution* privateer, Capt. Barber, under the name of Arthur Douglas, proceeded with the ship from London to this port [Liverpool], went aloft to furl the sails, &c., when called upon, was frequently mustered amongst the marines at the time they exercised the small arms, and in short executed the office of a landsman [unskilled sailor] in all shapes with alacrity, was on Saturday last discovered to be a woman by one of her mess-mates.' 'Tis said that he found out her sex on the passage, and that she, to prevent a discovery, then promised to permit him to keep her company when they arrived here; but as soon as they came into port refused his addresses. The officers in general give her a very modest character, and say by her behaviour that she must have had a genteel education. She has changed her clothes, but will not satisfy any of them with her name or quality; only that she left home on account of a breach of promise of her lover. 'Tis remarkable that during their passage down, on the appearance of a sail, she was eager to be fighting, and no ways affected with fear or sea sickness.' The ballad, too, has a bellicose lady, but it is clearly fanciful. This text appeared in the log of the ship, *Nellie*, of Edgartown, Massachusetts, in 1769. Like the many other versions since popular across Britain and America, it derives from 'The Female Sailor's Garland' printed between 1712 and '20, which describes 'The passionate Love between *William Taylor* and fair *Elizabeth*, whose Love he having gain'd & preparing for Marriage, he was maliciously press'd from his Friends and Bride as they were going to perform the Marriage Rites, how *Elizabeth* put her self in Man's apparel, and enter'd her self on board a Ship of her own Name, where she perform'd Seaman's Labour to a Miracle; with an Account how at last she was discover'd, and how the Noble Captain, thro' Pity of their Misfortunes, sent for & enquir'd of the neighbouring Ships, till he found her Love, whom he got released, with an Account, how he brought them to *London*, where he see them marry'd, to their great Joy and Satisfaction.'

54   *Spanish Ladies*

Farewell and adieu to you, Spanish ladies,
Farewell and adieu to you, ladies of Spain;
For we have received orders to sail to old England,
But we hope in a short time to see you again.

We'll rant and we'll roar like true British sailors,
We'll rant and we'll roar across the salt seas;
Until we strike soundings in the Channel of old England:
From Ushant to Scilly 'tis thirty-five leagues.

Then we hove our ship to, with the wind at sou'-west, my boys,
Then we hove our ship to, for to strike soundings clear;
Then we filled the main topsail and bore right away, my boys,
And straight up the Channel of old England did steer.

So the first land we made it is called the Deadman,
Next Ram Head off Plymouth, Start, Portland and the Wight;
We sailèd by Beachy, by Fairly and Dungeness,
And then bore away for the South Foreland light.

Now the signal it was made for the grand fleet to anchor,
All on the Downs that night for to meet;
Then stand by your stoppers, see clear your shank-painters,
Haul all your clew garnets, stick out tacks and sheets.

Now let every man take off his full bumper,
Let every man take off his full bowl;
For we will be jolly and drown melancholy,
With a health to each jovial and true-hearted soul.

This was a Royal Navy song, originally sung aboard ships homeward bound
from the Mediterranean. Then it was adopted by merchant seamen, and used as

Ushant] anglicization of Ouessant, an island off the west of Finisterre   Dead-
man] in Cornwall; now called Dodman Point   Ram Head] now called Rame
Head   Start] Start Point is in Devon, near Dartmouth   Portland] Portland
Bill, in Dorset   the Wight] Isle of Wight   Beachy] Beachy Head, near
Hastings, in Sussex   Fairly] now Fairlight Down; also near Hastings   Dun-
geness] in Kent   South Foreland] near Dover

a capstan shanty; the whalermen had their own version. The earliest text I have seen is from the *Nellie*'s logbook of 1769, but the triumphant enumeration of Channel landmarks is mangled, probably through mishearing or misunderstanding by American sailors, and reads: 'The first land we made it was called the deadman Then Ramhead of Plymouth doth start London white Sailed East past Beachy Folley and Underneys Until we roused the Forlan light.' The text from Captain Marryat's *Poor Jack* (1840) has been used here, together with a tune in a minor key from Chappell, though modern sailors use the major. Melville had the song sung aboard the *Pequod*, and in *White Jacket* (1850) remarked that it was 'a favourite thing with British man-of-war's men'. Even by 1906, according to Stone, it was 'still much sung in the navy', and Clements, who heard it from merchant seamen at about the same time, found the last verse 'as literally exact as a mathematical formula' and said of the whole that apart from 'Rolling Home' (116), 'no sweeter song ever gave expression to the homing instinct of the human heart'.

55 *A New Song, called the Frolicsome Sea Captain, or Tit for tat*

All you that delight in a frolicsome song,
I'll tell you a story before it be long.
It's of a sea captain, a frolicsome spark,
Who played with a sailor's fair wife in the dark.

John Linson the sailor was callèd by name;
His wife was a fair and beautiful dame.
On board she would go her brisk husband to see;
Thinks the captain: 'My girl, you're a supper for me.'

The captain his chops did water full sore.
One day he commanded all women on shore;
And every sailor on board he must be,
Whilst he this fair charmer would go for to see.

Young beautiful Molly took leave of her dear,
And after her the captain he quickly did steer;
And after her the captain he quickly went home,
And began for to make a lamentable moan.

'You fairest of creatures take pity on me,
And keep a little secret I'll tell unto thee;
The charms of your beauty my favour has won,
And if you deny me I'm surely undone.'

'Forbear, noble captain, your suit it is vain.
My husband's a sailor that ploughs on the main,
And you are his captain; so be not so base,
For we both shall rue it if he knew the cause.'

'Here's fifty bright guineas, my joy and delight,
I'll give you to lie with you all night.
His horns he may take for a venture at sea,
And I'll use him well in every degree.'

The sight of the gold did tempt this fair dame
That soon she consented to play at the game.
The captain so surely lay with her that night,
And he paid her the fifty good guineas so bright.

His bedfellow pleased him so well to the life
He oftentimes kissed her and left his own wife.
At length the young sailor heard this by and by,
But he kept it as snug as a pig in a sty.

One day he resolvèd to know what was done;
In the dusk of the evening went into the room,
And under the bed he lay both snug and warm
Till she sent for the captain, thinking little harm.

She said: 'My dear jewel, my husband's on board.'
'I doubt it', said the captain. She said: 'By my word,
He gave me a kiss and bade me goodnight.'
Then said the captain: 'I'll enjoy my delight.'

They stripped off their clothes and into bed goes,
And began to jumble in a huzzy hoze.
They tumbled the sailor so under the bed
That soon he found the captain had hornèd his head.

He lay snug and warm till they were fast asleep,
Then from under the bed he gently did creep;
He put on the captain's laced breeches and coat,
His shoes and his stockings to make up the joke.

venture] on occasion, sailors were allowed to do a small amount of trading on their own account, and goods so carried were called 'ventures'   huzzy hoze] probably an invented phrase, but the meaning is clear

127

He dressed himself up from top to toe,
And home to the captain's lady he did go.
He knocked at the door with courage so bold,
Dressed all in his glittering robes of gold.

The maid let him in; being late in the night,
The girl half asleep she reached him a light.
He said: 'Where's your mistress?' She said: 'She's in bed.'
'Come, open my chamber door quickly,' he said.

To be stark drunk himself he did frame.
The lady said: 'Captain, you run your own game.
Sometimes all the night you from me do roll,
And when you come home you're as drunk as an owl.'

He leapt into bed, and the candle put out.
The lady she turned her backside in a huff.
He mumbled and grumbled as sots they will do,
He pulled her and hauled her for to buckle to.

'You'll tear my lace smock,' said the lady so fair.
'Your breath smells so strong of the ale, wine and beer,
I can't turn to you, so seize me no more.
I suppose you have been carousing all night with a whore.'

He made her no answer, but played with her knees;
At length this young lady began to be pleased.
So he tit for tat with the captain did play,
And slept in her arms till the break of the day.

When the lady awoke and beheld his face,
Then she cried out in a pitiful case.
He said: 'My dear charmer, be not in a fright,
For the captain hath been with my wife all the night.'

He told her the story, and when she did hear
With wonder the lady began for to stare.
She laughed till her sides she did hold at the joke,
For to think how the captain did fret for his coat.

Said the lady: 'I'll go in my coach, I protest,
And see how he looks in his tarpollian dress.'

tarpollian] tarpaulin; that is, sailor's

The sailor put on his embroidered array,
So both to the captain they straight took their way.

Then up the stairs they both nimbly tripped.
The captain in his short jacket was fixed.
He stared at them both, but said never a word;
Said the sailor: 'I thought you had been on board.'

Jack lift up his cane and gave him a stroke.
'Zounds', said the captain, 'Jack, pull off my coat.'
'Husband,' said the lady, 'pray where might you be,
When he got your coat and came home to me?

'I am sure it has causèd a woeful mistake.'
'Sure', said the captain, 'you have not horned my pate.'
'Dear husband,' said she, 'I say little for that,
For if he did you know it was but tit for tat.'

'Here are fifty bright guineas. Jack, pull off my coat.
Of this to the sailors may be your report.
There is many can match us, you very well know,
So we are cuckolds, boys, all in a row.'

☞ The themes of cuckoldry, the biter bit, and the use of darkness to enable a man
to substitute himself in bed for another combine here to produce a song which
was widely popular in the eighteenth and nineteenth centuries, to judge by the
large number of different printings, though, curiously, there seems no record
from oral tradition. This text comes from a chapbook published in Belfast in
1769.

56 *Captain Glen's Unhappy Voyage to New Barbary*

There was a ship and a ship of fame
Launched off the stocks, bound to the main
With a hundred and fifty brisk young men,
Was picked and chosen every one.

William Glen was our captain's name;
He was a brisk and a tall young man,
As bold a sailor as went to sea,
For he was bound to New Barbary.

The first of April we did set sail,
Blest with a pleasant and prosperous gale,
For we were bound to New Barbary
With all our whole ship's company.

We had not sailèd one league, but two,
Till all our whole ship's jovial crew
They all fell sick, but sixty-three,
As we went to New Barbary.

One night the captain he did dream
There was a voice which said to him:
'Prepare you and your company.
Tomorrow's night you must lodge with me.'

This waked our captain in a fright,
It being the third watch of the night;
Then for his boatswain he did call,
And told to him his secrets all.

'When I in England did remain
The holy sabbath I did profane;
In drunkenness I took delight,
Which does my trembling soul affright.

'There's one thing more I do rehearse,
Which I shall mention in this verse:
A squire I slew in Staffordshire,
All for the love of a lady fair.

Barbary] the coastal region of North Africa. The name derives from that of the
Berber inhabitants.

'Now 'tis his ghost, I am afraid,
That hath to me such terror bred.
Although the king has pardoned me
He's daily in my company.'

'O worthy captain, since 'tis so,
No mortal of it e'er shall know.
So keep this secret in your breast,
And pray to God to give you rest.'

They had not sailed a league, but three,
Till raging grew the roaring sea;
There rose a tempest in the skies,
Which filled our hearts with great surprise.

Our mainmast sprung by the break of day,
Which made our rigging all give way;
Which did our seamen sore affright,
The terrors of that fatal night.

Up then spoke the foremast man,
As he did by the foreyard stand.
He cried: 'The Lord receive my soul';
So to the bottom he did fall.

The sea did wash both fore and aft
Till scarce one sail aboard was left;
Our yards were split and our rigging tore,
The like you never saw before.

The boatswain then he did declare
The captain was a murderer,
Which did enrage the whole ship's crew:
Our captain overboard we threw.

Our treacherous captain being gone,
Immediately there was a calm;
The winds did calm and the raging sea,
As we went to New Barbary.

fatal] fateful

131

Now when we came to the Spanish shore
Our goodly ship for to repair,
The people all were amazed to see
Our dismal case and misery.

But when our ship was in repair,
To fair England our course did steer;
But when we came to London Town
Our dismal case we then made known.

Now many wives their husbands lost,
Whom they lamented to their cost,
Which caused them to weep bitterly,
These tidings fom New Barbary.

A hundred and fifty brisk young men
Did to our goodly ship belong;
Of all our whole ship's company
Our number was but sixty-three.

Now seamen all where'er you be,
I pray a warning take by me;
As you love your life, have a care
You never sail with a murderer.

'Tis never more I do intend
For to cross o'er the raging main,
But I'll live in peace in my own country,
And so I end my tragedy.

☞ The idea of a ship's being endangered by the presence aboard of a guilty Jonah-like figure inspired several powerful songs, from 'William Grismond's Down-fall' to 'The Banks of Green Willow'. Of 'Captain Glen' John Masefield writes that it is 'an example of the terrible fo'c'sle ballad, which the old sailors sometimes sing when they are cheerful. It is not good poetry, but I know no poem which has so deep an effect, when sung as the sailors sing it, in a steady, clear, slightly changing tone, which brings out, as the chorus in a tragedy, with ever-increasing presage, the line "As we went to New Barbary".' It was sung all over the British Isles and North America, under various titles, including 'Sir William Gower', 'The Cork Trader' and 'The New York Trader'. The text given here dates from about 1770.

Bold Princess Royal

On the fourteenth of February we sailed from the land
In the bold *Princess Royal*, bound for Newfoundland.
We had forty bright seamen, our ship's company,
So boldly from the east'ard to the west'ard bore we.

We had not been sailing scarce days two or three
When a man from our topmast a sail he did see;
Come bearing down on us to see where we bore,
And under her mizen black colours she wore.

'Great God,' cried our captain, 'what shall we do now?
Here comes a bold pirate to rob us I know.'
'Oh no,' cried our chief mate, 'that shall not be so.
We will shake out our reef, my boys, and away from him we'll go.'

It was the next morning at the dawning of day,
This lofty, large pirate shot under our lee.
'Whence came you?' cried the pirate. We answered him so:
'We are out of fair London, bound for Callao.'

'Then back your main topsails and heave your ship to,
For I have a letter to send down to you.'
'If I back my main topsails and heave my ship to,
It will be for some pilot, not alongside of you.'

He chased us to the east'ard all that livelong day,
He chased us to the west'ard but he couldn't make no way.
He fired shots after us but none did prevail,
And the bold *Princess Royal* soon showed him her tail.

Callao] in Peru   to send down to you] some versions have 'to send home by you'

'Oh now', cried our captain, 'that pirate is gone,
Go down for your grog, my boys, go down every one.
Go down for your grog, my boys, and be of good cheer,
For while we've got sea room, bold lads, never fear.'

☞ Joanna Colcord suggests, without supporting argument, that this dates from the time of the American War of Independence, or shortly before. Bob Roberts believed that the ship, a fast packet plying between Harwich and Holland, and later converted to cargo-carrying, was the last to be attacked by a pirate in the western approaches. The song was only occasionally seen in print (not at all before the nineteenth century), but it was popular in Britain (especially East Anglia) and North America, with versions seldom varying much. This set comes from the shepherd, John Copper (1817–98), of Rottingdean, Sussex, via his family tradition.

58   *Jack Tar*

'Come brave honest Jack Tar, once more will you venture?
Press warrants they are out: I would have you to enter,
Take some Spanish prize, as we've done before O.'
'Yes, and be cheated of them all, as we were in the last war O.'

'No man that sails with me shall e'er be abusèd,
So Jack come and enter, you shall be well usèd.
You shall be boatswain's mate, Jack, so boldly come and enter,
And not like a dog be hauled on board of the tender.'

'Dear captain,' he said then, 'don't talk of your pressing.
It's not long since I gave six of them a dressing.'
'I know that very well, Jack; the truth I must grant you.
You are a brave, heart fellow, and that makes me want you.'

'Dear captain,' he said then, 'if the truth I do tell you,
I got so much the last war that it quite filled my belly,
For your damned rogues of officers they use men so cruel
That a man-of-war is worse than hell or the devil.

'There is the master a-swearing, the boatswain a-growling;
The midshipman howling out: "Take that fore-bowling".

58 venture] rhymes with enter   last war] the reference is perhaps to the Seven
Years' War, which ended in 1763

If you speak but one word you're a mutinous rascal,
Both your legs laid in irons, and tried by a court martial.

'Now, boys, we are pressed away from our own habitation,
And we leave wife and children in grief and vexation.
We venture our sweet lives in defence of our nation,
And we get nothing for it but toil and vexation.'

☞ Jack Tar's confident rebuttal of the suggestion that he should again volunteer
probably dates from the early years of the American War of Independence,
which began in 1775. It appears in 'Tibby Fowler', a garland without imprint, of
which the title song, later appropriated by Burns, appeared in a two-verse form
in Herd's collection of 1776.

59   *The Man-of-War's Garland*

Come all ye valiant seamen,
And each jolly tar,
And let us try our fortune
On board a man-of-war;
For the Yankees broke our peace, boys,
In the lands of Virginia,
But Royal George of England
Is governor by sea.

Though both the French and Spaniards
They seem to join in league
For to assist the Americans,
And rob us of our trade;
But we will show them play, boys,
As we have done before,
And we'll make the dogs to tremble
On board a man-of-war.

There's many in our nation
Who dare not show their face,
But lurks among the skulkers,
Which proves to their disgrace;
But if any jolly sailor
Will enter volunteer,
He now may be advancèd
On board a man-of-war.

There's riches to be got, boys,
While we are on the main,
And many a rich prize
From the Spaniards we have ta'en;
We strip them of their Indian gold,
Which they do bring from far,
And we'll make the dogs to tremble
On board a man-of-war.

The Dutch are so deceitful,
'Tis them we will not trust,
For by their cowardly action
Many brave men are lost.
The Dutch we will not trust, boys,
Lest they should us ensnare,
But we'll boldly face our enemies
On board a man-of-war.

We always are a terror,
Wherever we do come,
Likewise the French and Spaniards,
They tremble at our name.
The Dutch, the Swedes, the Portuguese,
With us they have no share,
For we sweep the seas where'er we come
On board a man-of-war.

We make our trumpets sound, boys,
Our colours we do hoise;
We make our great guns rattle
In the taking of a prize.
We make our great guns rattle,
And the smoke it turns to air;
We boldly face our enemies
On board a man-of-war.

But when our action's over
We drink both beer and wine,
And on our enemy's plunder
We sumptuously do dine.
Our prizes then we do divide,
To every man a share;

hoise] hoist

136

Thus live we jolly seamen
On board a man-of-war.

But when the war is ended,
And we get safe on shore,
We make the trumpets sound, boys,
And the cannons they do roar.
Our colours then we do hoist up,
And pendant in the air,
To show that Britain has gained the day
On board a man-of-war.

Here's a health unto King George, boys,
To him that wears the crown,
Likewise to British tars, boys,
That pull the rebels down.
Here's a health unto all mariners
And each brave jolly tar
That boldly faced their enemies
In the time of the war.

☞ This unabashed piece of special pleading may be contrasted with the previous song. It is the title-piece in a garland printed (or more likely, reprinted) in 1796, when it no doubt once more helped to obtain recruits for the navy, as it had in the American War.

60   *On the Late Engagement in Charles*
Town River

Good people of old England, come listen unto me,
All you who live at home at ease and from all dangers free,
What I'm a-going to mention and to you shall declare,
Concerning part of our fleet as they a-cruising were.

It is of a late action, as for a truth we hear,
As part of our British fleet for Charles Town they did steer.
As we the river sailed along the provincials they begun;
The *Bristol*, most unfortunate, she on the bar did run.

Then from the town and batteries they fired on us amain,
With red hot shell all from the shore on board of us they came;

And seeing us lie on the bar their intentions was so,
Our gallant ship for to blow up and prove our overthrow.

But through God's providence so great prevented their desire,
Though with their shot that came so hot they set us twice on fire;
But soon we out the flames did put; our gallant seamen brave
They did their best endeavours their precious lives to save.

The gallant *Bristol* well behaved, though she was in distress,
And all the ships in company kept firing in excess.
Our cannons briskly we displayed; our shot like hail did pour
Amongst the blacks and Indians so numerous on the shore.

We drove them from their batteries and made them to retreat;
Likewise the town soon shatterèd with our gallant fleet.
We gave them a warm reception, and that they know so well,
Because against old England great they strongly did rebel.

We engagèd many hours, for the best part of the day;
Our brave commander he was killed all in the bloody fray.
Two hundred more brave men was killed, th' engagement proved so
    sore;
Upon the decks, poor souls, they lay all in their purple gore.

Now to conclude and make an end, Lord send it was o'er,
In love and unity to live as we have done before.
Success unto all Britons bold that's by land or sea
Who now is venturing their lives in North America.

☞ Charles Town (now Charleston) in South Carolina was attacked on 28 June
1776 by a British fleet commanded by Commodore Peter Parker. The town was
held by 6,000 militiamen, and a half-finished fort on Sullivan's Island in the
harbour was defended by a small garrison. After a day's cannonade Parker was
obliged to abandon the assault, having lost one ship, the *Actaeon*. John Morris,
the captain of the flagship, *Bristol*, was mortally wounded and there were over a
hundred more casualties. The song comes from a (presumably) contemporary
publication, *The Shepherd's Garland*. The Americans had their own cheerful
version of the events in the form of a 'New War Song' which purported to be
written by Sir Peter Parker.

The Silk Merchant's Daughter

There was a rich merchant in London did right,
Had one only daughter, her beauty shined bright;
She lovèd a porter, and to prevent the day
Of marriage they sent this poor young man away.

Oh now he is gone for to serve his king,
It grieves the lady to think of the thing.
She dressed herself up in rich merchant's shape;
She wandered away her true love for to seek.

As she was a-travelling one day, almost night,
A couple of Indians appeared in her sight;
And as they drew nigh her, oh this they did say:
'Now we are resolvèd to take your life away.'

She had nothing by her but a sword to defend,
These barbarous Indians murder intend,
But in the contest one of them she did kill,
Which causèd the other for to leave the hill.

And as she was a-sailing over the tide
She spied a city down by the seaside.
She saw her dear porter a-walking the street;
She made it her business her true love to meet.

'How do you do, sir. Where do you belong?
I'm a-hunting a diamond, and I must be gone.'
He says: 'I'm no sailor, but if you want a man
For [your] passage over I'll do all I can.'

[your] passage] text has 'my passage' by mistake

Then straightway they both went on board.
Says the captain to the young man:
'What did you do with your sword?'
On account of long travel on him she did gaze:
'Once by my sword my sweet life did save.'

Then straightway to London their ship it did steer;
Such utter destruction to us did appear.
It was out on the main sea, to our discontent,
Our ship sprung a leak, and to the bottom she went.

There was four-and-twenty of us contained in one boat;
Our provision gave out and our allowance grew short.
Our provisions gave out, and death drawing nigh,
Says the captain: 'Let's cast lots for to see who shall die.'

Then down on a paper each man's name was wrote;
Each man ran his venture, each man had his note.
Amongst the whole ship's crew this maid's was the least;
It was her lot to die for to feed all the rest.

'Now', says the captain, 'let's cast lots and see
Amongst the ship's crew who the butcher will be.'
It's the hardest of fortune you ever did hear,
This maid to be killed by the young man, her dear.

He called for a basin for to catch the blood
While this fair lady a-trembling stood,
Saying: 'Lord, have mercy on me, how my poor heart do bleed
To think I must die, hungry men for to feed.'

Then he called for a knife his business to do.
She says: 'Hold your hand for one minute or two.
A silk merchant's daughter in London I be;
Pray see what I've come to by loving of thee.'

Then she showèd a ring betwixt them was broke.
Knowing the ring, with a sigh he spoke;
'For the thoughts of your dying my poor heart will burst;
For the hopes of your long life, love, I will die first.'

Says the captain: 'If you love her, you'll make amend;
But the fewest of number will die for a friend.

called for a basin] to catch the blood so that it could be drunk

140

So quicken the business, and let it be done';
But while they were speaking they all heard a gun.

Says the captain: 'You may now all hold your hand.
We all hear a gun, we are near ship or land.'
In about half an hour to us did appear
A ship bound for London, which did our hearts cheer.
It carried us safe over and us safe conveyed;
And then they got married, this young man and maid.

☞ Like 'A Sea Song' (45), this occurs in Tim Connor's notebook of 1778, though
the version given here was noted by Cecil Sharp in North Carolina in 1916. The
ultimate source seems to be a lengthy and picaresque broadside of the
eighteenth century. Credulity is stretched to the limits and beyond in both
longer and shorter versions of the ballad, but it contains the well-loved motifs of
parental opposition to a marriage which would cut across class divides, and of
female disguise in the quest of a banished lover. In addition, the central episode
concerns cannibalism by castaway mariners, which was not only a recurrent
theme in ballads (see also 69 and 91) but a documented practice in real life.

62   *The Yankee Man-of-War*

'Tis of a gallant Yankee ship that flew the stripes and stars,
And the whistling wind from the west-nor'-west blew through the
   pitchpine spars.

With her starboard tacks aboard, my boys, she hung upon the gale;
On an autumn night we raised the light on the Head of Old
   Kinsale.

It was a clear and cloudless night, and the wind blew steady and
   strong,
As gaily over the sparkling deep our good ship bowled along;
With the foaming seas beneath her bow the fiery waves she spread,
And bending low her bosom of snow she buried her lee cathead.

There was no talk of short'ning sail by him who walked the poop,
And under the press of her pond'rous jib the boom bent like a
   hoop;
And the groaning waterways told the strain that held her stout
   main-tack,
But he only laughed as he glanced abaft at her white and foamy
   track.

The mid-tide meets in the channel waves that flow from shore to
   shore,
And the mist hung heavy upon the land from Featherstone to
   Dunmore;
And the sterling light in Tuskar Rock where the old bell tolls each
   hour,
And the beacon light that shone so bright was quenched on
   Waterford Tower.

The nightly robes our good ship wore were her whole topsails three,
Her spanker and her standing jib—the courses being free.
'Now lay aloft, my heroes bold, not a moment must be passed';
And royals and top-gallant sails were quickly on each mast.

What looms upon our starboard bow? What hangs upon the breeze?
'Tis time our good ship hauled her wind, abreast the old Saltees,
For by her ponderous press of sail and by her consorts four
We saw our morning visitor was a British man-of-war.

Up spake our noble captain then, as a shot ahead of us passed:
'Haul snug your flowing courses. Lay your topsail to the mast.'

Head of Old Kinsale] peninsula in the south-west of Ireland   fiery] with
phosphorescence   Featherstone] there seems to be no township of this name in
Ireland   Dunmore] on Waterford Harbour   Tuskar Rock] some ten miles off
the south-eastern tip of Ireland   Waterford Tower] Ronald's Tower, Waterford
Saltees] islands

Those Englishmen gave three loud hurrahs from the deck of their
   covered ark,
And we answered back by a solid broadside from the decks of our
   patriot bark.

'Out booms, out booms,' our skipper cried; 'out booms, and give
   her sheet';
And the swiftest keel that ever was launched shot ahead of the
   British fleet,
And amidst a thundering shower of shot, with stun sails hoisting
   away,
Down the North Channel Paul Jones did steer just at break of day.

☞ John Paul, later known as John Paul Jones, and later still as Paul Jones (1747–
92), was a Scots merchant captain who fled to Virginia after killing one of his
seamen who had attacked him, and later served as an officer in the American and
Russian navies. He made two famous sorties into British waters during the
American War of Independence, sailing from French ports, the first in 1778 and
the second in 1779. In February 1778 he sailed north from Nantes with a roving
commission, then across the south and up the east coast of Ireland. In a few April
days he captured a merchant ship off Wicklow, chased a revenue cutter between
the Isle of Man and Scotland, sank a schooner off the Mull of Galloway, raided
Whitehaven and Kircudbright, and finally defeated and captured a British
sloop-of-war, the *Drake*, off Carrickfergus. His ship was the *Ranger*, which
sometimes gives its name to this song. Curiously, none of the incidents of 1778
figures in it (the escape through superior sailing was in Jones' earlier command,
the *Providence*, in 1776, from HMS *Solebay*, in American waters), and its grasp
of Irish geography is unconvincing. Yet the song was popular with generations of
seamen, not only in America but also in Britain, partly because of its impeccable
display of nautical terminology, partly because of its spirited and rousing
qualities. Jones's second campaign, which culminated in a spectacular victory
off Flamborough Head, was also remembered in song for well over a century
afterwards.

63   *The Greenland Men*

An excellent new song composed by 18 Greenland men in the Swan *tender's
hold in Leith Roads, June 2nd, 1780*

To the tune 'We'll go no more to Greenland in a ship that has no guns'

62 North Channel] between Ireland and Scotland
63 Leith] near Edinburgh

On board the noble *Ann*, twenty-seventh of March, from Shields to
   Greenland we set sail,
The wind it blowing fair with a sweet and pleasant gale.
We had not sailèd many days when Fair Isle we did see,
But on the next day morning, in with a privateer fell we.

     We'll go no more to Greenland in a ship that has no guns.

She bore down upon us, and upon our quarter she did come;
She hoisted French colours, and to windward fired a gun.
This greatly did surprise us, and to quarters we did go.
It never shall be said, my boys, but the noble *Ann* will face the foe.

All hands being at quarters, to work we did begin;
The first broadside she gave us, down our topsails did come.
Our captain called: 'Don't be afraid, but fight away like men;
It never shall be said, my boys, that we will run from them.'

Our guns being few in number, the number being but five,
To fire them it is needless till we can him espy.
He played upon our bow and quarter; the shot it came like hail.
To get our guns to bear upon him made us both curse and rail.

Our guns set for the best advantage, alongside they did come.
We said we need not fire till execution [could] be done.
As soon as they bore upon him we immediately let drive,
And wounded three of his Irishmen. 'Tis a pity we left them alive.

Our captain walked the quarterdeck like a lion stout;
Cried: 'Don't let it be said, my boys, we cowardly give it out.'
Our running ropes, sails and rigging being all shot away,
Our ship in this condition could neither wear nor stay.

We fought them five glasses, but found it all in vain;
We see she carries eighteen guns, and we're sure for to be taken.
Our captain cried: 'What must we do? To strike it will be best.
The cutter never will leave us until they see us lost.'

Then, seeing us an inferior force, they unto us did shout,
Saying, 'You poor English dogs, why don't you give it out?'
We found it was in vain to fight; down colours we did haul.
'Hoist our your boat and come aboard', [unto] us they did call.

Shields] now divided into North and South Shields (Tyne and Wear)   Fair Isle]
in between the Orkney and Shetland Islands

Oh then our captain went aboard, and part of our noble crew.
They beat the captain on the head and swore they would run him
    through.
Now into their hold they put us, bound into irons strong,
And for twelve days they kept us where we were thick and throng.

The first meal that they gave us was calavances and salt beef,
Which made us curse fortune, and wish for some relief;
We lying in this condition, for Ireland Captain Ray in did push
Unto the Irish Channel where he was bound to cruise.

They had not cruisèd many days, but only four or five,
Until they spied the *Friends* brig, and soon made her a prize;
But cruising two days longer in breast of Boron Head,
Which proved to our advantage, they took the *Jenny* brig.

Ransom being made for her, it being all agreed
For to knock off our irons and put us aboard with speed,
We're now on board the *Jenny*. To Glasgow she is bound;
And to secure us from the press we landed in a Highland sound.

Now to our joy and comfort we're landed all on shore,
And to Newcastle we are bound, to see our friends once more.
But travelling through the Highlands, the people, very poor,
They scarce would admit us to come within their door.

We being in this condition we travelled long and sore,
But as we came to the southward more pity they did show;
At last, meeting with one John Robson, who provèd very kind,
And for three days he kept us and maintained us like a friend.

After this refreshment on our journey we do proceed,
But, coming near to Edinburgh, we met a rogue indeed,
Who pretended to be our friend, but [with] an evil eye,
For then he did deceive us, as we in the barns did lie.

Next morning after two o'clock fifty of Neper's gang
Came with sword and pistol to take ten naked men.
They finding us able seamen, as we knew very well,
They gave us such an offer as is a shame to tell.

Now we are all taken, and to Leith we do come
Before Captain Neper to receive our doom.

in breast of] abreast of   Boron Head] ? Malin Head

We were that night in two barns as we were ne'er before,
Or we had broke some of these ruffians' heads and made them for
  to roar.

He told us we might enter if that we would pay
Forty shillings a man to the rogue that did us betray;
But Neper's high offer we rejected with disdain,
But we'll fight for our king against France and against Spain.

But I hope in short time sweet peace will be restored,
And the devil will have Neper though we're in the hold.
When peace is restored, to Leith we will come,
To pay Neper and his men for what they have done.

Come all you jolly seamen that to Greenland do go,
We wish you good success although we go no more,
For we are forced to serve the king on board of a man-o'-war,
But expects to return with gold and silver store.

☞ Although I have been unable to trace the *Ann* of Shields, the song has the ring of truth. Certainly, the area was famous for its energetic resistance to the pressgang. In 1759 a Shields man was killed in a struggle with the gang, and in the following year thirty men fought their way out of a tender at Sunderland. In 1760 sixty men took over a tender at sea and sailed her into Scarborough 'and made their escape, leaving the lieutenant and his men battened down under hatches'. There were further escapes from pressgang vessels in 1771 and 1777, and at Sunderland in 1783 sailors 'having got liberty to go on shore, through the temporary cessation of impressment at the close of the first American war, resolved to take summary and condign vengeance on the persons who had informed against them and their mates while the pressgang was in active operation. The informers who were caught were mounted upon stout poles or stangs, and carried through the principal streets, exposed to the insults of the populace. The women, in particular, bedaubed them plentifully with rotten eggs, soap suds, mud, &c'. In 1793 seamen at Shields, Newcastle, Sunderland, Blyth, and smaller ports 'entered into resolution to resist any attempt to press them', and as a consequence there were many violent incidents. In a curious twist of the female sailor theme, a Newcastle man was rescued by his sister from the gang after being allowed to visit him in the rendezvous. During the few minutes they were left alone, 'they managed to exchange clothes, and, on the door being opened, the young man, "snivelling and piping his eye", walked off unmolested in female attire, while his sister remained to fill the situation of a

    we might enter if that we would pay] instead of being pressganged the men would be treated as volunteers and paid a bounty, provided they would be willing to give part of it to the man who had betrayed them.

British tar'. The escape filled the gang with 'rage and disappointment' but the girl won local admiration, was given 'several pounds' by complete strangers, and 'was soon restored to her liberty by order of the magistrates'.

64 *The Rolling Sailor*

Don't you see the ships a-coming?
Don't you see them in full sail?
Don't you see the ships a-coming
With the prizes at their tail?
 Oh, my little rolling sailor,
 Oh, my little rolling he;
 I do love a jolly sailor,
 Blithe and merry might he be.

Sailors they get all the money,
Soldiers they get none but brass;
I do love a jolly sailor,
Soldiers they may kiss ---.
 Oh, my little rolling sailor,
 Oh, my little rolling he;
 I do love a jolly sailor,
 Soldiers may be damned for me.

How can I be blithe and merry,
And my true love so far from me,
When so many pretty sailors
Are pressed and taken to the sea?
 Oh, my little rolling sailor,
 Oh, my little rolling he;
 I do love a jolly sailor,
 Blithe and merry may he be.

Oh, I wish the press were over
And all the wars were at an end;
Then every bonny sailor laddie
Would be merry with his friend.
    Oh, my, &c.

When the wars they are all over
And peace and plenty come again,
Then every bonny sailor laddie
Will come sailing o'er the main.
    Oh, my, &c.

I hope the wars will soon be over
And all our sailors once come home,
Then every lass would get her lad
And every wife her son again.
    Oh, my, &c.

☞ James Gardner went to sea in his father's ship at the age of five, in 1775. Six years later he heard the first two verses of this song when he was at the naval academy at Gosport: 'I was standing on Gosport beach when the prisoners were landed from some of the prizes taken by Rear-admiral Kempenfelt (the ablest tactician in the navy), who with only twelve sail of the line by a masterly manoeuvre captured most of the convoy from the French admiral, Count de Guichen, who had nineteen sail of the line, and frustrated the expedition. A party of soldiers assembled on the beach to escort them to Forton prison, a lieutenant of the navy and several midshipmen also attending, when a *posse* of women rushed out of Rime's "noted alley" and, pointing to the soldiers, sang the following beautiful ditty. Then, catching hold of the lieutenant and midshipmen, they began to hug and kiss them, and it was time before they could get out of their clutches. They then began to pelt the soldiers, who took it very patiently and seemed very glad when the order was given to march with the Frenchmen.' The remaining verses are taken from the twenty-five of a garland text, 'The Sailor Laddie'. The song remained in oral tradition in Britain and America, and was also adapted to suit other professions, including tailors (probably as a joke), colliers, and fishermen.

65   *Jackie Tar*

When Jack had pulled the oar and the boat was gone,
And the lassie on the shore with her head hanging down,
The tears stood in her eyes and her bosom heaving sighs:
'Farewell, my dear', she cries, 'with your trousers on.'
'Farewell', said he, 'I go to sea, and you must stay behind;
But do not grieve, for while I live I ever will be kind,
And when I come to land you will meet me on the strand,
And welcome Jackie Tar with his trousers on.'

Now peace is proclaimed and the wars are all o'er;
The fleets they are moored and the sailors come ashore.
Now you may see her stand with a glass into her hand
To welcome Jack to land with his trousers on.
While up on high, she catched his eye with all her lovely charms;
Her face he knew and straight he flew and caught her in his arms.
Her hand he kindly pressed as he held her round the waist,
And he kissed the bonny lassie with his trousers on.

'O Jack, where have you been since you went from me?
And what have you seen upon the raging sea?

trousers] as opposed to the breeches worn ashore at the time

I mournèd for your sake while my heart was like to break,
For I thought I'd never see my Jack with his trousers on.
And while you stayed I sighed and prayed to Neptune and to Mars
That they would prove kind and send you home safe from the wars;
And now to my request they have been pleased to list,
And sent you to my breast with your trousers on.'

'I have sailed the seas for you to the Torrid Zone,
From the confines of Peru to Van Diemen's Land,
From the Bay of Baltimore to the coast of Labrador,
But now I'm safe on shore with my trousers on.
I have beat the storms in many forms upon the raging main,
I have fought the foes with deadly blows and many a hero slain;
I have heard the cannons roar, I have rolled in blood and gore,
But now I'm safe on shore with my trousers on.

'I have been aloft when the winds have blown,
And I have been aloft when the bombs were thrown;
But like a sailor bold I have now come from the hold
With my pockets full of gold and my trousers on.
And now no more from shore to shore I'll plough the raging seas,
But free from strife as man and wife we'll live in peace and ease.'
To the church this couple hied and the priest the knot has tied,
And the sailor kissed his bride with his trousers on.

J. Pitts, Printer, Wholesale Toy and Marble Warehouse, 6 Great St Andrew Street, Seven Dials (London)

☞ The sheet was printed between 1819 and 1844, but the ballad probably dates from soon after the end of the American War in 1783. Four oral versions turned up in Aberdeenshire in the early twentieth century, though unfortunately the tunes were not noted. A sailor's hornpipe rhythm was clearly intended for the song, and the hornpipe, 'Jack Tarr', is given here. It was otherwise known as 'The Cuckoo's Nest'.

66   *The Ship is all Laden*

The ship is all laden and ready for sea;
The foy boat is coming, away let us be.
Come hoist up your topsails, we'll go without fail;
The wind's west-nor'-west and it blows a fresh gale.

65 Torrid Zone] ? the Tropics   Van Diemen's Land] Tasmania
66 foy-boat] see commentary

The skipper goes forward and there takes his stand,
Both growling and grumbling and giving command;
Haul this rope, haul that rope, he doesn't know which,
And when he has time gives his breeches a hitch.

The men are all groggy. We can't find a boy;
Billy Wilson's too lazy to work for his foy.
A rope is fast here and a rope is fast there;
The foy boat's away—smash my wig if I care.

Such wrangling, such jangling, such cutting of ropes;
Such squalling and bawling and staving of boats;
Such cracking of bowsprits, such rattling of rails,
Such smashing of sterns and such tearing of sails.

Our owner comes down with his wig on one side;
He blows like a grampus to see such a tide.
'Bowse, bowse, boys, the capstan'—hang me if I care—
I'll have her to sea, if she strikes on the bar.

He's from the low quay then he's at the pier end,
And then to the ale house to drink with a friend.
We'll leave him there drinking his bumbo of rum;
We are stuck in the narrows, the tide it is done.

The ship is safe moored and all hands gone ashore
To court all the pretty girls that they adore;
They dance with their sweethearts and what not beside,
And if they think fit they will court them next tide.

☞ In the rivers of north-eastern England during the age of sail foy-boats towed
vessels to sea when wind or weather was adverse, or kedge-hauled them. This
was the practice of carrying a ship's kedge-anchor some distance ahead and
dropping it into the water, after which the men on board hauled in the anchor
cable so as to pull the ship forward, up to her anchor. The process was repeated
as many times as necessary. By the late eighteenth century there were some 150
foy-boats on the River Wear at Sunderland, where this song, 'softened down,
and deprived of many marine imprecations', was noted in 1789.

   groggy] drunk   bumbo of rum] rum mixed with sugar, water, and nutmeg

Duke William

Duke William and a nobleman, heroes of England's nation,
Got up one morn by two o'clock to take a recreation.
Unto the suburbs they did go in sailor's dress from top to toe;
Then said Duke William: 'Let us know what usage have poor
    sailors.'

Then all in their warlike dress they hastened to an inn, sir.
The landlady she did refuse, but by good words they did prevail.
'Walk in, my lads. Be not afraid,' the landlady she then did say.
'Walk in, my lads. Be not afraid. We love a jolly sailor.'

Then up the stairs she showed them. Duke William he did say:
'Go get you down, kind landlady; bring up white wine and red, sir.'
Before the white wine was drunk out a pressgang that was bold and
    stout
The lower rooms they searched about to find out the bold sailors.

'We do belong to George,' said Will. 'Come show us your
    protection.'
'We have not at all,' the duke replied. 'Don't cast on us reflection.'
With that the lieutenant he did say: 'Come, brothers, go without
    delay.
Of us you shall not make a prey; my warrant is for sailors.'

protection] document giving immunity from impressment

To a tender they did haul them; the captain he did meet, sir.
The duke replied: 'Kind gentlemen, take care of all your sheep, sir.'
With that the captain he did say: 'I am your shepherd, I declare
I'll let you know, you saucy bear. Go down amongst the sailors.'

The nobleman he did go down. Duke William he refusèd,
Which made the sailors frown on him and sorely him abusèd.
'Where must I lie?' his highness said. 'Must I have a featherbed?'
'You're fat enough,' they all replied. 'Pig in among the sailors.'

Duke William then he did go down unto his comrade, sir,
Which made Duke William for to stare on many a gallant sailor.
In going down his trousers tore; he callèd for a tailor.
The captain said: 'You saucy are. There's nothing but bold sailors.

'For your sauce, you saucy are, we're sure to have you flogged, sir.'
Unto the gangway they hauled him to strip him like a dog, sir.
'Come strip,' they cried. The duke replied: 'I don't like your laws
    by far, sir.
I ne'er will strip for to be whipped, so strip me if you dare, sir.'

Then instantly the boatswain's mate began for to undress him,
And instantly he did espy a star upon his breast, sir.
Then on their bended knees did fall, and straight for mercy they
    did call.
The duke replied: 'Base villains all for using these poor sailors.

'No wonder that my father can't get men to manage shipping,
For using these poor sailors so, and always them a-whipping;
But for the future sailors all shall have good usage great and small.'
The sailors all with one huzza cried: 'Heavens bless Duke William.'

He ordered all new officers that stood in need of wealth, sir,
And left the jolly crew some gold that they might drink his health,
    sir.
They left the boat and sailed away. The sailors all with one huzza
Cried: 'Blessed be that glorious day on which was born Duke
    William.'

John Harkness, Printer, Preston

☞ William (1765–1837), the third son of George III, was known as the Duke of
Clarence from 1789 until his accession to the throne as William IV in 1830. He
served in the Royal Navy from 1779 until 1790, rising from midshipman to rear-

admiral. He therefore knew perfectly well 'what usage have poor sailors', but the ballad is in the romantic tradition of the monarch's travelling incognito among his subjects before revealing his identity, punishing injustice and rewarding virtue. Its date is uncertain, but it probably appeared after 1790 and before 1815. It was frequently reprinted, and a solitary version, of which the tune is given here, was recovered from oral tradition as late as 1905.

68　　　　　　*The Fisher Lad of Whitby*

My love he was a fisher lad and when he came on shore
He always steered to me to greet me at the door,
For he knew I loved him well, as anyone could see,
And oh but I was fain when he came a-courting to me.

It was one lovely morning, one morning in May,
He took me in his boat to sail out on the bay;
Then he told me of his love as he sat by my side,
And he said that in a month he would make me his bride.

That very afternoon a man-of-war came in the bay,
And the pressgang came along and took my lad away;
Put irons on his hands and irons on his feet,
And they carried him aboard to fight in the fleet.

My father often talks of the perils of the main
And my mother says she hopes he will come back again;
But I know he never will, for in my dreams I see
His body lying low at the bottom of the sea.

The ships come sailing in and the ships they sail away,
And the sailors sing their merry songs out on the bay;
But for me, my heart is breaking, and I only wish to be
Lying low with my lover deep down in the sea.

When the house is all still and everyone asleep
I sit upon my bed and bitterly I weep;
And I think of my lover away down in the sea,
For he never, never more will come again to me.

☞ This Whitby girl's view of the pressgang is paralleled in Mrs Gaskell's novel, *Sylvia's Lovers* (1863) which is set during the French Wars in the same town.

68 fain] glad

The Ship in Distress

You seamen bold that plough the ocean,
What dangers landsmen do never know.
The sun gangs over old England's nation;
No tongue can tell what you go through.
Through bitter storms in the height of battle,
Now mark you well what I do say,
Where thund'ring cannons loudly rattle
There's no back door to run away.

Of a merchant ship there was a captain;
A long time they had been drove on sea.
The weather proved to them so uncertain,
Which brought them to extremity.
Nothing on board poor souls to nourish,
Nor to strengthen their feeble arms;
The whole ship's crew were nearly starving,
The men were nothing but skin and bone.

The cats and dogs how they did eat them,
Hunger proving to them severe;
Captain and men of one direction
They all of them went equal shares.

gangs] goes

At length, at length the hour came on them,
The hour came on them most bitterly.
Poor fellows all stood titter totter,
Casting lots which of them should die.

The lot was cast on one poor fellow
Which had a wife at home on shore,
But to think of eating our fellow creatures
It was that which grieved us ten times more.
'I am willing to die,' this young man answered,
'But to the topmast haste away,
For perhaps some help you may discover
While I unto the Lord do pray.'

The captain said he spied a vessel
About a league from us or more.
Some signals of distress were fired
And soon for us away she bore;
And soon we got provisions plenty,
And far from all such deadly fear.
To see such pity they took upon us
You could not help but shed a tear.

But now we're happy in old England
And far from all such deadly fear
We'll drink unto our wives and sweethearts
And unto all we love so dear.
May God protect all jolly sailors
And all that plough the raging main;
May they never see no more such trials
And never know the like again.

☞ The theme of cannibalism for survival re-emerges in this powerful and passionate song. The ritual of drawing lots was practised in reality, as is seen from an entry in the *Gentleman's Magazine* of 1759: 'Letters have been received by the American mail, giving an account of the sufferings of Capt. Baron and his crew in the *Dolphin* sloop, bound from the Canaries to New York; they had been from the Canaries 165 days, 116 of which they had nothing to eat.... The captain and people declare that they had not had any ship provisions for upwards of three months; that they had eaten their dog, their cat, and all their shoes, and, in short, everything that was eatable on board. Being reduced to the last extremity, they all agreed to cast lots for their lives, which accordingly they did; the shortest lot was to die, the next shortest to be the executioner. The lot fell

titter totter] one version has 'in a torture', but the phrase conveys agonising hesitation.

upon one Antony Galatio, a passenger; they shot him through the head, which they cut off and threw overboard; they then took out his bowels and eat them, and afterwards eat all the remaining part of the body, which lasted but a very little while.' It is difficult precisely to date the song, but one version was learnt by a singer born in 1831 from his grandfather, which indicates the late years of the eighteenth century, or perhaps earlier. George Butterworth noted in 1907 the words and tune given here.

70   *The Fishes' Lamentation*
      A New Song

In came the herring, the king of the sea.
I think it high time our anchor to weigh.

   For it's hazy weather, blowing weather.
   When the wind blows it's stormy weather.

Then in came the salmon as red as the sun.
He went between decks and fired a gun.

Then in came the oyster with his sharp shell,
Crying: 'If you want a pilot I'll pilot you well.'

Then in came the flounder with his wry mouth.
He went to the helm and steered to the south.

Then in came the shark with his sharp teeth:
'Let go the clew-gallants, haul in the main sheet.'

Then in came the dolphin with his crooked beak:
'Pull in the main sheet, let go the main tack.'

157

Then in came the cod with his chuckle head.
He went to the main chains and sounded the lead.

Then in came the suck-pin so near the ground:
'Pray, Mr Cod, do you mind the wind.'

Then in came the whiting with her glowing eyes:
'Take in the clew-gallants, let go the main ties.'

Then in came the sprat, the least of them all.
He stepped between decks and cried: 'Hold, boys, all.'

Then in came the mackerel with his sly look:
'Pray, Mr Herring, do you want a cook?'

Then in came the guardfish with his long snout.
He stepped between decks and turnèd about.

Then in came the smelt with his sweet smell:
'All hands go to dinner and I'll ring the bell.'

Then in came the crab with his crooked claws:
'I'll never go to sea with such lubbers as these.'

Then in came the lobster with his black cloak:
'All hands go to sleep and I'll go to smoke.'

☞ The song of fishes jumping aboard and performing incongruous acts or issuing commands dates (I estimate) from the late eighteenth century. It was widely sung by sailors who relished the opportunities for improvisation, both in the varieties of fish (other versions include the skate, hake, plaice, and even the conger eel) and in their actions and orders. Kipling tells us in *Captains Courageous* (1896) that fishermen on the Grand Banks sang it as a forecastle song. In the United States it was known as 'The Boston Come-all-ye', but elsewhere normally as 'Windy old Weather'. Captain Whall has a version called 'The Fishes' which was sometimes sung 'with each man in turn taking a verse and expected to give a new fish each time'. He adds that 'in later days it has been used as a shanty to the tune of "Blow the man down", and using the original chorus of the Black Ball Line song'. In England it was a particular favourite with East Anglian fishermen, and the tune given here comes from Bob Roberts (1907–82), whose version begins: 'As we were a-fishing off Haisborough [Happisburgh] Light, Shootin' and haulin' and trawlin' all night. It was windy old weather, stormy old weather. When the wind blows we all pull together.'

chuckle] clumsy   suck-pin] possibly the sucking-fish or remora

A Sailor's Life

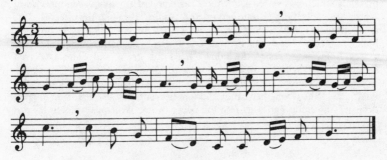

A sailor's life is a merry life:
They rob young girls of their heart's delight,
Leaving them behind to sigh and mourn:
They never know when they will return.

Here's four-and-twenty in a row;
My sweetheart cuts the brightest show.
He's proper, tall, genteel withal,
And if I don't have him I'll have none at all.

'O father, fetch me a little boat
That I might on the ocean float,
And every queen's ship that we pass by
I'll make enquire for my sailor boy.'

We had not sailed long upon the deep
Before a queen's ship we chanced to meet.
'You sailors all, come tell me true,
Does my sweet William sail among your crew?'

'Oh no, fair lady, he is not here,
For he is drownèd, we greatly fear.
On yon green island as we passed by
There we lost sight of your sailor boy.'

She wrung her hands and she tore her hair,
Much like a woman in great despair.
Her little boat 'gainst a rock did run:
'How can I live now my William is gone?'

genteel] ? gentle

☞ 'The Sailor Boy', 'The Sailing Trade', 'The Sailor Boy and his faithful Mary', 'The Faithful Lovers', and 'Sweet William' are some of the other titles used for this song which was widely known in Britain and, if anything, even more so in North America. It has also turned up in Australia. Although the queen's ships are mentioned it is likely that the song originated not in the time of Victoria but in that of George III, during the war with France. The text frequently attracted verses from other songs, including 'Died for Love' and 'The Deceived [Disappointed] Sailor' (39), but this version, from Henry Hills of Lodsworth, Sussex, keeps close to some of the uncontaminated broadside texts. One has this final verse: 'She wrung her hands and tore her hair, Just like a woman in great despair. She flung her body into the deep, In her William's arms to lay fast asleep'.

72   *The Greenland Whale Fishery*

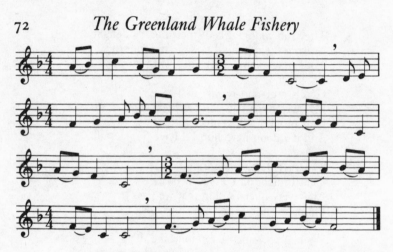

I cannot stay all on the shore
As I am so deeply in debt;
To Greenland we will go, brave boys,
Some money for to get, brave boys,
Some money for to get.

So when we had reached fair Liverpool,
And our goodly ship to man;
And there our names they were all taken down,
And for Greenland we were bound, brave boys,
And to Greenland we were bound.

And when we had safely reached Greenland,
And the goodly ship to moor;

And so soon we should wish ourselves back again
All along with the girls on the shore, brave boys,
All along with the girls on the shore.

For Greenland is a barren place,
It's a place that you seldom see;
For there's ice and snow where the whalefish blow,
And daylight's seldom seen, brave boys,
And daylight's seldom seen.

So our bosun up aloft he did go
With his spỳing-glass in his hand:
'There's a whale, there's a whale, there's a whalefish, brave boys,
And he blows on every swell, brave boys,
And he blows on every swell.'

So the boat being launched and the hands got in,
And the whalefish laid in view;
But no one would resolve of the whole ship's crew
To steer where the whalefish blew, brave boys,
To steer where the whalefish blew.

So the whale being struck and the line paid out,
And he gave a dash with his tail.
He capsized the boat and we lost five hands,
And we did not catch that whale, brave boys,
And we did not catch that whale.

So bad news, bad news to our captain did go,
When we've lost five jolly, jolly tars;
And the worst, we have lost our 'prentice boy,
And it grieved him more than all, brave boys,
And it grieved him more than all.

'So come, up your anchor, my jolly tars,
For the winter star I see;
And it's time we did leave this cold country.'
So from Greenland we bore away, brave boys,
So from Greenland we bore away.

☞ The song may well have existed before 1794 but the earliest extant versions
begin: 'It was in the year of 'ninety-four In March the twentieth day Our gallant

whalefish] cf. 'walfisch' in German and 'walvis' in Dutch   But no one would
resolve of] 'And resolvèd was' is the more logical wording in some other versions.

tars their anchor weighed And for sea they bore away.' It was updated as it continued to be sung, and dates between 1801 and 1901 occur in later texts. Even though Greenland whaling was in steady decline after 1830, largely because of over-fishing, the song continued to be popular, both ashore and afloat. This version was noted in 1924 by the composer, E. J. Moeran, from Harry Cox (1885–1971) of Potter Heigham, Norfolk. The mention of Liverpool is interesting, for although this was the most important whaling port on the west coast in the late eighteenth century, with twenty-one ships, it declined to only two by the early nineteenth.

73   *The Tars of the* Blanche

You Frenchmen, don't boast of your fighting,
Nor talk of your deeds on the main;
Do you think that old England you'll frighten
As easy as Holland or Spain?
We listen and laugh while you threaten,
We fear not your wily advance;
The boasting *La Pique* has been taken
By the jolly brave tars of the *Blanche*.

We sailed from the Bay of Point Peter,
Four hundred and fifty on board;
We were all ready to meet them,
To conquer or die was the word.
While the cans of good liquor was flowing
We gave them three cheers to advance,
And courage in each heart was glowing,
For cowards ne'er sailed in the *Blanche*.

The night then advancing upon us
The moon did afford us a light;
Each star then with lustre was shining
To keep the French frigate in sight.
While the night breeze our sails fillèd gently
Our ship through the water did launch,
And the grog flew about in full bumpers
Among the brave tars of the *Blanche*.

The fight made the sea seem on fire;
Each bullet distractedly flew.

73 distractedly] destructively

Britannia her sons did inspire
With courage that damped the French crew,
Saying 'Cowards now surely must rue'.
While over them death turned his lance
Our balls did repeat as they flew;
'Fight on, my brave tars of the *Blanche*'.

When Falkner resigned his last breath,
Each gave a groan and a sigh;
Such sorrow was found at his death,
And tears fell from every eye.
Like Wolfe, then with victory crownèd,
At his death he cried: 'Ne'er mind my chance,
But like gallant heroes fight on,
Or expire by the name of the *Blanche*.'

Stout Wilkins his place soon supplièd,
And like a bold actor engaged;
And his guns with more judgement to guide,
By the loss of his captain enraged.
And who could his fury allay,
When *La Pique* alongside did advance?
Four our masts being all shot away
We grappled her close to the *Blanche*.

Our foremast and mizen being gone,
The French thought to make us their own.
And while *Vive la République* they sung—
I thought that they ne'er would have done—
We joinèd their song with dismay;
And music that made them to dance,
And not a false note did we play,
The harmonious tars of the *Blanche*.

When they found it in vain for to stand
They cried out for quarter amain;
Although advantage they had,
Still Britons are lords of the main.
So push round the grog, let it pass,
Since they've found us true-hearted and staunch.
Each lad with his favourite lass,
Drink success to the tars of the *Blanche*.

Wolfe] killed in the moment of victory over the French at Quebec in 1759   amain]
straightaway

☞ On 5 January 1795 the *Blanche* (38 guns) encountered the French man-of-war, *La Pique* (36 guns) off Pointe-à-Pitre, Guadeloupe. After a fierce struggle at close range which lasted for some hours the French crew surrendered at 5.15 a.m. Both ships were extensively damaged. Of the 279 men on the *Pique*, 76, including the captain, were killed, and 110 wounded. The *Blanche* had eight killed, also including the captain (the first lieutenant, Frederick Watkins, took command), and 21 wounded. 'A spirit of chivalry seems to have animated both parties,' wrote a naval historian; 'and the action may be referred to with credit by either.' The ballad is rather more partisan. It was printed, with some variations, in places as far apart as London, Portsea (now Southsea), Devonport, Hull, Newcastle, York, and Birmingham, but the text given here is taken from J. H. Dixon: 'The first time we heard it sung was by a charcoal-burner in the New Forest. It was a hot sultry summer's day in 1835, and tired with pedestrianing, we had just entered a small inn when our ears were regaled with the "Tars of the Blanche". The swarthy songster gave it with great spirit, and the chorus was well sustained, by five or six fine-looking fellows of the like occupation with himself.' Unfortunately, the tune has not survived.

74   *Song*

Whilst landmen wander, though controlled,
And boast the rights of freemen,
Oh, view the tender's loathsome hold
Where droops your injured seamen;
Dragged by oppression's savage grasp
From every dear connection,
'Midst putrid air, oh, see them gasp,
Oh, mark their deep dejection.

    Blush then, oh, blush, ye pension host
    Who wallow in profusion,
    For our foul cell proves all your boast
    To be but mad delusion.

If liberty be ours, oh say
Why are not all protected?
Why is the hand of ruffian sway
'Gainst seamen thus directed?
Is this your proof of British rights?
Is this rewarding bravery?
Oh shame to boast your tars' exploits,
Then doom those tars to slavery.

When just returned from noxious skies
On winter's raging ocean,
To land the sunburnt seaman flies,
Impelled by strong emotion.
His much-loved mate, his children dear,
Around him cling delighted,
But lo the impressing fiends appear,
And every joy is blighted.

Thus from each soft endearment torn,
Behold the seaman languish,
His wife and children left forlorn,
The prey of bitter anguish.
'Reft of those arms whose vigorous strength
Their shield from want defended,
They droop, and all their woes at length
Are in a workhouse ended.

Mark then, ye minions of a court
Who prate at freedom's blessing,
Who every hell-born war support,
And vindicate impressing.
A time will come when things like you,
Mere baubles of creation,
No more will make mankind subdue
The work of devastation.

☞ In April 1797 the seamen of the Channel Fleet at Spithead refused to put to sea. They demanded an increase in pay, a more equitable division of prize money, better victuals, more humane treatment for the sick and wounded, and shore-leave in port. Earl Spencer, First Lord of the Admiralty, and then Lord Howe travelled to Portsmouth to meet the elected delegates of the seventeen ships involved. A royal pardon for the mutineers was granted, and pay was increased (for example, an able seaman's wage went up from 24 shillings a month to a shilling a day), though the other demands were not met. The fleet sailed on 17 May, but towards the end of the month further mutinies broke out at the Nore, an anchorage in the mouth of the Thames, and at Yarmouth. This time, the government's attitude hardened, public opinion turned against the mutineers, and they were forced to surrender without having achieved anything. The leader, Richard Parker (for whom, see the next song), was one of 29 seamen hanged. Many others were flogged through the fleet. A great many songs and ballads were written during the mutinies, mainly by the men themselves. The text given here is one of several found in manuscript form aboard the *Repulse*, one of the Nore ships, after the mutiny.

President Parker

Ye gods above protect the widow, and with pity look on me.
Oh help me, help me out of trouble and out of all calamity,
For by the death of my dear Parker fate to me has proved unkind;
Though doomed by law he was to suffer I couldn't erase him from
    my mind.

Brave Parker was my lawful husband, my bosom friend I loved so
    dear;
And at the moment he was to suffer I was not allowèd to come
    near.
In vain I asked, in vain I strove, ay, three times o'er and o'er again;
But still they replied: 'You must be denied, and must return on
    shore again.'

I thought I saw the yellow flag flying, the signal for my husband to
    die.
A gun was fired as they required when they hung on the yard-arm
    so high.·
I thought I saw his hand a-waving, bidding me a last farewell;
The grief I suffered at this moment no heart can paint nor tongue
    can tell.

suffer] die

My fainting spirit I thought would follow the soul of him I loved
    most dear;
No friend or neighbour would come near me to ease me of my grief
    and care.
Then unto the shore my Parker was brought, most scornfully to be
    laid in the ground,
And for to get my husband's body an artful scheme I quickly found.

In dead of night when all was silent, and many thousands fast
    asleep,
I and three more went to the shore and to his grave did quietly
    creep.
With trembling hands we worked with shovel and digged his body
    from the cold clay,
And there I had a coach a-waiting to carry to London his body
    away.

And there I got him decently buried, and then the doleful task was
    done;
I soon did finish the doleful task that his imprudence had begun.
Oh farewell, Parker, thou bright genius, thou wert once my only
    pride;
Though parted now it won't be long till I am laid down by your
    side.

Ye gods above protect the widow, and with pity look on me.
Although my Parker was hung for mutiny there were worse men in
    the wars than he.
All you who hear my tender ditty do not laugh at me in disdain,
But look on me with an eye of pity, for it is now my only claim.

☞ Richard Parker (1767–97) assumed the title of 'President of the Floating
Republic' as leader of the mutiny at the Nore. The story of his life and death is
full of conjecture and short of fact. He was a Devonshire man, reputedly of
gentle birth. He became a midshipman in the navy, but went ashore at the end of
the American War of Independence with a considerable sum in prize money. He
tried to make a living in Edinburgh as a schoolmaster and golf ball maker, and
married a Scotswoman in 1793. Soon afterwards, he enlisted again, and was
once more rated midshipman, but later court-martialled, disrated, and discharged as unfit. However, in 1797, to avoid being gaoled for debt, he applied
for the £30 bounty available to volunteers, and was drafted to the *Sandwich* at the
Nore as an able seaman. A few months later he was hanged at the yardarm after
being court-martialled for mutiny. There is a story that the navy buried his body
on the shore between high and low tide marks, and that his wife secretly
removed it for proper interment. 'A New Song on Parker the Delegate' set out to

attack him ('I will not sing in Parker's praise, disgraceful is the story'), but there is no evidence of its having gained favour. By contrast, the sympathetic ballad on his death was widely published and sung. Firth called it 'one of the commonest of all ballads relating to the navy', and added that 'the frequency with which it was reprinted seems to show that popular feeling was inclined to regard Parker as a hero and a martyr'. Several versions were obtained from oral tradition in the late nineteenth and early twentieth centuries. This one comes from a Scots singer, Jamie Coul.

76 *A New Song on the Total Defeat of the French Fleet*

by Sir Horatio Nelson, near Rosetta, on the first of August last

Come all you valiant heroes and listen unto me.
I'll tell you of a bloody fight that was fought on the sea
Between brave Admiral Nelson and the proud Monsieur;
Such a fierce engagement's not been known for many years.

The French set sail from Toulon many months ago.
Brave Nelson he sailed after them in hopes to catch the foe;
Both night and day he chased them, for many hundred leagues,
But never could come up with them, so swift they ploughed the seas.

'Twas on the first of August, just at the close of day,
Brave Nelson espied them and began the bloody fray.
He formed the line of battle, their force he valued not;
While thundering cannons rattle, like hail did fly our shot.

Long time this fray it lasted, and many there was slain,
While the blood it poured from the decks and stained the watery
    main.
Brave Nelson he was wounded, likewise some hundred men,
But let's hope they will recover to beat the foe again.

So well our noble sailors their courage they did show
They struck the French with wonder and proved their overthrow.
Thirteen ships burnt, sunk or taken, as we are well informed,
And only four escaped bold Nelson's thunderstorm.

Now to conclude my ditty and then lay down my pen,
Here's a health to Admiral Nelson and all his valiant men.

Whene'er they meet the haughty foe, may they serve them so again,
And let them know we always will be masters of the main.

☞ Horatio Nelson (1756–1805) was promoted to rear-admiral and given a
knighthood in 1797 after the battle of Cape St Vincent. In 1798 he commanded
a fleet of fourteen ships in what came to be called the battle of the Nile. A fleet of
twenty vessels, commanded by Admiral Brueys, had successfully escorted a
French expeditionary force to Egypt, and was lying at anchor in shallow water off
Aboukir Island, near the Rosetta mouth of the Nile, when the British came on
the scene, on 1 August. After a ferocious battle, mainly in darkness, all the
French ships but four were found to have surrendered or been destroyed. There
was considerable damage on the British side, too, though no ships sunk. The sea
seemed full of scorched and mangled corpses, both French and British. Nelson
himself was slightly wounded in the temple, and temporarily blinded in his one
good eye. The news did not become public in London until October, which is
probably the date of the ballad sheet.

77 *The Boatie Rows*

O weel may the boatie row and better may she speed,
And leesome may the boatie row that wins the bairns' bread.
The boatie rows, the boatie rows, the boatie rows indeed,
And weel may the boatie row that wins my bairns' bread.
O weel may the boatie row and better may she speed,
And leesome may the boatie row that wins my bairns' bread.

I cast my line in Largo Bay and fishes I catched nine,
There was three to boil and three to fry, and three to bait the line.
The boatie rows, the boatie rows, the boatie rows indeed,
And happy be the lot o' a' who wishes her to speed.

O weel may the boatie row that fills a heavy creel,
And cleads us a' frae head to feet and buys our pottage meal.
The boatie rows, the boatie rows, the boatie rows indeed,
And happy be the lot o' a' that wish the boatie speed.

When Jamie vowed he would be mine and wan frae me my heart,
O muckle lighter grew my creel; he swore we'd never part.
The boatie rows, the boatie rows, the boatie rows fu' weel,
And muckle lighter is the load when love bears up the creel.

My kurtch I put upo' my head and dressed mysel' fu' braw,
I true my heart was douf an' wae when Jamie ga'ed awa';
But weel may the boatie row and lucky be her part,
And lightsome be the lassie's care that yields an honest heart.

When Sawney, Jock an' Janetie are up and gotten lear
They'll help to gar the boatie row and lighten a' our care.
The boatie rows, the boatie rows, the boatie rows fu' weel,
And lightsome be her heart that bears the murlain and the creel.

And when wi' age we're worn down, and hirpling round the door,
They'll row to keep us dry and warm as we did them before.
Then weel may the boatie row, she wins the bairn's bread,
And happy be the lot o' a' that wish the boat to speed.

[The last two lines of verses 2 to 7 are repeated]

leesome] sprightly   Largo Bay] on the north side of the Firth of Forth
creel] basket   cleads] clads   muckle] much   kurtch] kerchief
fu'braw] full fine   I true] I trow   douf an' wae] mournful and woeful
gotten lear] got learning   gar] make   murlain] basket   hirpling] hobbling

170

☞ The song, which was known to Robert Burns, was published by James Johnson in the fifth volume of his *Scots Musical Museum* (1799), with three different tunes. The words have often been ascribed to an Aberdeen jeweller, John Ewen (1741–1821), but according to Turnbull and Buchan, he merely abridged a seventeenth-century ballad 'The Fisher's Rant of Fittie', 'for the purpose of being sung by a Mr Wilson in the theatre of Aberdeen'. In its new form the song was reprinted in books and on broadsides, and circulated orally in Scotland until the twentieth century.

78 *Second of August*

A New Song composed by the wounded Tars at the Siege of Boulogne

On the second of August, eighteen hundred and one,
As we sailed with Lord Nelson to the port of Boulogne
For to cut out some shipping, which provèd in vain:
To our misfortune they were all moored with chain.

Our boats being well manned by eleven at night
To cut out their shipping, not expecting to fight;
But the grape from their batteries so smartly did play
That nine hundred brave seamen killed and wounded there lay.

We hoisted our colours and so bold did them spread,
With the British flag flying at the royal mast head;
For the honour of old England we'll always maintain
While bold British seamen plough the watery main.

78 grape] grapeshot

Exposed to the fire of the enemy we lay
While ninety bright pieces of cannon did play;
There many brave seamen did lay in their gore,
And the shots from the batteries most smartly did pour.

Our noble commander with his heart full of grief
Used every endeavour to afford us relief.
No ship could assist us as well he did know;
In this wounded condition we were tossed to and fro.

All you who relieve us the Lord will you bless
For relieving poor seamen in times of distress.
May the Lord put an end to all cruel wars,
Send peace and contentment to all British tars.

Printed by J. Kendrew, Colliergate, York

☞ With his flag in the frigate, *Medusa*, Nelson led a flotilla in an abortive attack in August 1801 on French invasion craft in Boulogne harbour. (After a reconnaissance early in the month, the action took place on 15 August.) There were heavy losses. Little provision was made at the time for wounded seamen; sometimes they were merely put ashore and left to fend for themselves as best they could. One expedient was to raise money by singing a ballad which would stimulate the generosity of the public. This sheet was widely printed, and remained in oral tradition in the north-east of England long after its original purpose had passed.

79   *Distressed Men of War*

Says Jack: 'There is very good news; there is peace both by land
and sea;
Great guns no more shall be used, for we all disbanded must be.'

Says the admiral: 'That's very bad news.' Says the captain: 'My
heart it will break.'
The lieutenant cries: 'What shall I do, for I know not what course
for to take?'

Says the purser: 'I'm a gentleman born. My coat is linèd with gold
And my chest is full of the same, by cheating of sailors so bold.'

Says the doctor: 'I'm a gentleman too, I'm a gentleman of the first
rank.
I will go to some country fair and there I'll set up mountebank.'

Says the steward: 'I'm sorry it's peace, for I love my ships as my
    life,
And by cheating of honest Jack Tar I have plenty of shiners so
    bright.'

Says the carpenter: 'I have a chest, a chest of very good tools.
I will go to some country fair and there I'll sell three-legged stools.'

Says the cook: 'I will go to that fair and there I will sell all my fat.'
Says Jack Tar: 'If I should meet you there, damn me, I'll pay you
    for that.

'For don't you remember the time our topsail stuck close to the
    tack,
And we all stuck fast in the sheet for want of some of that fat?'

Says the midshipman: 'I have no trade; I have got my trade for to
    choose.
I will go to St James' Park Gate and there I'll set blacking of shoes.

'And there I will set all the day at everybody's call,
And everyone that comes by: "Do you want my nice shining
    balls?"'

Says Jack: 'I will take to the road for I'd better do that than do
    worse;
And everyone that comes by I'll cry: "Damn you, deliver your
    purse".'

J. Davenport, 6 George's Court [London]

☞ Preliminary articles of peace between Britain and France were signed on 1
October 1801, and ratified at Amiens on 27 March 1802. Hostilities resumed on
17 May 1803. The ballad was printed by the end of 1802, since Davenport was
at St George's Court only until then, so it exactly coincides with the temporary
cessation of the war. It seems to have reached the fleet very quickly, for Gardner
records in his journal for 1801–2 the singing aboard HMS *Brunswick* of this
version of the first two verses: 'Jolly tars, have you heard of the news? There's
peace both by land and sea; Great guns are no more to be used, Disbanded we all
are to be. Oh! says the admiral, the wars are all over; Says the captain, my heart it
will break; Oh! says the bloody first lieutenant, What course of life shall I take?'

shiners] coins; probably guineas   fat] the fat skimmed off when meat was
boiled was regarded as the cook's perquisite, though it was also used for greasing the
running gear   St James' Park] in London   balls] of blacking

80

Nelson's Death and Victory

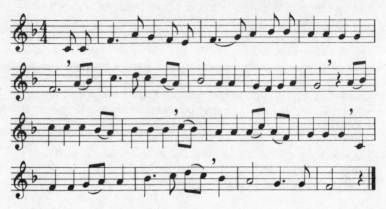

Ye sons of Britain in chorus join and sing:
Great and joyful news is come to our royal king.
An engagement we have had by sea
With France and Spain our enemy,
And we've gained the glorious victory
Again, my brave boys.

On the twenty-first of October at the rising of the sun
We formed the line for action, at twelve o'clock begun.
Brave Nelson to his men did say:
'The Lord will prosper us this day.
Give them a broadside, fire away,
My true British boys.'

Broadside and broadside our cannon balls did fly,
And small shot like hailstones on the deck did lie.
Their masts and rigging were shot away;
Besides, some thousand on that day
Were killed and wounded in the fray
On both sides, brave boys.

Heaven reward Lord Nelson and protect his men.
Nineteen sail of the combined fleet was sunk and taken in.
The *Achille* blew up amongst them all,
Which made the French for mercy call.

combined fleet] of France and Spain

Nelson was slain by a cannon ball:
Mourn, England, mourn.

Many a brave commander in tears he shook his head,
But yet their grief was no relief for Nelson he lay dead.
It was a fatal musket ball
Which caused our hero for to fall.
He cried: 'Fight on. God bless you all,
My brave British tars.'

Huzza, valiant seamen, huzza, we've gained the day,
Though lost a bold commander who on the deck did lay;
With joy we've gained the victory,
Before me dead I now do see.
'I die in peace, bless God,' said he,
'The victory is won.'

Let's hope this glorious battle will bring a peace,
That our trade in England may prosper and increase;
And our ships from port to port go free.
As before let us with them agree,
May this turn the heart of our enemy.
Huzza, my brave boys.

J. Kendrew, Printer, Colliergate, York

☞ The victory of Trafalgar in 1805, and with it the death of Nelson, produced a
spate of songs of all kinds. Several street ballads of the time went into oral
tradition, including this. A fragmentary version, starting with the second verse of
the broadside (of which the tune is given here) was noted by Anne Gilchrist in
1909 from James Bayliff, a carpenter from the Westmorland village of Barbon,
who was born in 1839. The song seems to have been based on 'Bold Sawyer',
written in 1758, and beginning: 'Come all ye jolly sailors with courage stout and
bold, Come enter with bold Sawyer, he'll clothe you all in gold. Repair on board
the old *Nassau*, As fine a ship as e'er you saw. We'll make the French to stand in
awe; She's manned with British boys.'

81

A New Song called the Victory

I am a youthful lady, my troubles they are great;
My tongue is scarcely able my troubles to relate.
Since I have lost my true love, that was ever dear to me;
He is gone to plough the ocean across the raging sea.

Many a pleasant evening my love and I have met;
He clasped me round my slender waist and gave me kisses sweet.
I gave him both my hand and heart; he vowed to marry me;
But I did not know my love would go on board the *Victory*.

My parents could not endure my love because he was poor,
Therefore he dare not presume to come within the door;
But had he been some noble lord or man of high degree
They'd never 'a' sent the lad I love on board the *Victory*.

Thirteen of the pressgang they did my love surround,
And one of the cursèd gang he laid bleeding on the ground.
My love was overpowered, and he fought most manfully,
Till he was obliged to yield, and go in the *Victory*.

Each night when in my slumbers I can't find any rest;
The lad I love so dearly runs in my aching breast.
Sometimes I dream I do enjoy my love's sweet company,
And closely locked in his arms on board the *Victory*.

His teeth were white as ivory, his hair in ringlets hung,
His cheeks like blooming roses all in the month of June.
He is lively, tall and handsome in every degree;
My heart lies in his bosom on board the *Victory*.

Here's a health unto the *Victory* and crew of noble fame,
And glory to the noble lord, bold Nelson was his name.
In the battle of Trafalgar the *Victory* cleared the way,
And my love was slain with Nelson upon that very day.

J. Wheeler, Printer, Manchester

☞ The *Victory* was commissioned in 1778 and became Nelson's flagship in 1803.
She is now preserved at Portsmouth. It seems strange that the death of a lover is
mentioned only in the last line of a song about him. Originally, perhaps, the
subject was his enforced absence (through the pressgang), and one version,
printed by Such, ends in this way: 'Now since that I am robbed of the lad that I
adore, My prayer will be offered up for him for evermore. It will be my daily
prayer wherever that may be, That providence will protect me till he comes
home from sea.' After the battle of Trafalgar the earlier version might have been
changed to record the lover's death. The argument about origins cannot be
conclusive, since no early text seems to have survived; Wheeler's dates from
between 1838 and 1845. The elaborate tune is from a version noted as recently
as 1951 in Nova Scotia.

82   *Pleasant and Delightful*

It was pleasant and delightful one midsummer's morn
When the green fields and meadows they were covered with corn,
And the blackbirds and thrushes sang on every green tree,
And the larks they sang melodious at the dawn of the day.
And the larks they sang melodious, and the larks they sang
    melodious,
And the larks they sang melodious at the dawn of the day.

Said the sailor to his true love: 'I'm bound far away,
I am bound to the East Indies where the loud cannons roar.
I am bound to the East Indies where the loud cannons roar,
And I'm going to leave my Nancy, she's the girl I adore.
And I'm going to leave my Nancy', &c.

A ring from her finger she then instantly drew,
Saying: 'Take this, dearest Willie, and my heart will go too.'
And whilst he was embracing her tears from her eyes fell,
Saying: 'May I go along with you?' 'Oh no, my love, farewell.'
Saying: 'May I go along with you', &c.

Said the sailor to his true love: 'I can no longer stay,
For our tops'ls they are hoisted and our anchor is a-weigh.
Our big ship she lies waiting for the next flowing tide,
And if ever I return again I will make you my bride.
And if ever I return again', &c.

☞ The giving of rings or other tokens such as one half of a broken ring was not only
of romantic but of practical significance when years of separation and hardship
could greatly transform a lover's physical appearance. A Mr Willie Miller sang
this song, which is still a favourite in East Anglia, at the *Eel's Foot*, Eastbridge,
Suffolk, in 1947. It dates back at least to between 1809 and 1815 when it was
issued as 'The Sailor and his Truelove' by Jennings of Water Lane, off Fleet
Street in London. A later adaptation substituted a soldier for the sailor and went
into oral tradition as 'The Soldier and his True Love'.

The Servant of Rosemary Lane

When I was a servant in Rosemary Lane
I gained the goodwill of my master and dame,
Till at length a young sailor came there for to lie,
Which was the beginning of my misery.

He called for a candle to light him to bed,
He called for a napkin to tie round his head;
To tie round his head as he used for to do,
And he vowed and he swore I should come to bed too.

In the middle of the night this young man grew bold
And into my lap he threw handfuls of gold,
Saying: 'Take this, my dear, and more you shall have.
I'll be a friend to you as long as I live.'

So we tumbled and tossed by the light of the moon;
We rose the next morning all in the same tune.
The very next morning this young man arose
And dressed himself out in his tarpaulin clothes.

'Alas,' then I cried, 'oh, I am undone.
He has left me with child of a daughter or son;
And if 'tis a girl she shall stay at home with me,
And if 'tis a boy he shall plough on the sea.

'With his long-quartered shoes, check shirt and blue jacket,
On the quarterdeck he shall stand like a bold British tar;

tarpaulin] sailor's

So I'll dry up my milk as you shall plainly see,
And pass for a maid in my own country.'

Printed and sold by Jennings, No. 13, Water Lane, Fleet Street, London

☞ At first sight this is the story of an innocent girl betrayed, which may indeed be the song's message. Yet Rosemary Lane (now called Royal Mint Street) was in a part of London, near the Tower, where brothels abounded, and the girl's chief embarrassment seems to be the potential baby. A racy derivative, the mock-cautionary 'Bell-bottomed Trousers', remained popular at least until the Second World War. Jennings was printing at Water Lane between 1809 and 1815. The tune was noted from the Sussex singer, Henry Burstow, in 1983.

84 *A Copy of Verses on Jefferys the Seaman*

You captains and commanders both by land and sea,
Oh do not be hard-hearted; refrain from cruelty.
It is of Jefferys the seaman who though not cast away
Was left upon a dismal rock by his captain, they say.

  Think of Jefferys the seaman's hard fate.

For eight days and nights he in misery did remain,
Without any food or nourishment himself for to maintain;
Dejected, in a wretched state, his fate he did deplore,
For some good Christians to convey him to his native shore.

At length kind providence gave ear unto his mournful strain:
An American vessel to his assistance came.
John Dennis's humanity soon set him free,
And very soon released him from his captivity.

It really is surprising he could so cruel be
Unto his fellow creature; lost to humanity
And any Christian feeling; that such corrections there be,
It is a pity such should have a command either by land [or] sea.

But now he is arrivèd unto old England's shore,
And I think he is very much to blame to go to sea any more.
The gentry pity his fate; as his suffering he explores
He is glad to have the happy sight of his native land once more.

His mother in amazement, almost distracted, run,
When she viewed the situation of her dear only son,

Quite meagre and almost starving with hunger and fatigue,
This sight it caused his agèd mother's heart then for to bleed.

J. Pitts, Printer, 14 Great St Andrew Street, Seven Dials

☞ Robert Jeffery was a native of Polperro in Cornwall. In the summer of 1807, at the age of eighteen, he joined a privateer, the *Lord Nelson*, at Plymouth. A week later, when the ship docked at Falmouth, he was taken by the pressgang and made armourer's mate on the 18-gun brig-sloop, *Recruit*, which then sailed for the West Indies. Later, the captain, the Honourable Warwick Lake, ordered Jeffery to be put on the blacklist as a petty thief and skulker, and then as the ship passed by the uninhabited island of Sombrero, 80 miles south-west of St Christopher, he decided to maroon him. As soon as the *Recruit* reached the Leeward Islands and Rear-admiral Cochrane, the commander-in-chief, heard of the incident, he immediately sent Lake back to collect Jeffery, but there was no trace of him when the ship once more reached Sombrero on 11 February 1808. Fortunately for Jeffery, he had been picked up by an American schooner, the *Adams*, on his ninth day of living off rainwater and limpets, and taken to her home port of Marblehead, Massachusetts. There, Jeffery worked at his trade of blacksmithing until the British government received news from the American press of his rescue and arranged for his repatriation. In October 1810 he was discharged from the navy and received not only his backpay but a substantial sum in compensation raised by the friends of Lake. In the meantime, in February 1810, Lake had been court-martialled and dismissed the service for marooning him. The ballad seems to have been published at the time of Jeffery's return to England, and the last verse is fanciful, since this was almost three years after his ordeal.

85   Shannon *and* Chesapeake

The *Chesapeake* so bold out of Boston we've been told
Came to take the British frigate neat and handy, O.
All the people of the port they came out to see the sport,
And the bands were playing 'Yankee doodle dandy, O'.

The British frigate's name which for the purpose came
Of cooling Yankee courage neat and handy, O,
Was the *Shannon*—Captain Broke. All her crew were hearts of oak,
And at fighting they're allowed to be the dandy, O.

Now before the fight begun the Yankees with much fun
Said they'd take the British frigate neat and handy, O;
And after that they'd dine, treat their sweethearts all with wine,
And the band should play up 'Yankee doodle dandy, O'.

We no sooner had begun than from their guns they run,
Though before they thought they worked 'em neat and handy, O.
Brave Broke he waved his sword, crying, 'Now, my lads, we'll
    board,
And we'll stop their playing "Yankee doodle dandy, O".'

We no sooner heard the word than we all jumped aboard,
And tore down the colours neat and handy, O;
Notwithstanding all their brag o'er the glorious British flag,
At the Yankee mizen-peak it looked the dandy, O.

Here's a health to Captain Broke and all the hearts of oak
That took the Yankee frigate neat and handy, O;
And may we always prove that in fighting and in love
The true British sailor is the dandy, O.

☞ During the first years of the British–American War of 1812–15 American ships
had many successes, though British naval superiority later reasserted itself. The
USS *Constitution*, now preserved at Boston, was victorious in a number of
actions, including that of 19 August 1812 against the British frigate, *Guerrière*.
One of four ballads on this success was to the tune of 'The Pretty Lass of Derby'
(or 'The Landlady of France', which was perhaps merely another name for the
same tune). It began: 'It ofttimes has been told how the British seamen bold
Could flog the tars of France to neat and handy, O. But they never found their
match till the Yankees did them catch. Oh the Yankee boys for fighting are the
dandy, O'. In 1813 the British reworked the same song to mark a victory of their
own. On 1 June Captain James Lawrence of the USS *Chesapeake* (36 guns), in
defiance of orders and with an untrained crew, rashly accepted a challenge to
come out of Boston harbour and fight the *Shannon* (38 guns), which her captain,
Philip Bowes Vere Broke, had in seven years of command made into a highly

efficient fighting machine. After two broadsides the *Chesapeake* was a shambles, and 146 of her crew were dead (including Lawrence) or wounded. Broke led a boarding party on to the ship, which surrendered. The action lasted only fifteen minutes. Of the *Shannon*'s crew 85 were killed or wounded, including Broke, who never served at sea again. He was made a baronet after the action, and a rear-admiral in 1830. The news of the victory was received with rapture in England, and at least two street ballads celebrated. Of these, one, beginning 'On board the *Shannon* frigate', remains in oral tradition to the present day. '*Shannon* and *Chesapeake*' does not seem to have appeared as a printed ballad. It was popular at Rugby in the time of Thomas Hughes, and was included in the song book of Harrow School. Captain Whall gives a version which he heard sung at sea. A traditional text from Firth, after Sir J. K. Laughton, is given here, with a copy of the tune from a music sheet of 'Peggy of Derby O'.

86 *The* Flying Cloud

My name is Edward Hollander, as you may understand.
I was born in the city of Waterford in Erin's lovely land.
When I was young and in my prime, and beauty on me shone,
My parents doted on me, I being their only son.

My father bound me to a trade in Waterford's fair town,
He bound me to a cooper there, by the name of William Brown.
I served my master faithfully for eighteen months or more,
Till I shipped on board of the *Ocean Queen*, belonging to Tramore.

86 Waterford] on the south-eastern coast of Ireland   Tramore] to the west of Waterford

When we came unto Bermuda's isle, there I met with Captain
   Moore,
The commander of the *Flying Cloud*, hailing from Baltimore.
He asked me if I'd ship with him on a slaving voyage to go
To the burning shores of Africa where the sugar cane does grow.

It was after some weeks' sailing we arrived off Africa's shore,
And five hundred of these poor slaves, my boys, from their native
   land we bore.
We made them walk in on a plank and we stowed them down
   below;
Scarce eighteen inches to a man was all they had to go.

The plague and fever came on board, swept half of them away;
We dragged their bodies up on deck and hove them in the sea.
It was better for the rest of them if they had died before
Than to work under brutes of planters in Cuba for ever more.

It was after stormy weather we arrived off Cuba's shore,
And we sold them to the planters there to be slaves for ever
   more;
For the rice and the coffee seed to sow beneath the broiling sun,
There to lead a wretched, lonely life till their career was run.

It's now our money is all spent we must go to sea again,
When Captain Moore he came on deck and said unto us men:
'There is gold and silver to be had if with me you'll remain,
And we'll hoist the pirate flag aloft and we'll scour the Spanish
   main.'

We all agreed but three young men who told us them to land,
And two of them was Boston boys, the other from Newfoundland.
I wish to God I'd joined those men and went with them on shore,
Than to lead a wild and reckless life serving under Captain
   Moore.

The *Flying Cloud* was a Yankee ship of five hundred tons or more;
She could outsail any clipper ship hailing out of Baltimore.
With her canvas white as the driven snow and on it there's no
   specks,
And forty men and fourteen guns she carried on her decks.

It's oft I've seen that gallant ship with the wind abaft her beam,
With her royals and her stunsails set, a sight for to be seen,

With the curling wave from her clipper bow a sailor's joy to feel,
And the canvas taut in the whistling breeze logging fourteen off the
    reel.

We sank and plundered many a ship down on the Spanish main,
Caused many a wife and orphan in sorrow to remain;
To them we gave no quarter but gave them watery graves,
For the saying of our captain was that dead men tell no tales.

Pursued we were by many a ship, by frigates and liners too,
Till at last a British man-o'-war, the *Dungeness*, hove in view.
She fired a shot across our bow as we sailed before the wind,
Then a chainshot cut our mainmast down, and we fell far behind.

Our crew they beat to quarters as she ranged up alongside,
And soon across our quarterdeck there ran a crimson tide.
We fought till Captain Moore was killed and twenty of our men,
Till a bombshell set our ship on fire, we had to surrender then.

It's next to Newgate we were brought, bound down in iron chains,
For the sinking and the plundering of ships on the Spanish main.
The judge he found us guilty; we were condemned to die.
Young men, a warning by me take and shun all piracy.

Then fare you well old Waterford and the girl that I adore;
I'll never kiss your cheek again or squeeze your hand no more.
For whisky and bad company first made a wretch of me.
Young men, a warning by me take and shun all piracy.

☞ The antecedents of this song are mysterious. It was first mentioned in print as
recently as 1916, yet seems to derive from a much earlier period. Joanna
Colcord, whose version is reprinted here, suggests that it dates 'from
somewhere between the years 1819 and 1825, when the West Indies were finally
cleared of pirates by the joint efforts of the United States and several of the
European naval powers'. She adds that Baltimore was the third most important
American port at that time. However, William Doerflinger has argued that the
song is based on a booklet entitled *Dying Declaration of Nicholas Fernandez*, which
probably appeared in 1830. Despite a careful investigation, H. P. Beck was
unable to establish the historicity of the song, but it undoubtedly reflects the
history of the pirate-slaver ships of the first third of the nineteenth century. It
was widely popular in North America, especially with lumberjacks (the ability to
sing it being a prerequisite, it was said, of employment in the Michigan lumber
camps), but despite its Irish and English connections, turned up only once in
Britain—in Aberdeenshire.

logging fourteen] fourteen knots

The North Country Collier

At the head of Wear Water about twelve at noon
I heard a maid a-talking, and this was her tune:
'There are all sorts of callings in every degree,
But of all sorts of callings a collier for me.

'You may know a jolly collier as he walks on the street,
His clothing is so handsome and so neat are his feet;
With teeth as white as ivory and his eyes as black as sloes,
You may know a jolly collier wherever he goes.

'You may know a jolly collier, he's a swaggering young blade;
When he goes a-courting of his buxom fair maid
With his lips he so flatters her and spends his money free;
You may know a jolly collier wheresoever that he be.

'You may know a jolly collier as he sails the salt sea;
As he ploughs the wide ocean he sets his sails three:
The foresail for to lift her and the mainsail to drive,
And the pretty little crojick for to make her steer wild.

'I'll build my jolly collier a castle on a hill
Where neither duke nor squire can work me any ill;
For the queen can but enjoy the king and I can do the same,
And I am but a sheep-girl and who can me blame?'

☞ From the seventeenth to the nineteenth centuries coal was carried from Newcastle and Sunderland to London and the south on collier brigs, whose sailors were also called colliers. The song, from Masefield's *Garland*, seems to derive from a broadside, 'A Sailor for me; or the Saucy Colliers', which was issued by J. Pitts between 1819 and 1844. In turn, this is based on 'Molly's Lamentation for her Sailor', published in 1781, of which one verse reads: 'You may know my jolly sailor wherever he goes, He's so neat in his behaviour and so kind to his love. His teeth are white as ivory, his eyes black as sloes, You may know my jolly sailor wherever he goes.'

Wear Water] the River Wear enters the sea at Sunderland.   crojick] cross-jack, the lowest square sail set on the mizen mast of a square-rigged ship. Colliers were normally brigs (with two square-rigged masts), but this one is ship-rigged (with three masts).

Homeward Bound

Now to Blackwall Docks we bid adieu,
To Suke and Sal and Kitty too;
Our anchor's weighed, our sails unfurled,
We are bound to plough the watery world.
    Huzza, we are outward bound.
    [*Huzza, we are outward bound*].

Now the wind blows hard from the east-nor'-east,
Our ship will sail ten knots at least;
The purser will our wants supply,
And while we've grog we'll never say die.
    Huzza, &c.

And should we touch at Malabar
Or any other port as far
The purser he will tip the chink,
And just like fishes we will drink.
    Huzza, &c.

And now our three years it is out,
It's very near time we backed about;
And when we're home and do get free,
Oh won't we have a jolly spree.
    Huzza, [*we are homeward bound.*
    Huzza, we are homeward bound].

Malabar] in the south of India

And now we haul into the docks
Where all those pretty girls come in flocks,
And one to the other they will say:
'Oh here comes Jack with his three years' pay'.
   Huzza, &c.

And now we haul to the *Dog and Bell*
Where there's good liquor for to sell.
In comes old Archer with a smile,
Saying: 'Drink, my lads, it's worth your while,
   For I see you are homeward bound,
   [I see you are homeward bound].

But when our money's all gone and spent,
And none to be borrowed nor none to be lent,
In comes old Archer with a frown,
Saying: 'Get up, Jack, let John sit down,
   For I see you are outward bound,
   [I see you are outward bound'].

☞ 'In sailing ship days this song was a prime favourite,' writes Whall, 'and was sung all over the world.' British variants mention Katherine's, Liverpool, London, Milbay, Millwall, Bristol, and Sunderland Docks, and American, Pensacola, and Boston Town. The song was sung both for recreation and for work (at the capstan or pumps), and is one of the few shanties to have appeared as a street ballad. Hugill suggests that it originated in the navy and may be 'of great age', but there is no trace of it before printings of the 1820s. The text given here is from a broadside, and the tune from an ex-sailor, W. Bolton, for whom, see 94.

89   *The Smuggler's Victory*

Come all you Sussex heroes with courage stout and bold,
And listen unto these lines I have penned, which quickly I'll unfold.
It's of a glorious victory which was fought the other day
Between a party of preventive men and the smugglers brave, huzza.

   The preventive men run on the beach, thinking they had a prize,
   But the Sussex heroes with their bats began to tan their hides.

89 bats] thick ash poles, about six feet long

It was on the twenty-seventh of November, my boys, from Boulogne
    we set sail,
Bound for the Sussex coast, brave boys, with a sweet and pleasant
    gale;
And when we came to land, brave boys, our vessel we hove to;
Our tub boat then we sent on shore though our company was but
    few.

It was near the town of Bognor our tubs we tried to land,
But soon we were surrounded by a party of preventive men;
With cutlasses and firearms they began to fire away,
But our party with their bats, my boys, began to thrash away.

The preventive men said to one another: 'Now here is a rich prize:
About one hundred tubs of spirits, tea and tobacco likewise;
Besides if we can take the men, you know there's twenty pounds,
So we will swear black is white, my boys; we don't care who sinks
    or drowns.'

Then like the savage tigers those Philistines did run,
With cutlasses and firearms their bloody work begun.
Two of our men they shot, and wounded three more,
But from the beach we took them up all in their bloody gore.

Our party, seeing two of our men shot, a signal then was gave,
Determined for to fight, my boys, and our cargo for to save.
The preventive men, seeing them fall, they thought they got the day,
But in less than ten minutes the Philistines run away.

The preventive men took to their heels, and some on the beach did
    lay,
While every man took up his tubs and boldly walked away.
The Philistines stood a-trembling, you would have laughed if you
    had been there,
To see the Philistines how they began to shed their tears.

Then drink success to all fair traders that lived both far and near,
But as for all informers, shave their heads and cut off their ears;
For an informer is worse than a thief, the truth to you I say,
To banish them from England for life to Botany Bay.

---

tub boat] small boat carrying tubs of contraband goods ashore   Bognor] in
Sussex   twenty pounds] reward   Philistines] officers of justice   fair traders]
south-country smugglers' name for themselves

So now my song is ended, I will conclude my ditty,
And drink success to all fair traders in a thumping glass of brandy;
And down with all informers, so merrily let us sing,
Success to our wives and sweethearts and God save the king.

Written by and printed for William Smith, Isle of Wight

☞ Smuggling was rife during the Revolutionary and Napoleonic Wars with
France, and it dramatically increased for a time afterwards. The ballad, which
may be based on a real incident, probably dates from the early 1820s.

90 *Sally Munro*

Come all you young maidens I pray you attend
Unto these few lines that I have here penned,
To all the sad troubles that I did undergo
Since I became acquainted with sweet Sally Munro.

James Dickson's my name, I'm a blacksmith by trade,
And in the town of Ayr I was born and bred.
From that town to Belfast I late did go;
'Twas there I got acquainted wi' sweet Sally Munro.

I loved this young lassie as dear as my life;
It was my intention to make her my wife,
But though dearly I loved her, her parents said 'No',
Which caused me to mourn for young Sally Munro.

I unto this lassie a letter did send,
It was by a comrade whom I thought a friend;
But instead of a friend he proved to me a foe,
For he never gave the letter to my Sally Munro.

He told her old parents to beware of me:
He said I had a wife in my own country.
Then said her old parents: 'Since we've found it so,
He never shall enjoy his sweet Sally Munro.'

I said if she'd come to Urie with me,
In spite of her parents there married we'd be.
She said: 'No objections have I there to go,
If you only prove constant to Sally Munro.'

'Here is my hand, love, and here is my heart;
Till death separate us we never shall part.'
Next day in a coach we to Urie did go,
And there I got married to young Sally Munro.

It was at Newry Point the ship *Newry* lay
With four hundred passengers ready for sea.
We both paid our passage to Quebec also;
'Twas there I embarked wi' my Sally Munro.

On the fourteenth of April our ship did set sail
And hove down the Channel with a sweet pleasant gale.
The parting of friends caused some salt tears to flow,
But I was quite happy wi' my Sally Munro.

When dreading no danger we met with a shock
When all of a sudden our ship struck a rock.
Three hundred and sixty went all down below,
And in among the number I lost Sally Munro.

Many a man on that voyage lost his life
And children they loved far dearer than life,
Yet I was preserved and my salt tears do flow.
Oh I mourn when I mind on my Sally Munro.

It was from her parents I stole her away,
Which will check my conscience till my dying day;
But she said: 'No objections have I now to go',
And now I'll keep sighing for Sally Munro.

☞ The *Newry* was wrecked at Porth Oer on the Lleyn Peninsula in North Wales on
the night of 16–17 April 1830. It seems that James Dickson and Sally Munro

Urie] Newry   Newry Point] Warrenpoint

were real people. Gavin Greig wrote that 'in none of our ballads is the note of sincerity more strong and convincing'. He had eleven versions from Aberdeenshire, of which one, from a Mrs McKenzie of Peterhead, is given here. Others have turned up in England, Ireland, and America.

The Banks of Newfoundland (I)

Oh may you bless your happy lot that lies secure on shore,
Free from the billows and the blast that round poor seamen roar.
It's little you know the dangers that we were forced to stand
For fourteen days and fourteen nights on the Banks of
    Newfoundland.

Our good ship never crossed before the stormy western seas;
The raging seas came tumbling down, soon beat her into staves.
She being of green unseasoned wood, little could she stand,
For the hurricane had met us on the Banks of Newfoundland.

[Our captain and mate including with twelve of the ship's crew,
Ten passengers we had on board, made up just twenty-two;
Some had their wives and families on their dear native strand,
Intending soon to cross again the Banks of Newfoundland.

But we were all benumbed with cold from the day we left Quebec;
Except that we had walked about we were frozen to the deck,

But we were all hardy Irishmen that our good ship manned.
Our captain doubled each man's grog on the Banks of
  Newfoundland.

The tempest blew from the sunset to the cold wintry dawn;
When she fell on to leeward two of her masts were gone.
Our captain says: 'My brave boys, we must inventions plan
For to hoist a sign[al] of distress on the Banks of Newfoundland.'

If you had seen our doleful state your hearts would been oppressed;
It blew a most tremendous gale with the wind from the south-west.
Some of our men jumped overboard, said they would rather swim to
  land,
But alas, it was five hundred miles from the Banks of
  Newfoundland.]

We fasted for three days and nights when our provisions they ran
  out,
And on the morning of the fourth we sent the lots about.
The lot fell on the captain's son and you may understand
We spared him for another day on the Banks of Newfoundland.

No sails appeared. Reluctantly, we ordered him prepare;
We gave him just another hour to offer up a prayer,
But providence was always kind, kept blood from every hand,
When an English vessel hove in sight on the Banks of
  Newfoundland.

When we were taken off the wreck we were more like ghosts than
  men;
They clothed us and they used us well and brought us home again,
But four of our brave Irish boys ne'er saw their native land,
And our captain lost his legs by frost on the Banks of
  Newfoundland.

[Of all the gallant seamen was of our brave ships's crew
There live but five to tell the tale, and passengers but two.
For them their friends may shed salt tears on their dear native
  strand;
The mountain waves run o'er their graves on the Banks of
  Newfoundland.]

☞ In dire extremity cannibalism seems to have been accepted as part of the custom
of the sea, and there are plenty of documented examples. 'The Banks of

Newfoundland' is the title of two distinct songs, the other of which is given as 119 below. This one, dealing with narrowly-averted cannibalism, was printed on several English broadsides but has turned up in oral tradition only in Ireland, the Shetland Isles (as recently as 1971) and North America. The version here, taken down from an Antrim man in 1934, has been supplemented from a broadside without imprint which was probably issued in the 1830s by Joseph Russell of Birmingham.

92   *The Rambling Sailor*

I am a sailor stout and bold,
Long time I have ploughed the ocean
To fight for my king and country too,
For honour and promotion.
I said: 'Brother sailors I will bid you adieu.
I will go no more to the seas with you,
I will travel the country through and through,
And still be a rambling sailor.'

When I came to Greenwich town,
There were lasses plenty.
I boldly steppèd up to one
To court her for her beauty.

194

I said: 'My dear, be of good cheer.
I will not leave, you need not fear.'
I will travel the country through and through,
And still be a rambling sailor.

When I came to Woolwich town,
There were lasses plenty.
I boldly steppèd up to one
To court her for her money.
I said: 'My dear, what do you choose?
There's ale and wine and rum punch too,
Besides a pair of new silk shoes
To travel with a rambling sailor.'

When I awoke all in the morn
I left my love a-sleeping.
I left her for an hour or two
Whilst I go courting some other;
But if she stays till I return
She may stay there till the day of doom.
I'll court some other girl in her room,
And still be a rambling sailor.

And if you want to know my name,
My name it is young Johnson.
I have got a commission from the king
To court all girls that are handsome.
With my false heart and flattering tongue
I court all girls both old and young;
I court them all and marry none,
And still be a rambling sailor.

H. Disley, Printer, St Giles [London]

☞ The notion of sailors' fickleness in love was widely held, and frequently
expressed in song. This ballad was often printed from the 1830s to the '50s, and
then went into oral circulation, though apparently only in England. There were
adaptations to suit the rambling soldier, miner, 'suiler' (in Ireland: 'beggar-
man'), and also the female rambling sailor. 'The Rambling Sailor' seems to have
had a forerunner, 'The Jolly Sailor', which dates perhaps from 1810 or earlier.
The verses end not with a 'rambling' but with a 'roving' or 'rolling' sailor, and
Johnson's commission is received not from the king but from 'Venus the queen'.
The tune here is from a Somerset singer.

Fare ye well, lovely Nancy

var. (a) all verses but first

'Fare ye well, lovely Nancy, for now I must leave you.
I am bound to th' East Indies my course for to steer.
I know very well my long absence will grieve you,
But, true love, I'll be back in the spring of the year.'

'Oh, 'tis not talk of leaving me, my dearest Johnny,
Oh, 'tis not talk of leaving me here all alone;
For it is your good company that I do admire:
I will sigh till I die if I ne'er see you more.'

'In sailor's apparel I'll dress and go with you,
In the midst of all dangers your friend I will be;
And that is, my dear, when the stormy wind's blowing,
True love, I'll be ready to reef your topsails.'

'Your neat little fingers strong cables can't handle,
Your neat little feet to the topmast can't go;
Your delicate body strong winds can't endure.
Stay at home, lovely Nancy, to the seas do not go.'

Now Johnny is sailing and Nancy bewailing;
The tears down her eyes like torrents do flow.
Her gay golden hair she's continually tearing,
Saying, 'I'll sigh till I die if I ne'er see you more.'

Now all you young maidens by me take warning,
Never trust a sailor or believe what they say.

First they will court you, then they will slight you;
They will leave you behind, love, in grief and in pain.

☞ In 'Adieu, my lovely Nancy' a sailor expresses his reluctance to go to sea because of the joint dangers of war and battle, promises to write letters while he is away, and looks forward to returning. In 'Fare ye well, lovely Nancy' we have moved on in time: the war is over, and the departing sailor is faced only with hard work and a struggle with the elements. Nevertheless, he has to dissuade Nancy from following him in disguise. This theme has a pedigree going back at least to the 1680s, and ballads such as 'The Seaman's Doleful Farewell', 'The Undaunted Seaman', and 'The Undaunted Mariner'. The last of these begins 'Farewell, my dearest Nancy, for this day I must leave thee', and all have verbal similarities with 'Fare ye well, lovely Nancy', which appeared in its turn on broadsides and also circulated traditionally in America, Australia, Ireland, and Britain. The version given here was sung to Vaughan Williams by a Hampshire man, George Lovett, in 1909.

94 *Ratcliffe Highway*

As I was a-walking down Wapping
I stepped into Ratcliffe Highway,
And there I went into an alehouse
To spend all that night and next day.

Two charming young girls sat beside me.
They asked if I'd money to sport.
'Bring a bottle of wine, change a guinea.'
'I see you are one of the sort.'

The bottle was placed on the table
With glasses for every one;
When I asked for the change of my guinea
She gave me the verse of a song.

The old woman she flew in a passion,
And placed her two hands on her hip,
Saying: 'Young man, you don't know our fashion.
You think you're on board of your ship.'

'If that is your fashion, to rob me,
It's a fashion I don't much admire.
So tip me the change of my guinea,
Or a broadside into you I'll fire.'

The bottle that stood on the table
I quick at her head did let fly,
And down on the ground she did tumble
And loudly for mercy did cry.

The gold watch that hung on the mantel
I into my pocket did slip;
And, darn my old shoes, didn't I trick her,
And soon got aboard of my ship.

Our anchor being weighed at our bow, boys,
Our tops'ls being well sheeted home,
We soon bid adieu to fair London
And all the flash girls in the town.

☞ Ratcliffe Highway, close to London Docks, was described by Henry Mayhew as
'a reservoir of dirt, drunkenness and drabs'. William Bolton, who was born in
1840, said that 'in his young days it was a favourite diversion among sailors
ashore to take a walk down the Highway, and if their hearts were not cheered by
the sight of some fight or disturbance already going on, to set about creating one
without delay'. Starting at the age of twelve, Bolton spent fourteen years in the
Royal, then twenty-one in the Merchant Navy, before retiring to Southport,
where Anne Gilchrist met him in 1906. He knew a score of shanties and
forebitters, including 'Ratcliffe Highway', which he described as 'a great
favourite with sailors'. It was published on broadsides, starting perhaps with
Pitts' version in 1830, as 'Rolling down Wapping'.

95   *Loss of the* Amphitrite

Come list you gallant Englishmen who ramble at your ease
While I unfold the horrors and the dangers of the seas;
It's of a ship, the *Amphitrite*, with a hundred and eight females
And children, crew and cargo, all bound for New South Wales.

'Twas on August twenty-fifth we sailed from Woolwich shore,
Leaving our friends behind us whose hearts were grievèd sore;
Along the shore away we bore till friends were out of sight,
Who, crying, said: 'Adieu, poor girls, on board of the *Amphitrite*.'

We sailed away without delay and arrived off Dungeness,
But when we came off Port Boulogne then great was our distress.
On Friday morning the fourth day, oh, what a wretched sight:
We, crying, said: 'Adieu, poor girls, on board of the *Amphitrite*.'

Our captain found she was near aground, her anchor he did let go,
Crying: 'Set your main and topsails, boys, or soon your fate you'll
    know.'
The raging sea ran mountains high, the tempest did unite;
Poor souls in vain did shriek with pain on board of the *Amphitrite*.

At three o'clock in the afternoon we were put to a stand;
Our fatal ship she ran aground upon a bank of sand.
Poor children round their parents hung, who tore their hair with
    fright,
To think that they should end their days aboard the *Amphitrite*.

Our moments they were ending fast and all prepared to die;
We on our bended knees did fall and loud for mercy cry.
Our ship she gave a dreadful roll and soon went out of sight.
Oh the bitter cries that rent the skies on board the *Amphitrite*.

Great praise belongs unto the French who tried us all to save.
Our captain he was obstinate to brave the stormy wave,
But he went down among the rest all in the briny sea,
The rocks beneath the pathless deep his pillow for to be.

The crew were tossed and all were lost but two poor lads and me,
For on a spar we reached the shore and dared the raging sea;
But one exhausted by the waves he died that very night,
So only two were saved of the crew of the fatal *Amphitrite*.

So now the *Amphitrite* is gone, her passengers and crew.
Oh think upon the sailor bold that wears the jacket blue;
God grant relief to end their grief of those distracted quite,
Lamenting sore for those no more on board the *Amphitrite*.

London H. P. Such, Machine Printer and Publisher, 177, Union Street,
Borough

set your main and topsails] should be 'furl'

☞ The *Amphitrite* sailed from London on 28 August 1833, with 136 people on board. The total was made up by 106 female convicts and 12 of their children, a surgeon-superintendent and his wife, and a crew of 16. On 30 August the vessel went aground off Boulogne, but the captain declined assistance, thinking she would float clear with the tide. When the tide came in, at about eleven at night, the *Amphitrite* was quickly pounded to pieces by the waves. The only people to reach the shore alive were three sailors, of whom one died shortly afterwards. The ballad purports to have been written by one of the survivors, but there is nothing in it which could not have been gleaned from a news report of the event. A solitary version from oral tradition, close to the broadside but calling the ship the *Anford-Wright*, turned up in Virginia in 1917, though the tune was not noted.

96   *Bold Adventures of Captain Ross*

Air, 'Tars of the *Blanche*'

Come listen awhile with attention,
You seamen and landsmen likewise,
While I of a hero will mention,
Which England, famed England, should prize.
Bold Ross was our noble commander,
His equal was ne'er seen before;
But mark what us sailors went under
When we sailèd from old England's shore.

We sailed to the Pacific Ocean,
Our hearts both undaunted and free;
Bold Ross cheered us all with the notion
That we should all prosperous be;
But our mainmast was soon smashed to pieces,
While we hauled in the ship, *Fury*'s, store.
Said Ross: 'Now the tempest increases,
'Tis for honour of old England's shore.'

Long time in tempestuous weather,
'Midst rocks, ice and water were we;
We were staunch, bold, and vowed to each other
To die or the North Pole to see.

   96 ship, *Fury*'s store] the *Fury*, Parry's exploration ship, had been wrecked in Prince Regent's Inlet in 1825 by the ice. Equipment and stores were landed and stockpiled for the use of later expeditions.

Ross espied from the ship's starboard quarter
The land that did add to their store,
Crying: 'Look out, my boys, for fresh water.
We're far from old England's shore.'

Our hardships we bore and were ready
To follow our brave captain's call,
Who was bold, was undaunted but ready:
His study alone was us all.
While we roamed o'er the cold stormy regions
On wilds that were ne'er trod before;
No cot, house or church or religion
Like those upon old England's shore.

You may talk about Parry and Cook, boys,
Who tried these cold regions to find;
Only a short trip they took, boys,
Then left the bright magnet behind.
Bold Ross left the British flag flying,
Which no one could e'er do before;
Then light-hearted, though nearly dying,
Came with glory to old England's shore.

'Twas thought that no one since creation
Would find it until time did end,
But King William's name of this nation
So proud on that magnet does bend.
So build for bold Ross a fine pillar
And cast it with gold letters o'er;
Bold Ross braved the wind, ice and billows,
In triumph reached old England's shore.

This hero, the pride of our nation,
Gained honour; likewise his ship's crew,
May they rise into dignity's station
For being undaunted and true.
Bold Ross as a pledge of honour
With the lord mayor of London did dine,
And they gave him three cheers in a bumper,
Drank to trade and to commerce in wine.

Parry] Sir William Edward (1790–1855) made several expeditions to the Arctic
between 1818 and 1827.   Cook] James (1728–79) best-known for his work (and
death) in the South Seas, also surveyed the coasts of Newfoundland between 1763 and
1768.

Printed by W. Taylor, 16, Waterloo Road, near the Victoria theatre. Country Dealers and Shops supplied at wholesale prices.

☞ The Scotsman, Captain (later Rear-Admiral) John Ross (1777–1856), having explored Baffin Bay in 1818–19, went on a second voyage of discovery in 1829. In the paddlesteamer, *Victory*, he travelled to the north of Canada, where the ship was icebound for three years. During this time the Boothia Peninsula and King William Island were surveyed, and Ross's second-in-command and nephew, James Ross, discovered the magnetic north pole. In the summer of 1832 the expedition took to the ship's boats, and was picked up in Barrow's Strait by a whaler. On returning to London in 1833, Captain John Ross was knighted. James Ross went on further expeditions between 1839 and 1849.

97 *The Female Cabin Boy,*
or, the Row among the Sailors

Tune, 'Female Drummer'

It's of a pretty female as you shall understand;
She had a mind for roving into a foreign land.
Attired in sailor's clothing she boldly did appear,
And engaged with the captain to serve him for a year.

She engaged with the captain as cabin boy to be;
The wind it was in favour so they soon put out to sea.
The captain's lady being on board she seemed it to enjoy,
So glad the captain had engaged the pretty cabin boy.

So nimble was that pretty maid, and done her duty well,
But mark what followed often the thing itself will tell.
The captain with that pretty maid did ofttimes kiss and toy,
For he soon found out the secret of the female cabin boy.

Her cheeks appeared like roses with her side-locks curled;
The sailors often smiled and said: 'He looks just like a girl';
By eating captain's biscuits her colour did destroy,
And the waist did swell of pretty Nell, the pretty cabin boy.

As through the Bay of Biscay their gallant ship did plough,
One night among the sailors there was a pretty row.
They bundled from their hammocks, it did their rest destroy,
And they swore about the groaning of the handsome cabin boy.

'O doctor, O doctor,' the cabin boy did cry.
The sailors swore by all was good the cabin boy would die.
The doctor ran with all his might, and smiling at the fun,
For to think a sailor lad should have a daughter or a son.

The sailors when they heard the joke they all began to stare;
The child belonged to none of them they solemnly did swear.
The lady to the captain said: 'My dear, I wish you joy,
For either you or I betrayed the handsome cabin boy.'

So they all took a bumper and drank success to trade,
And likewise to the cabin boy, though neither man nor maid;
And if the waves should rise again the sailors to destroy,
Why then we must ship some sailors like the handsome cabin boy.

Williams, Printer, No. 47, Queen Street, Portsea. Bills and Cards Printed
Cheap

☞ 'The Female' or 'Handsome Cabin Boy' appeared at least a dozen times on broadsides, starting probably after the end of the French Wars. The text given here was printed between 1833 and 1847. The witty treatment of the well-loved female sailor theme was widely popular with singers, but seldom published in collections until very recent years.

often] after   waves] in some versions, 'wars'

98

The Fancy Frigate

It is of a fine frigate, dare not mention her name,
And in the West Indies she bore great fame
For cruel hard usage in every degree;
Like slaves in a galley we plough the salt sea.

At four in the morning the game is begun:
To the cockpit the waisters for buckets must run;
For fore and main topmen so loud they do bawl,
For sand and for stones both large and small.

O Master Make-clever, you know very well,
He comes upon deck and cuts a great swell.
It's: 'Bear a hand here, boys, and bear a hand there';
And round the gangway he takes a broad stare.

Half a dozen he starts, and so he goes on;
You're sure of a hiding, boys, every one.
For soldier nor sailor he cares not a damn,
But he'll hide you as long as you're able to stand.

Our decks being washed and our sheets being home,
Stand by your hammocks, boys, every one;
Seven turns with your lashings so equal must show,
And all of a size, boys, and through the hoop go.

stones] holystones   hide you] thrash you

Our hammocks being stowed and our breakfast done,
We're ranked in divisions with our white hats all on;
With our speeguls and lashings so black they must shine,
With our white frocks and trousers we must all be a line.

Our division officer then takes his round;
Not a hole, not a spot on your clothes must be found.
For an hour or more in this form we must be;
Our ropes they are flemished either in harbour or at sea.

Our divisions being over the next thing comes on:
Jack o' Clubs here is calling for swabs in his song;
Three or four dry swabs each cook they must find,
And the bright iron hoops on the mess-kids must shine.

There is pulling and hauling all the four hours round;
On deck or below there's no peace to be found.
Either paint room or store room you're sure for to clear,
To find out what blacking or paint is to spare.

'Pass the word for the painter', fore and aft is the cry.
Neither booms nor gangway I would have you draw nigh;
Nor yet in the ports I would have you be found:
For six dozen or more your name will go round.

Our boarding pikes and cutlasses are bright as the sun,
Our shot racks are copper, boys, every one,
Our pumelins and handspikes and belaying pins also;
With our bright iron stanchions we cut a fine show.

Neither coamings nor hatchway I'd have you go near,
From the bell or cook's funnel I'd have you keep clear;
Nor yet in the galley I'd have you to go,
For a black thunder squall will take you in tow.

Now, my brave boys, comes the best of the fun:
All hands to make sail, going large, is the song.
From under two reefs in our topsails we lie,
Like a cloud in the air in an instant must fly.

white hats] straw hats   four hours] a watch   ports] gun ports
six dozen] lashes   pumelin] knob on the breech of a cannon

There's topsails, topgallant sails and staysails too,
There is stunsails on both sides, aloft and below;
There's royals and skysails, stargazers so high:
By the sound of one pipe everything it must fly.

Now, my brave boys, comes the best of the fun:
About ship and reef topsails in one.
Our hands go aloft when the helm it goes down,
Lower away topsails when the mainyard goes round.

Trace up and lie out and take two reefs in one;
In a moment of time all this work must be done.
Man your head braces, your halliards and all,
And hoist away topsails when it's 'Let go and haul'.

As for the use of tobacco, all thoughts leave behind:
If you spit upon deck then your death warrant's signed;
If you spit overboard either gangway or stern
You are sure of six dozen by the way of no harm.

But worse than all this, I have known them to stop
A week's wine or grog if you spill but one drop.
Either forward or aft I would have you keep clear,
Or the bell or cook's funnel will fall to your share.

Come all brother seamen wherever you be,
From all fancy frigates I'd have you keep clear.
Take compassion all on us and never forget
Those poor pipeclay rangers, so callèd of late.

☞ An alternative opening for this song is: 'It's of a fine frigate, *La Pique* was her name'. There were three navy ships of that name. The first was a French vessel taken into the service after its capture in 1795 (see 73). The name was transferred to another prize, formerly the *Pallas*, in 1807, and then passed on in 1834 to a new 36-gun ship which was probably the *La Pique* of the song. The spit and polish described are typical of the long years of *pax britannica*, and although seamen's uniform was not officially instituted until 1857, the dress, and in particular the tropical rig, described here accords with that customarily worn during the first half of the century. The song remained well known for many generations, and was adapted to fit at least one other ship, the *Dreadnought* (114).

bell or cook's funnel will fall to your share] to clean   pipeclay] for whitening

99

Three Jolly Fishermen

We are three jolly fishermen, we are three jolly fishermen,
We are three jolly fishermen, while the merry, merry bells do ring.

(Solo) *Make haste, make haste.*
(Tutti) *You be too late.*
(Solo) *What fish, my dear?*
(Tutti) *I cannot wait.*
(Tutti) *For me fine fry of herring, me bonny silver herring.*
Mind how I sell them while the merry, merry bells do ring.

We cast our nets upon the rocks, &c.

We sell them three for fourpence, &c.

With white and speckled bellies, &c.

☞ Steve Gardham recorded this from Thomas Calvert of Runswick Bay, North
Yorkshire, in 1971. The song, which seems to have been a particular favourite in
the Whitby area (though Cecil Sharp had a version from Middlesex, attached to
a dance), was issued on a broadside printed in 1837–8 by W. and T. Fordyce,

Newcastle, under the title of 'Caller Herring'. This in turn loosely derives from a song of the same name by Lady Carolina Nairne (1766–1845), published in 1824 to a tune by Nathaniel Gow (1777–1831), based on 'the original Cry of the Newhaven fish wives, Selling their fresh Herrings in the streets of Edinburgh'. Gow's tune was issued as a shilling music sheet for piano in *c.*1802.

100 *Grace Darling*

'Twas on the Longstone Lighthouse there dwelt an English maid,
Pure as the air around her, of danger ne'er afraid.
One morning just at daybreak a storm-tossed wreck she spied.
Although to try seemed madness, 'I'll save the crew,' she cried.

And she pulled away o'er the rolling seas, over the waters blue.
'Help, help': she could hear the cry of the shipwrecked crew;
But Grace had an English heart: the raging storm she braved;
She pulled away 'mid the dashing spray, and the crew she saved.

They to the rocks were clinging, a crew of nine, all told;
Between them and the lighthouse the seas like mountains rolled.
Said Grace: 'Come help me, father. We'll launch the boat,' said
   she.
''Tis madness', said her father, 'to face that raging sea.'

One murmured prayer: 'Heaven guard us'; and then they were
   afloat.
Between them and destruction the planks of that frail boat.
Then said the maiden's father: 'Turn back, or doomed are we.'
Then up spoke brave Grace Darling: 'Alone I'll brave the sea.'

They rode the angry billows and reached the rock at length;
They saved the shipwrecked sailors: in heaven alone their strength.
Go tell the wide world over what English pluck can do,
And sing of brave Grace Darling who nobly saved the crew.

☞ Grace Darling (1815–42) achieved lasting fame for her part in a heroic rescue. On 7 September 1838 the paddle-steamer, *Forfarshire*, bound from Hull to Dundee, was wrecked on the Farne Islands, close to the coast of Northumberland. William Darling was the keeper of the Longstone Lighthouse, which stood on one of the islands. He wrote this report to Trinity House, London: 'On the morning of the 7th September, it blowing gale with rain from the north, my daughter and me being both on the alert before high water securing things out of doors, one quarter before five my daughter observed a vessel on the Harker's rock; but owing to the darkness, and spray going over her, could not observe any person on the wreck ... until near 7 o'clock, when, the tide being fallen, we observed three or four men on the rock. . . . We immediately launched our boat, and was enabled to gain the rock, where we found eight men and one woman, which I judged rather too many to take at once in the state of weather, therefore took the woman and four men to Longstone. Two of them returned with me, and succeeding in bringing the remainder, in all nine persons, safely to the Longstone about 9 o'clock.' Even put in these sober terms the achievement of travelling in an open boat on mountainous seas over a distance of a mile each way was magnificent, and William and Grace Darling were both awarded the Royal Humane Society's gold medal. Grace Darling herself had a waltz, a quadrille, and a galop composed in her honour, and also a song, by Felix McGlennan, which is still in print. This was reproduced as one of several street ballads on the rescue, and also circulated orally, despite (or perhaps because of) the extreme lengths to which it takes poetic licence. The version given here was sung by Walter Pardon of Knapton, Norfolk, in 1974. The song has also turned up in Australia and Ireland (where Grace acquired 'an Irish heart').

As I strolled out one evening upon a dark career
I spied a lofty clipper ship and for her I did steer.
I hoisted up my signals which she so quickly knew,
And when she saw, to my surprise, she suddenly hove to.

She had a dark and rolling eye and her hair hung down in ringalets;
She was a nice girl, a proper girl, but one of the rakish kind.

'Oh, sir, you must excuse me for being out so late,
For if my parents knew of it how sad would be my fate.
[My father is a preacher, a good and pious man;
My mother is a Methodist, and I'm a true Briton.']

I took her to a public house and treated her to wine,
But little did I think she belonged to the rakish kind.
I handled her, I handled her, but found to my surprise
She was nothing but a fire ship rigged up in a disguise.

[Come all you able seamen that plough the raging main,
That get a little money by the cold, wind and rain,

I'd have you shun those fiery ships or you will surely rue,
Or else you'll get your cobbles sprung and set on fire too.]

☞ The extended sexual metaphor of a man's boarding a vessel and then finding she
is a fire ship is as least as old as the seventeenth century. The version given here
is sung by Bill ('Pop') Hingston (b. 1914), of Dittisham, Devon, whose text has
been completed from a broadside issued by Jackson and Son of Birmingham
between 1839 and 1851 under the title of 'Black and Rolling Eye'. The song was
sung at sea as a forebitter and also as a pumping shanty. It is rare, both in print
and in oral tradition.

102 *Liverpool Girls*

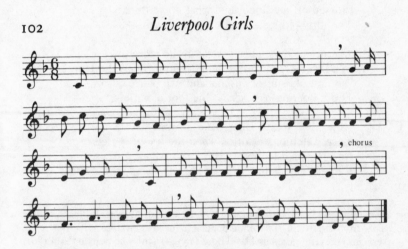

When I was a youngster I sailed with the rest
On a Liverpool packet bound out to the west.
We anchored a day in the harbour o' Cork,
Then put out to sea for the port o' New York.

> *And it's ho, ro. Ho, bullies, ho.*
> *The Liverpool gir-ils have got us in tow.*

For thirty-two days we was hungry and sore;
The wind was agin us and gales they did roar,
But at Battery Point we did anchor at last
Wi' the jib boom hove in and the canvas all fast.

102 Battery Point] seaward tip of Manhattan Island

The boarding house masters was off in a trice,
And shouting and promising all that was nice;
And one fat old crimp he got cottoned to me,
And said I was foolish to follow the sea.

Says he: 'There's a job as is waiting for you
Wid lashings o' liquor and nothing to do.
Now, what d'ye say, lad, will you jump her too?'
Says I: 'Ye old beggar, I'm damned if I do.'

But the best of intentions they never go far
After thirty-two days as the door of a bar.
I tossed off me liquor and what do ye think?
The dirty old rascal had drugs in me drink.

The next I remember I woke in the morn
In a three skysail yarder bound south round the Horn,
With an old suit of oilskins and two pair o' socks,
And a flooring o' bricks at the foot o' me box.

Now all ye young sailors take warning by me,
Keep watch on yer drink when the liquor is free,
And pay no attention to runner or whore
When yer hat's on yer head and yer feet's on the shore.

☞ According to Hugill, this 'favourite capstan song in Liverpool ships' probably
dates from the 1840s, 'since it was popular in the Western Ocean Packets'. This
version comes from Captain David Bone (1874–1959), who went to sea in 1891.
He comments: 'The preparation of the ground tackle is a sign that the end of a
voyage is not far away. Anchors and cables have to be got ready, and in the
laborious work of heaving up and ranging the cable on deck, the capstan is used.
"The Liverpool Girls" is a good chanty for the job, particularly if the wind is
blowing fair and fresh, for then the girls are said to have got hold of the towrope.'
He adds, writing in 1931: 'The last line of the sixth verse was not quite as
respectable as I have printed it. In the true version it would indicate that the
singer had sustained damage on a voyage to Cytherea.'

crimp] boarding house or tailor's runner who specialized in persuading seamen to jump
ship in port.

Leave her, Johnny

Oh the times was hard and the wages low,
Leave her, Johnny, leave her;
And the grub was bad and the gales did blow,
And it's time for us to leave her.

Leave her, Johnny, leave her,
Oh leave her, Johnny, leave her,
For the voy'ge is done and the gales can blow,
And it's time for us to leave her.

I thought I heard the Old Man say,
'Ye can go ashore and take yer pay'.

Oh her stern was foul and the voy'ge was long;
And the winds was bad and the gales was strong.

And we'll leave her tight and we'll leave her trim,
And heave the hungry packet in.

Oh leave her, Johnny, leave her with a grin,
For there's many a worser we've sailed in.

And now it's time to say goodbye,
For the old pierhead's a-drawing nigh.

☞ This shanty was sung at the end of a voyage, at the halliards (in which case, without the chorus), at the capstan when warping into dock, or at the pumps so as to leave the ship dry. Hugill says that it was used for pumping even during a voyage, but Bullen writes: 'It sums up all the hatred of a ship that had been accumulating during the voyage. To sing it before the last day or so on board was almost tantamount to mutiny and was apt even at the latest date to be fiercely resented by captain and officers.' The version given here, from Bone, seems unlikely to have excited much resentment, but singers drew on a pool of literally dozens of verses, such as: 'Oh sing that we, boys, will never be In a hungry bitch the likes of she' or 'We'll leave her tight and we'll leave her trim, We'll heave the hungry bastard in' or 'Well the old Man's a bugger and the mate he's a Turk And the bosun he's a bastard with the middle name of work'. The shanty was sung on both sides of the Atlantic, from the 1840s until the end of sail, and even afterwards, for Colcord says that striking stokers from a transatlantic liner marched ashore singing it at New York in the 1920s. The song has since, like many other shanties, enjoyed a new lease of life in convivial circumstances ashore.

104 *George Jones*

Good people all come listen to my melancholy tale,
My dying declaration which I have penned in jail.
My present situation may to all a warning be,
And a caution to all seamen to beware of mutiny.

George Jones is my name, I am from the county Clare;
I quit my aged parents and left them living there.
I being inclined for roving at home I would not stay,
And much against my parents' will I shipped and went to sea.

My last ship was the *Saladin*, I shudder at her name;
I joined her in Valparaiso on the Spanish Main.
I shipped as cabin steward, which proved a fatal day:
A demon came aboard of her which led us four astray.

I agreed to work my passage, the ship being homeward bound
With copper ore and silver and over thousand pounds;
Likewise two cabin passengers on board of her did come:
The one was Captain Fielding, the other was his son.

He did upbraid our captain before we were long at sea,
And one by one seduced us into a mutiny;
The tempting prize did tempt his eyes, he kept it well in view,
And by his consummate art he's destroyed us all but two.

On the fourteenth night of April I am sorry to relate
We began his desperate enterprise. At first we killed the mate;
Next we killed the carpenter and overboard him threw;
Our captain next was put to death with three more of his crew.

The watch were in their hammocks when the work of death begun.
The watch we called. As they came up we killed them one by one.
These poor unhappy victims lay in their beds asleep;
We called them up and murdered them and hove them in the deep.

There were two more remaining still below and unprepared.
The hand of God protected them that both their lives were spared.
By them we're brought to justice and both of them are free;
They had no hand in Fielding's plan, nor his conspiracy.

An oath was next administered to the remainder of the crew,
And like a band of brothers we were sworn to be true;
This was on Sunday morning when the bloody deed was done,
When Fielding brought the Bible and swore us every one.

The firearms and weapons all we threw into the sea.
He said he'd steer for Newfoundland, to which we did agree,
And secret all our treasure there in some secluded place;
If it was not for his treachery that might have been the case.

We found with Captain Fielding (for which he lost his life)
A brace of loaded pistols, likewise a carving-knife;
We suspected him for treachery, which did enrage the crew;
He was seized by Carr and Galloway and overboard was threw.

His son exclaimed for mercy, as being left alone,
But his entreaties were soon cut off, no mercy there shown.
We served him like his father was who met a watery grave,
So we buried son and father beneath the briny wave.

Next it was agreed upon before the wind to keep;
We had the world before us then, and on the trackless deep.
We mostly kept before the wind as we could do no more,
And on the twenty-eighth of May we were shipwrecked on the shore.

We were all apprehended and into prison cast,
Tried and found guilty, and sentence on us passed.
Four of us being condemned and sentenced for to die,
And the day of execution was the thirteenth of July.

Come all you pious Christians who God is pleased to spare,
I hope you will remember us in your pious prayer.
Make appeals to God for us, for our departing souls.
I hope you will remember us when we depart and mould.

Likewise the pious clergymen who for our souls did pray,
Who watched and prayed along with us whilst we in prison lay,
May God reward them for their pains, they really did their best,
They offered holy sacrifice to God to grant us rest.

And may the God of mercy who shed his blood so free,
Who died upon the holy cross all sinners to set free.
We humbly ask his pardon for the gross offence we gave,
May he have mercy on our souls when we descend the grave.

We were conveyed from prison unto the gallows high,
Ascended on the scaffold whereon we were to die.
Farewell, my loving countrymen, I bid this world adieu.
I hope this will a warning be to one and all of you.

They were placed upon the fatal drop, their coffins beneath their
    feet,
And the clergy were preparing them their maker for to meet.
They prayed sincere for mercy whilst they humbly smote their
    breast;
They were launched into eternity, and may God grant them rest.

☞ The extraordinary events narrated here took place in 1844. An English ship, the
Saladin, of Newcastle-upon-Tyne, was about to sail to London from Valparaiso,

in Chile. Her captain, 'Sandy' Mackenzie, agreed to give passage home to a Captain Fielding and his son whose ship had been confiscated by the authorities in Peru because of their involvement in some illegality. The *Saladin* was carrying a ton of silver bars and a large amount of cash, and the Fieldings conceived a plan to take over the ship, sail to Newfoundland, and make off with the treasure. They persuaded four members of the crew to join them, and killed Captain Mackenzie and several others. Then, fearing for their own lives, the four mutineers forced Carr and Galloway, two members of the crew who had taken no part in the mutiny, to throw the Fieldings overboard. This left them without a navigator, but they managed to follow the plan to go to Newfoundland. However, they sailed too close, the vessel went aground, and the facts of the mutiny came out. The four men involved were put on trial, and hanged at Halifax, Nova Scotia.

105 *Heave away, my Johnny*

As I was going out one day down by the Clarence Dock,
  Heave away, my Johnny, heave away;
As I was going out one day down by the Clarence Dock,
  Hand away, my jolly boys, we're all bound to go.

I overheard an emigrant conversing with Tapscott,
I overheard an emigrant conversing with Tapscott.

'Good morning, Mr Tapscott'. 'Good morning, sir', said he.
'Have you got any ships bound for New York in the States of Amerikey?'

'Oh, yes, I have got packet ships. I have got one or two.
I've got the *Josey Walker*, besides the *Kangaroo*.

'I've got the *Josey Walker* and on Friday she will sail,
With all four hundred emigrants and a thousand bags o' meal.'

Now I am in New York and I'm walking through the street,
With no money in my pocket and scarce a bit to eat.

Bad luck to *Josey Walker* and the day that she set sail,
For them sailors got drunk, broke into my bunk, and stole out all
    my meal.

Now I'm in Philadelphia and working on the canal;
To go home in one o' them packet ships I'm sure I never shall.

But I'll go home in a National boat that carries both steam and sail,
Where you get soft tack every day and none of your yellow meal.

☞ Until at least the middle of the nineteenth century passengers travelling to
America had to take their own provisions. An Irish ballad, 'Yellow Meal', tells
about the theft of this eponymous food by the crew of the *Joshua A. Walker*. It
must date from before 1815, since the vessel was wrecked off Nova Scotia in that
year. It was taken up by sailors and used as 'a genuine brake-windlass shanty'
(Hugill). A chorus was added, and with the passage of the years different ships
and docks were mentioned. Tapscott must have been introduced between the
mid-1840s and the mid-50s. He was an American broker working in Liverpool
who arranged passages to Australia and especially America. Part of his trade was
in the provision of passages prepaid for others by emigrants already in America,
the money being transmitted by his brother, who worked in New York. They
were, according to Coleman, 'systematic villains, whose frauds began with their
advertisements', which deliberately exaggerated the tonnages of the ships
named. Their business nevertheless flourished. In the first six months of 1851
alone they booked westward passages for 20,000 English and Irish emigrants.

106   *The* Flying Dutchman

105 meal] pronounced 'male'   National boat] ship of the National Line

'Twas on a dark and stormy night well southward of the Cape,
And from a stiff nor'-wester we'd just made our escape.
Like an infant in his cradle rocked, the breeze lulled us to sleep,
While peacefully we ploughed along the bosom of the deep.

At last the helmsman gave a shout of terror and of fear,
As if he had just gazed upon some sudden danger near.
We looked all round the ocean and there upon our lee
We saw the *Flying Dutchman* come bounding through the sea.

'Take in all flowing canvas, now,' our watchful master cried,
'For this for our ship's company great terror does betide.'
The billows tossed all white with foam and dangerous did appear,
As the wind sprang to a hurricane and auld Van Dyke came near.

Here comes the *Flying Dutchman*, comes fast through the hissing
   spray,
And proceeding by the tempest he heads for Table Bay.
With bird-like speed he's borne along before the howling blast,
But he never can cast anchor there, for the Bay, alas, he's passed.

Moan, ye *Flying Dutchman*, moan, for horrible is thy doom:
The ocean round the stormy Cape it is thy living tomb;
For there Van Dyke must beat about for ever, night and day;
He tries in vain his oath to keep to anchor in Table Bay.

☞ The story goes that a Dutch captain, Vanderdecken, swore that he would beat
into Table Bay in the teeth of a gale which he attributed to the wrath of God. As a
punishment for his temerity he was doomed for ever to wander the seas off the
Cape of Good Hope. George Boughton went to sea in the *Archos* from
Sunderland in 1882 at the age of twelve. Like many seamen he firmly believed in
the *Flying Dutchman*. He wrote in his autobiography: 'This spectre, the ghost of a
full-rigged ship in full sail, white and transparent, looms up suddenly in the
black darkness, tearing along at a crazy speed on a reckless course, all her sails
and gear aloft plainly visible, a terror and danger to ordinary innocent seamen,
threatening to run into them with disastrous consequences of an unknown
nature. How many mysteries of the sea may be the result of her nocturnal

villainies, vessels missing with all hands, and not the slightest trace of her fate?
Sailors shudder to think of her, and dread falling in with her.' The song, with a
tune by John Orlando Parry to words by Richard Ryan, was first published in
1848. It soon appeared on English broadsides, and also travelled to America.
The version given here was noted in 1943 from an eighty-four-year-old Irish
singer, Jack Murphy, of Broadway, near Wexford, to the tune of 'The Banks of
Newfoundland' (91). He also believed in the spectral Dutchman, though he had
forgotten his name.

107 *The Sailor's Alphabet*

A's for the anchor that swings at our bow,
B's for the bowsprit through the wild seas do plough.
C for the capstan we merrily around,
D are the davits we lower our boats down.

Sing high, sing low, wherever you go,
Give a sailor his tot and there's nothing goes wrong.

Now E for the ensign that flies at our peak,
F is for the focsle where the good sailors sleep.
G for the galley where the cooks hop around,
H are the halliards we haul up and down.

Now I is the iron the ship is made of,
J for the jib which moves her along.
K is the keel at the bottom of the ship,
L is the lanyards that never do slip.

220

Now M is the mainmast so neat and so strong,
N for the needles which never go wrong.
O for the oars we row our boats out,
P for the pumps that we keep her afloat.

Q for the quarterdeck where officers do stand,
R is the rudder that steers us to land.
S for the sailors which move her along,
T for the topsails we pull up and down.

U for the Union which flies at our peak,
V for the victuals which the sailors do eat.
W for the wheel where we all take our turn,
X,Y,Z is the name on our stern.

☞ The alphabet song is of considerable antiquity: one version, beginning 'A was an archer and shot at a frog', was published during the reign of Queen Anne. Soldiers, fishermen, sailing bargemen (see 142), lumbermen in North America, sheepshearers in Australia, all have versions. In the case of sailors the song seems to have originated in the Royal Navy, possibly in the eighteenth century, and spread to merchantmen, where it was sung both as a forebitter and a pumps shanty. The version given here probably dates, because of its reference to 'the iron the ship is made of', from the middle of the nineteenth century or later. It comes from Johnny Doughty (b. 1903), of Rye, Sussex, who served in the Royal Navy and also worked as a fisherman.

108 *Blow the Man Down*

1st version

Come all you young fellows who follow the sea,
To me weigh, heigh, blow the man down,
Now please pay attention and listen to me:
Give me some time to blow the man down.

I'm a deep water sailor, just come from Hong Kong;
If you give me some whisky I'll sing you a song.

On a trim Black Ball Liner I first served my time;
On a trim Black Ball Liner I wasted my prime.

When a big Black Ball Liner's preparing for sea
You'd split your sides laughing, such sights you would see.

Here's a big Black Ball clipper just leaving her dock,
While the boys and the girls on the pierhead do flock.

There are tinkers and tailors, shoemakers and all,
For you'll seldom find sailors aboard the Black Ball.

Now when a Black Baller gets clear of the land
Our bosun soon roars out the word of command.

'Come quickly, lay aft to the break of the poop,
Or I'll help you along with the toe of my boot.

'Pay attention to orders, now you, one and all,
For, see, right above you there flies the Black Ball.

''Tis larboard and starboard, on deck you will sprawl,
For kicking Jack Rogers commands the Black Ball.'

(Spoken) *Belay*.

2nd version

I'll put on my boots and I'll blow the man down,
   Way, hey, blow the man down.
I'll put on my boots and I'll blow the man down,
   Gimmie some time to blow the man down.

As I was a-walking down fair London Street,
A charming young lady I chanced for to meet.

I fired off my bow gun to make her heave to;
She backed her main topsail, the signal she knew.

I hailed her in English and asked her the news:
'This morning from Sally Port, sir, bound for a cruise.'

Then I hove out my tow rope and took her in tow,
And away to the grog-shop poor Jack he did go.

Then he wanted to board her without more delay.
'Come along, then, young man, if you're able,' said she.

Then she took me to a house of ill fame;
It was the sign of the ship in Water Lane.

She had some whisky and I had some rum.
She asked me if I would see her home.

We went home together and to bed we did go,
But what we did there I'm sure I don't know.

[We had a drink, maybe two, three or four,]
And in the morning when I awoke [I was stretched on the floor].

☞ The American Black Ball Line was started in 1816, with little ships of between three and five hundred tons, commanded in many cases, it was said, by former privateersmen. They sailed regularly, whatever the weather, leaving New York on 1st and 16th of each month, averaging six weeks to Liverpool and three weeks on the return voyage. They also sailed from Boston and Philadelphia and to London and Le Havre. Later, the size of ships increased, and the fastest ever westward passage by a sailing ship from Liverpool to New York was accomplished in 1843 by the *Yorkshire*, of a thousand tons. It took sixteen days. The emblem of the line was a crimson swallowtail flag with a black ball in the centre, and the same device was painted on the ships' foretopsails. Other lines had other symbols: Red Star, Black Cross, Swallowtail, White Diamond. By 1865 three-quarters of emigrants leaving British ports for America were travelling on steamships, and the Black Ball Line was wound up in 1878. The crews, known as 'packet rats', were driven extremely hard, and discipline was maintained by brute force. 'Blow the Man Down', 'blow' being synonymous with 'knock', was used for topsail halliards. It was (and possibly still is) the best known of all shanties. It was certainly current by the 1850s (Carpenter met two sailors, both over ninety, who had heard it in 1854 and 1855), though it may date from earlier. It had the extraordinary power of attracting sets of words from different songs, at least six, including 'The Fishes' Lamentation' (70) and 'Ratcliffe Highway' (94) (see the second text here, which was noted in the 1920s by Carpenter from James Wright of Leith, who had spent 47 years at sea from 1864, ten of them as a packet rat sailing between Glasgow and America).

Sally Port] at Portsmouth

The City of Baltimore

Come all ye true-born Irishmen, a story I will tell,
Concerning Denis McCarthy, in Liverpool Town did dwell.
'Twas down the northern docks one day he happened for to stay;
On a western ocean steamboat he stowed himself away.

After four long days and four long nights in the chain locker he was
    found,
[The Irish lad was stowed away, leaving his native ground.
The Irish lad was stowed away, leaving his native shore
On board of a western ocean boat, *The City of Baltimore*.]

The mate he came up on the deck, and to the crew did say:
'Where is that Irish son of a gun who stowed himself away?'
'I'm here,' says bold McCarthy, 'and as I've said before,
I'll fight any man that's fore or aft *The City of Baltimore*.'

The mate, he being a cowardly man, before him wouldn't stand;
McCarthy, being a smart man, 'twas at the mate he ran.
McCarthy, being a smart man, this bucko he did lower,
And he stretched him senseless on the deck of *The City of
    Baltimore*.

The second mate and the bosun came to the mate's relief;
McCarthy with his capstan bar he soon made them retreat.
His Irish blood began to boil and he like a lion did roar,
Saying: 'Skin and hair will fly this day on *The City of Baltimore*.'

The captain was a Scotchman, McDonald was his name;
When he had seen what McCarthy done, right for'ard then he
  came.
'Well done,' he cried, 'my gallant boy. I'll give you three cheers
  more.
You fought your way right fore and aft on *The City of Baltimore*.'

☞ *The City of Baltimore*, a vessel of 2,000 tons, was operated in the 1840s by the Inman Line, between Liverpool and New York. Ships were very carefully searched for stowaways before sailing. Anyone found when a ship was out to sea would be liable to be tarred and feathered and would certainly be made to work his passage. The song is rare. Apart from this version, from south-east Ireland, only two others have come to light, both in Canada.

110　　　*The First of the Emigrants*

Now I'm leaving old England, the land that I love,
And I'm bound out far across the sea.
Oh I'm bound to Australia, the land of the free,
Where there will be a welcome for me.

So fill up your glasses and drink what you please,
For no matter's the damage, oh, I'll pay.
So be aisy and free whilst you're drinking with me,
Sure, I'm the man you don't meet every day.

Now when I boarded my ship for to go
She was looking all snug and trim;
For I landed aboard with my bag and baggage,
And the mate he told me just where to go.

Now down to Gravesend, oh, soon we did go,
And the Customs they came on board,
And inspected us all and called out our names:
There was girls and boys all galore.

They let go of us and we soon sailed away
Down to the Nore and around.
Oh, the Foreland's in sight, oh, it became late at night,
But I was the man they didn't meet every day.

Now we sailed down the Channel of old England, and away
To the Ushant and far across the bay;
Oh, out into the Roaring Forties did stay,
And it's here were our westerly wainds.

Now I'll never forget the look on the Old Man's face
As he roared: 'All stuns'ls we'll set.'
Oh, we're bound to the island of St Helena,
And around the Cape of Good Hope we will get.

Now I ofttimes have wondered just what he meant
When he roared like a bull to the mate;
But the mate understood, and soon they were bound.
We're the men you don't meet every day.

Gravesend] port on the southern shore of the River Thames   Nore]
anchorage in the mouth of the river   Foreland] North Foreland, the easternmost tip
of Kent   Ushant] Ouessant, off Cape Finisterre   the bay] of Biscay   Forties]
here in North Latitude, though the term normally refers to the South   wainds] the
spelling probably indicates the archaic pronunciation of the word, to rhyme with 'finds'

We rounded the Cape with a fair waind abaft,
And soon we were running our easting down.
We were bound to the Semaphore and the southern shores,
And good lord, how the waind did roar.

Now we got round the Heads and into Sydney harbour,
Where the bays are all fine to look upon.
Oh the doctor he came on board and examined us,
And, 'What a fine crowd', the words he did say.

Now I've worked hard in Australia for thirty long years,
And today, sure, I'm homeward bound
With a nice little fortune for to call me own;
I'm bound home, but not the same way I came out.

Oh I'm sorry I'm leaving you all today,
For I'm homeward bound, don't you see?
But a different way to the way I came out;
I am going home on a steamboat, you see.

Then it's goodbye to one and it's goodbye to all,
For I'm bound home for England's merry country;
And my girl I will find, the one I left behind,
And I'll make her as happy as can be.

☞ After the discovery of gold in Australia in 1851 there was a huge increase in emigration from Britain. The song comes from Captain Patrick Tayluer, who said that it was sung by sailors 'to cheer up the emigrants as they came on board, or while the men hove in the mooring lines or brought the anchor to the hawsepipe'. The tune is derived from 'Believe me, if all those endearing young charms'.

running our easting down] travelling east towards Australia, with the prevailing winds   the Semaphore] telegraph and signal station on the South Head at Sydney the Heads] headlands on either side of the entrance to Sydney Harbour

Whip Jamboree

Now Cape Clear it is in sight
We'll be off Holyhead by tomorrow night,
And we'll shape our course for the Rock Light,
Oh Jenny get your oat cake done.

Whip jamboree, whip jamboree,
Oh you long-tailed black man, poke it up behind me,
Whip jamboree, whip jamboree,
Oh Jenny get your oat cake done.

Now my boys we're off Holyhead;
No more salt beef, no more salt bread.
One man in the chains for to heave the lead,
Oh Jenny get your oat cake done.

Now my lads we're round the Rock,
All hammocks lashed and chests all locked.
We'll haul her into the Waterloo Dock,
Oh Jenny get your oat cake done.

Cape Clear] in south-west Ireland   Holyhead] in the island of Anglesey
Rock Light] in the River Mersey   Waterloo Dock] in Liverpool

Now my lads we're all in dock
We'll be off to Dan Lowrie's on the spot;
And now we'll have a good roundabout,
Oh Jenny get your oat cake done.

☞ Hugill says that this was a homeward-bound shanty, 'sung at capstan or windlass'. The words varied with the ports approached: one version runs from the Lizard Light in Cornwall to Blackwall Docks in London, and another from Lundy Light to Bristol. The shanty seems to derive partly from 'Jenny, get your hoe cake done', a 'celebrated banjo song' sung in 1840 'with great applause at the Broadway Circus by J. W. Sweeny', and partly from 'Whoop, Jamboree', a Dan Emmett jig-song published in White's *Ethiopian Melodies* of 1851. This version was sung to Cecil Sharp in 1914 by John Short, aged seventy-six, town crier of the little port of Watchet in Somerset. He had spent over fifty years at sea under sail, mainly as a shantyman, and knew over fifty shanties. He had a 'tenacious memory', said Sharp, and his voice was 'rich, resonant and powerful, and yet so flexible that he can execute trills, turns and graces with a delicacy and finish that would excite the envy of many a professional vocalist'. Terry later took down the same shanty from the same singer, remarking that the word 'whip', 'as "coughed up" by Mr Short (with a shock of the glottis) sounded more like "whup".'

112 *Lady Franklin's Lament for her Husband*

You seamen bold that have oft withstood
Wild storms of Neptune's briny flood,
Attend to these few lines which I now relate,
And put you in mind of a sailor's dream.

111 Dan Lowrie's] playhouse in Paradise Street, Liverpool   roundabout]
? merrymaking

As homeward bound one night on the deep,
Slung in my hammock, I fell fast asleep.
I dreamed a dream which I thought was true
Concerning Franklin and his brave crew.

I thought as we neared to the Humber shore
I heard a female that did deplore.
She wept aloud and seemed to say:
'Alas, my Franklin is long away.'

Her mind it seemed in sad distress.
She cried aloud: 'I can take no rest.
Ten thousand pounds I would freely give
To say on earth that my husband lives.

'Long time it is since two ships of fame
Did bear my husband across the main
With a hundred seamen with courage stout
To find a north-western passage out.

'With a hundred seamen with hearts so bold
I fear have perished with frost and cold.
Alas,' she cried, 'all my life I'll mourn,
Since Franklin seems never to return.

'For since that time seven years are past,
And many a keen and bitter blast
Blows o'er the grave where the poor seamen fell,
Whose dreadful sufferings no tongue can tell.

'To find a passage by the North Pole
Where tempests wave and wild thunders roll
Is more than mortal man can do
With hearts undaunted and courage true.

'There's Captain Austen of Scarborough town,
Brave Granville and Penny of much renown,

Austen] Sir Horatio Thomas (1801–65) sailed in 1824 with Parry's third expedition in search of a north-west passage from the Atlantic to the Pacific and in 1850–1 commanded an unsuccessful expedition to find Franklin.   Granville] ? Captain Griffin of the *Rescue*, one of the ships engaged in searching for Franklin.   Penny] William Penny of Aberdeen, a whaling captain also involved in the search

With Captain Ross and so many more
Have long been searching the Arctic shore.

'They sailèd east and they sailèd west
Round Greenland's coast they knew the best;
In hardships drear they have vainly strove,
On mountains of ice their ships were drove.

'At Baffin's Bay where the whalefish blows
The fate of Franklin nobody knows,
Which causes many a wife and child to mourn
In grievous sorrow for their return.

'These sad forebodings they give me pain
For the long lost Franklin across the main,
Likewise the fate of so many before,
Who have left their homes to return no more.'

Harkness, Printer, 121 Church Street, Preston

☞ John Franklin was born at Spilsby, Lincolnshire, in 1786. He joined the navy, and was present at the battles of Copenhagen and Trafalgar. In 1818 and 1825 he made voyages to the Arctic, and was knighted in 1829. After several years' service as Governor of Tasmania he sailed for a third time to the Arctic in 1845 with the aim of discovering the elusive north-west passage round Canada. His two ships, the *Erebus* and the *Terror*, were sighted a few months later in Baffin Bay, then never seen again. Over the years, no fewer than 39 expeditions were sent in search, and only in 1859 was the fate of Franklin and his men discovered. A logbook was found in a cairn on King William Island with the information that Franklin had died in 1847. The ships had become icebound, and the crews had set off, towing supplies in boats used as sledges, to trek to safety. None of the 129 men had survived. In 1983 some bones were found which bore the marks of knives, which led to speculation that seamen in an attempt to survive had eaten parts of some of their dead comrades. In 1984 other bodies were found perfectly preserved in the ice where their shallow graves had been hacked. The enigma of Franklin's expedition and the eventual news of its fate gave rise to several ballads. The text given here, which was originally printed in 1853 or '54, entered oral tradition in England, Ireland, Scotland, and North America, and was sung both on shore and at sea.

Captain Ross] see 96. In 1850 he commanded a privately-organized expedition in search of Franklin.

Paddy West

Now as I took a walk down Grand Street I stepped into Paddy
  West's house.
He gave me a feed of American hash and he called it English
  scouse;
He said: 'Cheer up, me hearty. You just came in time
To put your name upon the book as quickly as you can sign.'

> *Put on your dungaree jacket and give the boys a rest.*
> *Think of the cold nor'-wester that we had in Paddy West's.*

As I went into Paddy West's house the gale began to blow.
He sent me up in the garret the main royal for to stow.
As I went up in the garret no main royal could I find
So I slewed around to the window and I furled the window blind.

scouse] stew

Paddy's wife stood in the kitchen, a bucket of water in her hand;
Paddy pipes all hands on deck all the stays'ls for to man;
Paddy's wife left hold that bucket and the water flew each way,
Saying: 'Clew up your fore topga'nts'ls, boys, we're taking in the
　　say.'

If there's any other young man that wishes to go to sea,
Let him step into Paddy West's house. He'll sign you right away.
He'll swear you are a sailor from the hour that you were born.
If he'll ask you: 'Were you ever at sea?' tell him: 'Three times
　　around Cape Horn.'

☞ Paddy West is believed to have kept a boarding house in Great Howard Street,
Liverpool, in the 1850s and '60s. He provided various forms of spurious training
for the sea, which enabled him to pass raw hands off as able seamen. He could
thus secure them a larger advance in wages, which he retained in lieu of rent, but
'Paddy Westers' came to be synonymous with poor seamen. When steamships
came in he had men shovelling piles of stones to and fro in his backyard for
experience in stoking. He also had ways of ensuring that men had 'crossed the
Line' (the equator) and rounded Cape Horn:

'And now we're off to the south'ard, boys, to 'Frisco we are bound',
And Paddy called for a piece of rope and passed it quickly round;
And I stepped across and back again and he says to me: 'That's fine.
When they ask you if you've been to sea you can say you've crossed the Line.

'And now the only thing to do before you sign away—
You've crossed the line and stowed the jib and been soaked with spray—
Is to step around the table there on which there is a horn,
And you can say you've rounded it ten times since you were born.'

The stories of Paddy West were widely told, and also embodied in a song which
served both as forebitter and capstan shanty, and seems to have been modelled
on 'The Banks of Newfoundland' (II) (119, below). The tune used here,
however, is a variant of 'Tramps and Hawkers'.

114　　　　　*The* Dreadnought

It is of a flash packet, she's a packet of fame,
She hails from New York and the *Dreadnought*'s her name;
She is bound to the westward where the stormy winds blow,
Bound away in the *Dreadnought* to the westward we'll go.

The time of her sailing is now drawing nigh.
'Farewell, pretty May', I must bid you goodbye;
'Farewell to old England and all those we hold dear',
Bound away on the *Dreadnought* to the westward we'll steer.

Oh the *Dreadnought* is heading out of Waterloo Dock
Where the boys and the girls on the pierheads do flock.
They will give us three cheers while the tears freely flow,
Saying: 'God bless the *Dreadnought* wheresoe'er she may go.'

Oh the *Dreadnought* is waiting in the Mersey so free,
Waiting for the *Independence* to tow her to sea,
For to round that black rock where the Mersey does flow,
Bound away in the *Dreadnought* to the westward we'll go.

Oh now the ship's sailing down the long Irish shore
Where the pilot he boards us as he oft done before.
Fill away your main topsails, board your foretop also,
She's the Liverpool packet, brave boys, let her go.

Oh the *Dreadnought* is howling down the wild Irish sea
Where the passengers are merry with hearts full of glee,
While the sailors like lions walk the decks to and fro,
Bound away in the *Dreadnought* to the westward we'll go.

Oh the *Dreadnought* is sailing the Atlantic so wide
Where the dark heavy seas roll along her black sides;
With the sails neatly spread and the red cross to show,
Bound away in the *Dreadnought* to the westward we'll go.

Independence] a tug

234

Oh the *Dreadnought* is becalmed on the banks of Newfoundland
Where the water's so green and the bottom is sand;
Where the fish in the ocean swim around to and fro,
Bound away in the *Dreadnought* to the westward we'll go.

Oh the *Dreadnought* has arrived in America once more;
We'll go ashore, shipmates, on the land we adore,
See our wives and our sweethearts, be merry and free,
Drink a health to the *Dreadnought* wheresoe'er she may be.

Here's a health to the *Dreadnought* and to all her brave crew,
Here's a health to Captain Samuels and officers too.
Talk about your flash packets, Swallowtail and Black Ball,
But the *Dreadnought*'s the clipper to beat one and all.

☞ If not the fastest of the Western Ocean packets, the *Dreadnought*, of the Red Cross Line, was arguably the best known. She was built at Newburyport, Massachusetts, and at 1,413 tons register was a large ship for the time. She once ran from the Mersey to Long Island Sound in 19 days, though she averaged just under 25 days eastbound and 22 westbound. She was wrecked off Cape Horn in 1869. Captain Samuel Samuels, who was in command for the first ten years, wrote in his autobiography, *From Forecastle to Cabin*: 'The Liverpool packet sailors were not easily demoralized. They were the toughest class of seamen in all respects. They could stand the worst weather, food and usage, and put up with less sleep, more rum and harder knocks than any other sailors.' So far, so good, but he added: 'They had not the slightest idea of morality or honesty, and gratitude was not in them. The dread of the belaying pin kept them in subjection. I tried to humanise their brutal natures but the better they were treated the more trouble my officers had from them.' The song may have derived from 'The *Fancy* Frigate' (98), which was current from some twenty years earlier. The two songs shared the tune of 'King John and the Abbot of Canterbury', and 'The *Dreadnought*' was also sung to versions of 'The Bold Princess Royal'. It was mainly a forebitter, but also used as a capstan shanty, sometimes to the tune of 'Goodbye, fare thee well'. The first printing seems to have been in 1896, when Kipling published three verses in *Captains Courageous*, with the comment that there were 'scores' more. The version here was noted by Helen Creighton as recently as 1951 in Nova Scotia.

115

Andrew Rose

Andrew Rose, the British sailor,
Now to you his woes I'll name.
'Twas on the passage from Barbados
Whilst on board of the *Martha Jane*.

> *Wasn't that most cruel usage,*
> *Without a friend to interpose?*
> *How they whipped and mangled, gagged and strangled*
> *The British sailor, Andrew Rose.*

'Twas on the quarterdeck they laid him,
Gagged him with an iron bar.
Wasn't that most cruel usage
To put upon a British tar?

'Twas up aloft the captain sent him,
Naked beneath the burning sun,
Whilst the mate did follow after,
Lashing till the blood did run.

The captain gave him stuff to swallow,
Stuff to you I will not name,
Whilst the crew got sick with horror,
While on board the *Martha Jane*.

'Twas in a water-cask they put him;
Seven long days they kept him there.
When loud for mercy Rose did venture
The captain swore no man should go there.

For twenty days they did ill-use him.
When into Liverpool they arrived
The judge he heard young Andrew's story:
'Captain Rogers, you must die.'

Come all ye friends and near relations
And all ye friends to interpose,
Never treat a British sailor
Like they did young Andrew Rose.

☞ The *Martha and Jane* was a Sunderland-owned barque which sailed from Hartlepool to Calcutta in 1856, and thence to Demerara. Homeward bound, she put into Barbados for repairs, and there Henry Rogers, a thirty-seven-year-old Swansea man, went on board to take command. There were also changes in the crew, and among those joining was an able seaman, Andrew Rose. While the ship was still in harbour the second mate, Charles Seymour, found fault with Rose's work, and gave him a beating. Rose jumped ship, but was brought back by the police. After the vessel had sailed he was beaten again by Seymour and also by the captain and by the first mate, William Miles. This treatment became almost a daily occurrence, but there were further cruelties. For singing a hymn Rose was gagged with an iron bolt for an hour and a half. The captain taught his dog to bite him, and even to tear out pieces of his flesh. The first mate sent him aloft naked to furl a sail, and whipped him up and down the rigging till the blood ran. On another occasion Rose was forced to get into a water cask, which was then headed up, with only the bunghole left open. It was then rolled round the deck, then lashed to the bulwarks for twelve hours. Finally, Rose was suspended from the mainmast by a rope round the neck until he almost suffocated. Two or three days later, Rose lost his reason, and then died. His body was dragged to the ship's side at the end of a rope and thrown overboard without ceremony. When the vessel reached Liverpool, on 9 June 1857, Rose's shipmates went to the police. The captain and his two mates were arrested, and stood trial at the assizes. The evidence of the seamen called by the prosecution was damning, and it was found that the ship's log was silent about most of the incidents, and put Rose's death down to his 'going rotten inside'. The three defendants were all found guilty, and, despite a recommendation to mercy from the jury, sentenced to death. The sentences of the two mates were later commuted to imprisonment, but not that of Captain Rogers. While waiting for death he vehemently proclaimed his innocence, maintaining that the account of his treatment of Rose had been 'much overdrawn'. On 12 September, the day of execution, a crowd of between twenty and thirty thousand people assembled to watch outside Kirkdale (now Walton) Gaol included many sailors. One said: 'My word, he'll be a different man on *that* quarterdeck than he was on the quarterdeck of the *Martha and Jane*.' Another shouted to Rogers: 'Luff, luff, and weather hell.' Rogers was unlucky only to the extent that he was far from being the only captain to cause the death of a sailor by brutality. Joanna Colcord says that American sailors would sing the song to taunt the British, but it was also sung by the British themselves.

Rolling Home

Call all hands to man the capstan, see the cable is all clear,
For tonight we'll sail for England and for England, sure, we'll steer.

> *Rolling home, rolling home, rolling home across the sea;*
> *Rolling home for dear old England, rolling home, dear land, to thee.*

Up aloft amidst the rigging loudly roars th' exulting gale;
Like a bird with outstretched pinions rolling on 'neath billowing sail.

Many thousand miles behind us, many thousand miles before,
Ancient ocean wave to waft us to that well-remembered shore.

☞ 'I have heard it in various parts of the world, and I think that on the whole it has given me more pleasure than any song I have ever heard. It has many stanzas, for I expect that many of its lovers have added to it.' So John Masefield wrote of 'Rolling Home', which was originally a poem written by Charles Mackay (1814–89) on 26 May 1858 while homeward bound from America as a passenger on the *Europa*. Its eight verses were indeed augmented by sailors. Hugill, who calls it 'the most famous homeward-bound song of them all', prints well over twenty, many with variants. Bob Roberts (1907–82) (for whom, see 142) heard this version sung in the forecastle of the barquentine, *Waterwitch*, coming up-Channel, when an American sailor remarked: 'Goddam, that song almost makes me wish I was a "limey".' He need not have worried, for there are versions in which 'dear old England' is replaced by New England, fair Columbia, and New York City, not to speak of bonny Scotland, dear old Ireland and even Deutschland Heimat. The song was also used as a capstan shanty.

The Wreck of the Royal Charter

var. (a)

Good people all attend I pray;
Now I'll relate a sad calamity
Of a dreadful shipwreck near Beaumaris town
Of the *Royal Charter* while homeward bound.

From far Australia with a pleasant gale
The *Royal Charter* for old England had sailed
With her human cargo, but the fates did rule
She never more would reach Liverpool.

For nine long hours this vessel brave
Was tempest-tossed on the stormy wave;
But in Moelfre Bay, without mast or sails,
She was drove in pieces on the coast of Wales.

On Wednesday morning I grieve to say
Her fore and mainmast were cut away;
Our mizentop fell with a heavy crash
As the raging waves o'er the ship did dash.

Now Captain Taylor with his seamen brave
Used all their efforts the ship to save,
But notwithstanding all they could do
The *Royal Charter* she broke in two.

Now broadside on she drove on shore;
The lightning flashed and the sea did roar.

Brave Captain Taylor was drowned, it's true,
With ninety-seven of his gallant crew.

The total number that lost their lives
Was four hundred and fifty-five;
Of women and children, we are assured,
Not one escaped out of all on board.

O God, 'tis frightful to think that crowds
Of drowning passengers clung to the shrouds;
To hear their shrieks on the stormy sea
As from the vessel they were washed away.

May the Lord look down on the deep distress
Of the widowed mother and the fatherless,
Likewise the parents of the seamen brave
Who in the *Royal Charter* met a watery grave.

☞ The *Royal Charter*, launched on the River Dee in 1855, was an iron sailing ship
of over 2,500 tons, with an auxiliary steam engine. On her maiden voyage to
Australia she made a record passage of 59 days between Plymouth and
Melbourne. She was wrecked in October, 1859, when homeward bound for
Liverpool with 493 passengers and crew, together with a cargo which included
four million pounds' worth of gold. She arrived off Point Lynas, the extreme
north-eastern tip of the island of Anglesey, at 9 p.m. on Tuesday, 25 October,
just as a violent storm blew up from the north-east. Both anchors were dropped,
but the cables parted, and the engine was not powerful enough to prevent the
ship from drifting on to the jagged rocks of Moelfre Bay. For some nine hours
the ship was battered on the rocks, until it broke up. A seaman called Joseph
Rogers managed to get a rope ashore, and by this means 39 people were saved.
All the rest perished. E. J. Moeran noted the song from James Sutton of
Winterton, Norfolk, in 1915.

118   *Blow Ye Winds*

They've advertised for whalermen, five hundred brave and true,
To fish for sperm on the whaling grounds of Chile and Peru.

Singing blow ye winds in the morning and blow ye winds high, O.
Clear away your running gear and blow ye winds high, O.

It's now we are at sea, my boys, the wind comes on to blow;
One half the watch is sick on deck, the other half below.

But as for the provisions, we don't get half enough;
A little bit of stinking beef and a little bag of duff.

Then there's the running rigging which you're supposed to know;
It's 'Lay aloft, you son of a whore, or overboard you go'.

The cooper's at the vice bench a-making iron poles;
The mate's upon the mainhatch a-blasting all our souls.

The skipper's on the quarterdeck a-squinting at the sails
When up aloft the lookout sights a bloody school of whales.

'Now clear away them boats, my boys, and after him we'll travel;
But if you get too near his flukes he'll flip you to the devil.'

Then our waist-boat got down and we made a good start.
'Lay on me now, you bleeders, for I'm hell for a long dart.'

Then the harpoon struck and the whale sped away,
But whatever he done, boys, he gave us fair play.

Now we got him turned up and we towed him alongside,
And we over with our blubberhooks and rob him of his hide.

Now the bosun overside the lift-tackle do haul,
And the mate there in the mainchains so loudly he do bawl.

duff] dough pudding

Next comes the stowing down, boys, to take both night and day.
'You'll have a tanner apiece, boys, on the hundred and ninetieth lay.'

Now we're all bound into Tumbez, that blasted whaling port,
And if you run away, my boys, you surely will get caught.

Now we're bound for Talcahuano, all in our manly power,
Where the skipper can buy a whorehouse for half a barrel of flour.

When we get home, our ship fast, and we get through our sailing,
A winding glass around we'll pass, and to hell with blubber whaling.

☞ Both American and British whalermen claimed this song as their own. In America it began ' 'Tis advertised in Boston, New York and Buffalo [or Albany], Five hundred brave Americans a-whaling for to go'. It was another of the songs sung both as a forebitter and a capstan or pumps shanty. The earliest text seems to be in the 1859 logbook of the *Elizabeth Swift*, of New Bedford, Mass. The version given here is from A. L. Lloyd (1908–82), who himself made a voyage on an Antarctic whaler in 1937–8.

119   *The Banks of Newfoundland* (II)

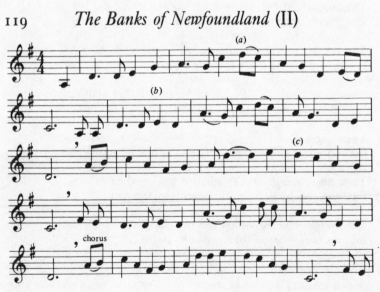

118 tanner] sixpence   lay] share in proceeds   Tumbez] Tumbes, Peru
Talcahuano] Talcahuana, Chile (pronounced 'Tackuanna')

You rambling boys of Liverpool I'll have you to beware;
When you go a-packet sailing no dungarees don't wear,
But have a monkey jacket all unto your command,
For there blows some cold nor'-westers on the Banks of
    Newfoundland.

> *We'll wash her and we'll scrub her down with holystones and sand,*
> *And we'll bid adieu to the Virgin Rocks on the Banks of*
>   *Newfoundland.*

We had one Lynch from Balla na Lynch, Jimmy Murphy and Mike
    Moor;
It was in the winter of 'sixty-two these sea-boys suffered sore.
They pawned their clothes at Liverpool and sold them out of hand,
Not thinking of the cold nor'-westers on the Banks of
    Newfoundland.

We had one lady passenger on board, Bridget Riley was her name;
To her I promised marriage, and on me she had a claim.
She tore up her flannel petticoats to make mittens for our hands,
For she couldn't see the sea-boys frozen on the Banks of
    Newfoundland.

Now, my boys, we're off Sandy Hook, and the land's all covered
    with snow.
The tug-boat will take our hawser, and for New York we will tow;
And when we arrive at the Black Ball Dock the boys and girls there
    will stand.
We'll bid adieu to packet-sailing and the Banks of Newfoundland.

☞ Cecil Sharp noted this in 1915 from a sixty-one-year-old seaman on board the
American liner, *St Paul*. Sharp was returning from one of his song-hunting trips
in the Appalachians, and 'the voyage home was unexpectedly brightened by the
discovery of an old chantey singer among the ship's crew. Permission was given

Balla na Lynch] Ballynahinch. There are three townships with this name in Ireland, two
in Tipperary, and one in County Down.   Sandy Hook] in Long Island Sound
Black Ball] American shipping line (see 108)

him to visit Cecil's cabin when off duty and day by day he appeared at the appointed hour, equipped with a sheet of newspaper which he solicitously spread on the bed before taking his seat on it'. The song, as forebitter and capstan shanty, was known on both sides of the Atlantic. It may derive from 'Van Diemen's Land', a ballad dating from 1829 or '30, which deals with poachers transported to the antipodes. In one Irish version there is a Bridget Reilly who 'gave us all good usage, boys, going to Van Diemen's Land'. Her namesake in 'The Banks of Newfoundland' did not take generosity quite so far. The song was published as a broadside by Hodges of London (1839–55) and Ross of Newcastle (1847–52). Oral versions give dates between 1844 and 1873, though the song was probably sung before then, and certainly afterwards.

120 *The Leaving of Liverpool*

Fare thee well to Prince's Landing Stage, River Mersey fare thee well.
I'm off to California, a place I know right well.

> *So fare thee well, my own true love.*
> *When I return united we shall be.*
> *It's not the leaving of Liverpool that grieves me*
> *But me darling when I think of thee.*

Now I'm off to California by way of the stormy Cape Horn,
And I'll send you a letter, love, when I am homeward bound.

Farewell to Lower Frederick Street, Anson Terrace and Park Lane;
Farewell, it'll be a long, long time before I see you again.

I shipped on a Yankee clipper ship, *Davy Crockett* is her name,
And Burgess is the captain of her, and they say she's a floating hell.

The tug is waiting at the old pierhead to take us down the stream;
Our sails are loosed and our anchor secure, so I'll bid you goodbye
   once more.

☞ The *David Crockett* was launched at Mystic, Connecticut, in 1853. From 1863,
under the command of Captain John A. Burgess, she regularly called at
Liverpool on voyages to and from California. Burgess was lost overboard on the
last trip before he was due to retire, in 1874, so the song must date from that
eleven-year period or soon afterwards. An American sailor, Dick Maitland,
bosun of the *General Knox*, was on deck one night in about 1885 when he heard a
Liverpool man singing it in the focsle. Many years later he sang the song to
Doerflinger, who published it in 1951. As a result it enjoys (and still does) a new
lease of life, especially in Ireland, where it can be widely heard, sung with
sweeping glissandi.

121   *Execution of Five Pirates for Murder*

Is there not one spark of pity for five poor unhappy men,
Doomed, alas, in London city on a tree their lives to end?
The dreadful crime which they committed on the raging, stormy sea,
By everyone must be admitted they each deserved to punished be.

> *Five poor unhappy sailors on the drop did trembling stand,*
> *And their lives did pay a forfeit for their deeds on board the* Flowery
>   Land.

Sometimes at sea there's cruel usage, and men to frenzy oft are
   drove;
They're always wrong[ed] by men in power, and that there's many a
   sailor knows.
But those unhappy seven sailors did commit a dreadful deed,
Killed and slaughtered, sad to mention, on board the *Flowery Land*,
   we read.

Great excitement through the nation this most sad affair has caused,
Sent across the briny ocean to be tried by English laws;

Seven tried and there convicted, and sentenced each to hangèd be
For the dreadful murders they committed while sailing on the
  raging sea.

For two of them they did petition; alas, there nothing could them
  save.
Sad indeed was their condition, to lie side by side in a murderer's
  grave.
Far away from friends and kindred they unpitied on the drop did
  stand;
Sad was the deed that they committed on board the fatal *Flowery
  Land*.

Thousands flocked from every quarter seven unhappy men to see,
Sailors from distant foreign nations suspended on a dreadful tree;
The fatal signal soon was given, the awful drop at length did fall.
It caused a groan, it caused a shudder; may God receive their guilty
  souls.

May this to sailors be a warning, the dreadful sight the world did
  see;
In London that fatal morning the seven died on Newgate's tree.
Was there not a tear of pity while trembling they in death did stand
To die for crimes in London city committed on the *Flowery Land*.

Their victims they did show no mercy, no time for to prepare did
  give;
They killed them in a barbarous manner, and though they were not
  fit to live
We pity to them on the gallows Englishmen could not deny.
Now, alas, their days are ended; they died on Newgate's gallows
  high.

H. Disley, Printer, 57, High Street, St Giles, London

☞ On 10 September 1863 while on a voyage to Singapore, seven seamen rose in
mutiny aboard the *Flowery Land* and killed the captain and five other men. They
were later brought to trial, and sentenced to death. Two were reprieved, but five
hanged outside Newgate Gaol on 22 February 1864. A huge crowd of spectators
was controlled by a thousand policemen. With one exception the sailors were
from Manila in the Philippines. Their names were: John Leone, Francisco
Blanco, Ambrosio Duranno, Marcus Watto and Miguel Lopez.

Roll, Alabama, Roll

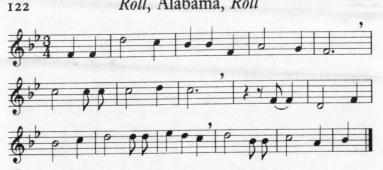

Oh, in eighteen hundred and sixty-one,
  Roll, Alabama, *roll*,
This ship her building was begun,
  Oh, roll, Alabama, *roll*.

When the *Alabama*'s keel was laid,
This ship her building was begun.

Oh, she was built in Birkenhead,
Built in the yard of Jonathan Laird.

And down the Mersey she rolled one day,
And across the western she ploughed her way.

With British guns, oh, she was stocked.
She sailed from Fayal, in Cherbourg she docked.

To fight the North Semmes did employ
Any method to kill and destroy.

But off Cherbourg the *Kearsarge* lay tight;
Awaiting was Winslow to start a good fight.

Outside the three-mile limit they fought,
And Semmes escaped on a fine British yacht.

The *Kearsarge* won. *Alabama* so brave
Sank to the bottom to a watery grave.

☞ During the American Civil War the Confederate ship, *Alabama*, a three-masted
schooner with auxiliary steam power, was built at Birkenhead with her identity

disguised as No. 290. She escaped to sea in 1862 hours before a British government detention order could be served, and was armed in the Azores with guns taken down from Liverpool. (The British government later paid over three million pounds in compensation to the United States.) During the next two years, under the command of Captain Raphael Semmes, she captured over sixty Northern vessels and sank one man-of-war. In June, 1864, she sailed into Cherbourg for a refit, and was trapped there by the USS *Kearsarge* (Captain J. A. Winslow). On 19 June she came out to fight, and the last battle between wooden warships ensued, under the eyes of some 15,000 spectators who lined the cliffs. The *Alabama* was sunk, but the survivors, including Semmes, escaped capture by being picked up by an English yacht, *Deerhound*. The battle was commemorated in a broadside entitled 'Great Naval Action between the *Kearsage* [sic] and the *Alabama*', but a halliard shanty on the same subject proved more lasting, and is still well known in folk-song circles. Hugill's version (reproduced here) comes from a New Zealand lady whose husband was a seaman on the *Alabama*. The British attitude to the two sides in the American Civil War was ambivalent. Here, the South is favoured, but in the forebitter, '*Cumberland*'s Crew', sympathies lie very much with the North.

123 *Strike the Bell*

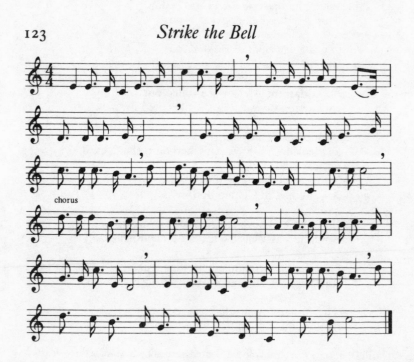

Aft on the poop deck and walking about,
There's the second mate so steady and so stout;
What he is a-thinking of he doesn't know himsel'—
We wish that he would hurry up and strike, and strike the bell.

> Strike the bell, second mate, let us go below;
> Look well to wind'ard, you can see it's going to blow.
> Look at the glass, you can see that it has fell—
> We wish that you would hurry up and strike, strike the bell.

Down on the maindeck and working at the pumps
There's the starboard watch all a-longing for their bunks;
Looking out to wind'ard they see a great swell,
They're wishing that the second mate would strike, strike the bell.

Aft at the wheel poor Anderson stands,
Grasping at the wheel with his cold, mittened hands;
Looking at the compass, oh, the course is clear as hell,
He's wishing that the second mate would strike, strike the bell.

For'ard on the focsle head a-keeping sharp lookout
Young Johnny's standing, ready for to shout:
'Lamps are burning bright, sir, and everything is well.'
He's wishing that the second mate would strike, strike the bell.

Aft on the quarterdeck the gallant captain stands,
Looking out to wind'ard with a spyglass in his hands.
What he is a-thinking of we know very well,
He's thinking more of shortening sail than striking the bell.

☞ A song entitled 'Ring the Bell, Watchman' was written by Henry Clay Work
(1832–84) to salute the end of the American Civil War. The tune was quickly
taken up, and new words fitted, such as 'Click go the Shears' in Australia and
'Strike the Bell' in England. The latter was sung as a pumps shanty by both
English and Scandinavian seamen.

strike the bell] to signal the time for the end of a watch   Young Johnny]
riding lights were usually maintained by the apprentices.

124

Off to Sea Once More

When first I landed in Liverpool I went upon the spree.
While money lasts I spent it fast, got drunk as drunk could be,
But before my money was all gone on liquor and the whores
I made up my mind that I was inclined to go to sea no more.
No more, no more, to go to sea no more,
I made up my mind that I was inclined to go to sea no more.

As I was walking down the street I met with Angeline.
She said: 'Come home with me, my lad, and we'll have a cracking
    time.'
But when I awoke it was no joke, I found I was all alone;
My silver watch and my money too, and my whole bloody gear was
    gone.
Was gone, was gone, my whole bloody gear was gone.
When I awoke, &c.

As I was walking down the street I met big Rapper Brown.
I asked him if he would take me in, and he looked at me with a
    frown.

He said: 'Last time you was paid off, with me you chalked no score,
But I'll take your advance and I'll give youse a chance to go to sea
  once more.
Once more, once more, to go to sea once more;
But I'll take', &c.

Sometimes we're catching whales, my lads, but mostly we get none,
With a twenty-foot oar in every paw from five o'clock in the morn;
And when daylight's gone and the night coming on, you rest upon
  your oar,
And, oh boys, you wish that you was dead or snug with the girls
  ashore.
Ashore, ashore, snug with the girls ashore,
And, oh boys, you wish, &c.

Come all you bold seafaring lads that listen to my song,
When you go a-big-boating, boys, I'll have you not go wrong.
You take my tip, when you come off a trip, don't go with any
  whore,
But get married instead and have all night in bed, and go to sea no
  more.
No more, no more, don't go to sea no more.
Get married, my lads, and have all night, &c.

☞ In the 1870s a large number of whaling ships were sailing from San Francisco to the Bering Sea, and the song probably dates from those years. Many versions begin: 'The first day I landed in 'Frisco, boys, I went upon the spree.' The boarding-house masters there would give a sailor credit against the advance of a month's pay for his next voyage, and would then ensure, if necessary by drugs, violence, or trickery, that he went on board his ship. Shanghai Brown (otherwise called Dixie, Jackie, or Rapper in different versions of the song) was a Norwegian crimp who was shanghaied himself on one occasion by brass-bounders (apprentices) from a British ship. It is said that he shipped his own father's corpse aboard an outward-bound ship as a dead-drunk seaman, thus collecting a ninety dollar advance for him and also avoiding funeral expenses. The song was sung as a capstan or pumps shanty and also (without chorus) as a forebitter. It was once 'known to every seaman', says Hugill, though it was first printed only in 1906 (partially), and infrequently after that. The version given here comes via A. L. Lloyd from a Welsh seaman, Ted Howard, of Barry.

125

The Holy Ground

Fare thee well, my lovely Dinah, a thousand times adieu.
We are bound away from the Holy Ground and the girls we love so
   true.
We'll sail the salt seas over and we'll return once more,
And still I live in hope to see the Holy Ground once more.
(Shouted) *Fine girl you are.* (Sung) *You're the girl that I adore,*
            And still I live in hope to see the Holy Ground once more.

Now when we're out a-sailing and you are far behind
Fine letters will I write to you with the secrets of my mind,
The secrets of my mind, my girl, you're the girl that I adore,
And still I live in hope to see the Holy Ground once more.

Oh now the storm is raging and we are far from shore;
The poor old ship she's sinking fast and the riggings they are tore.
The night is dark and dreary, we can scarcely see the moon,
But still I live in hope to see the Holy Ground once more.

It's now the storm is over and we are safe on shore
We'll drink a toast to the Holy Ground and the girls that we adore.

We'll drink strong ale and porter and we'll make the taproom roar,
And when our money is all spent we'll go to sea once more.

☞ The song, which may well be descended from 'Adieu, sweet lovely Nancy' (see note to 93), was sung in focsles and also at the windlass or capstan, but it is now chiefly heard in taprooms. The Holy Ground is the name for a fishermen's quarter at Cobh in Cork, and, by extension, for Ireland itself. The words 'Swansea Town' crop up in English versions: a correspondent of Hugill's wrote that this 'was always sung homeward bound in the little Welsh barques engaged in the copper ore trade of the [18]'70s and '80s'. There was also a 'Campbeltown' variant which was carried by Scots emigrants to North America, Australia, and New Zealand.

126 *The Wreck of the* Northfleet

Come listen all ye feeling people while this sad story I relate;
It's about a vessel called the *Northfleet* which met with such an awful fate.
Five hundred souls she had aboard her, lay anchored there, off Dungeness;
Bound for Australia was the vessel; they'd bid farewell with fond caress.

It was a big and foreign vessel came drifting with the channel tide,
Bore down upon the helpless *Northfleet* and crashed into her timbered side;
Nor did she stop to give assistance or repair the damage she had made,
While everyone aboard the *Northfleet* went down upon their knees and prayed.

> *God bless those widows and those orphans, comfort them where'er they be.*
> *May God in heaven above protect them from all the perils of the sea.*

The captain said: 'Now, to the lifeboats. Stand back you men, the women first.
I'll shoot the first that disobeys me.' They did not heed, but madly rushed.
The captain fired. His shot was fatal, and one poor fellow's life was slain,
While everyone aboard the *Northfleet* went down upon their knees and prayed.

The captain sent down for his first mate and bade him try and save his life,
And gave into his trustful keeping his young but newly-wedded wife.
'No, let me stay with you, dear husband.' 'No, no, my wife, that cannot be.'
She stayed aboard the sinking vessel; with him went to eternity.

> *God bless*, &c.

☞ On 22 January 1873 the wooden ship, *Northfleet*, lay at anchor off Dungeness, near the mouth of the Thames, waiting for a favourable wind. She was bound for Australia with 379 people on board, many of them navvies and their families travelling to Tasmania to work on the railway. She also had a cargo of iron. At 10.30 p.m. she was struck amidships by the Spanish steamship, *Murillo*, and sank within fifteen minutes. 320 people lost their lives. The *Murillo* did not stop, but was later arrested by the admiralty, and confiscated. The shipwreck inspired several street ballads, none of which included the detail about Captain Knowles' wife which appears in the version sung by Johnny Doughty (b. 1903) of Rye, Sussex. The remains of the *Northfleet* still lie at the bottom of the sea three miles off Dungeness. Until a few years ago the fishermen of the town used to sing of the wreck every Christmas.

127   *Rounding the Horn*

The gallant frigate, *Amphitrite*, she lay in Plymouth Sound,
Blue Peter at the foremast head for she was outward bound.
We were waiting there for orders to send us far from home;
Our orders came for Rio, and thence around Cape Horn.

Next day we weighed our anchor, boys, and waved goodbye all
    round,
And some of us we knew would never more see Plymouth Sound;
But still our hearts were light and gay, and when all was taut and
    snug
We foraged out the bumboat grog and each man filled his mug.

We drank success to Plymouth girls, to Kate and Poll and Sue,
And arguing o'er their various charms struck up a fight or two.
Jim Crab he landed Bonny Hodge a clout that made him snort,
And to this day his nose has got a heavy list to port.

When we arrived at Rio we prepared for heavy gales;
We set up all our rigging, boys, and bent on all new sails.

From ship to ship they cheered us as we did sail along,
And wished us pleasant weather in rounding of Cape Horn.

While beating off Magellan Strait it blew exceeding hard;
Whilst shortening sail two gallant tars fell from the topsail yard.
By angry seas the ropes we threw from their poor hands were torn,
And we were forced to leave them to the sharks that prowl around
    Cape Horn.

When we got round the Horn, my boys, we had some glorious days,
And very soon our killick dropped in Valparaiso Bay.
The pretty girls came down to us; I solemnly declare
They are far before the Plymouth girls with their long and curly
    hair.

They love a jolly sailor when he spends his money free;
They'll laugh and sing and merry, merry be, and have a jovial spree,
And when your money is all gone they won't on you impose,
They are not like the Plymouth girls that'll pawn and sell your
    clothes.

Farewell to Valparaiso, farewell for a while,
Likewise to all the Spanish girls all on the coast of Chile;
And if ever I live to be paid off I'll sit and sing this song:
'God bless those pretty Spanish girls we left around Cape Horn.'

☞ One of the last royal naval squadrons of square-rigged ships was one operating
in the Pacific. According to Sam Noble, who joined the navy in 1875 at the age of
sixteen, this song was 'a pure navy ditty'. The version which he and his
shipmates sang on HMS *Swallow* had a chorus tacked on from 'Away down Rio',
and began: 'Our ship had been inspected by the adm'ral all around, While lyin'
in Portsmouth Harbour, that large and beautiful town. We were waitin' there for
orders to sail away from home; Our orders were for Rio, and then around Cape
Horn.' The song spread, with other ports (Liverpool, Plymouth, Boston) being
mentioned, and the names of various ships, RN and merchant, English and
American, added (*Garibaldi, Amphitrite, Conway, Hero, California*). In addition,
fresh material was included, such as the deaths of seamen off Cape Horn.
William Bolton (for whom, see 94), who sang this version to Anne Gilchrist in
1907, told her that he had made up the second and third verses himself. Rio was
pronounced 'Rye-O', and Chile rhymed with 'while'.

The Unseaworthy Ship

Written by J. Smith, Denholme, near Bingley. Air, 'Driven from Home'

The doomed ship weighs anchor, out she is bound,
With cargo too heavy and timbers unsound.
A storm overtakes her, reef, reef every sail,
But all to no purpose, she's lost in the gale.
See the old vessel now tossed on the waves,
Telling the crew to prepare for their graves;
Sent out insured, with a hope she'd go down,
Not caring for widows and orphans at home.

Honour to Plimsoll, his labour will save
Thousands of brave men from watery graves.

257

May his movement all our support adorn;
His work will save thousands of lives yet unborn.

Out on the wild waves sailors must go,
Earning bread for their children—what perils they know.
In old, rotten craft which ship agents procure
Brave men they are lost in those vessels insured.
The captain is anxious the vessel to save
From the tempests which threaten a watery grave,
But all human efforts can't keep her afloat.
Oh God, she is sinking, out, out with the boat.

Down with the lifeboat, out on the waves,
Hoping to find land or sight some vessel's sail.
They pray to be saved but what can they do,
Surrounded by wild waves, that boat and her crew?
The storm it is raging, the billows they roll;
No help it is near for to save those poor souls.
The boat is upset, that brave crew is lost:
This, this is the price which our rotten ships cost.

Out, out, ye landsmen, out with a will.
Stand up in justice for Plimsoll's Great Bill;
Don't be rejected, it's on God's mission sent,
But up, all as one man, before Parliament.
The nation demands it, 'tis the widows' cry;
The sailors' poor orphans, we can't pass them by.
Let us work, every soul, to help brave Plimsoll through,
And then we may boast of our ships and their crews.

T. Pearson, Printer, 4 and 6, Chadderton Street, Manchester

☞ Samuel Plimsoll (1824–98), MP for Derby from 1868 to '80, was an ardent social reformer. The most famous of his campaigns was for improved safety at sea, and his main target was 'coffin ships', overloaded and unseaworthy vessels which were heavily insured so that when they were lost, as frequently happened, the shipowners and charterers made money. After failing in an attempt to introduce legislation in 1871, Plimsoll wrote his famous appeal to the nation, *Our Seamen* (1873), which helped to lead to the setting up of a royal commission. The load line which Plimsoll advocated was not recommended, and in 1875 he again put forward his own bill. The government, led by Disraeli, who was hostile to Plimsoll, proposed an inadequate alternative. Plimsoll's fury led to a famous scene in the House of Commons when he called other members villains. In the country there was tremendous support for him, and his temporary Unseaworthy

Ships Act became law in August 1875. His Merchant Shipping Act of the following year permanently embodied the Plimsoll Mark, and gave the Board of Trade powers of inspection. The struggle was marked by several street ballads, and also drawing-room songs such as 'Our Sailors on the Sea'.

129 *The Sailor's Christmas Day*

Come rouse ye, my lads, though no land we are near
We've old Christmas aboard us to give us good cheer.
We've our salt beef and grog, lads, and plum duff galore,
And a right gallant captain. What can men want more?

> *For our ship is our home, though it floats on the main.*
> *Your glasses fill ready and drink to old England again and again.*

The landsman may boast when he hails Christmas Day
He can call friends around him to dance and be gay,
But though lone on the ocean our hearts they are true
To the lasses that love us, for we love them too.

Now, lads, join with me and a bumper fill high
To those who most miss us when Christmas draws nigh,
To the darling old mother and father so grey,
Who will think of their loved ones at sea, lads, today.

Then messmates be merry. We'll dance and we'll sing,
And scrape the old fiddle till we crack every string.
Though his ship bears him fast to his home that's afar
Christmastide cheers the heart of a brave British tar.

☞ Richard Cotten served as a seaman on HMS *Comus* from 1879 until 1884, and then as a gunner for two years on HMS *Bacchante*, voyaging in the Far East and the Pacific. At Callao in June 1883 he bought himself a fine notebook into which he copied over thirty poems and songs, mainly nautical, some traditional and some perhaps written by him. He kept a journal in which he also noted songs, remarking on one occasion: 'Had a nice sing song on the forecastle just to let the gentry aft see we were alive.' Although he does not say so it is clear that the nostalgic Christmas song went to an adaptation of the tune 'Hearts of Oak'.

130

The Common Sailor

I am a man before the mast, I plough the trackless sea,
And on this simple subject, won't you please enlighten me?
Common sailors we are called. Pray tell me the reason why
This sneering adjective unto us which you so often reply
[This sneering adjective unto us which you so often reply?

    Don't call us common sailors any more, any more,
    Don't call us common sailors any more.
    Good things to you we bring, why call us common men?
    We're as good as any lubber on the shore.]

When speaking of a man on shore I never hear you say
He is a common this or that, be his calling what it may,
Be he a travelling tinker, a scavenger or sweep.
Then why term common unto those who travel on the deep?

For is it not your proudest boast that England rules the waves?
But could you say as much if none its dangers brave?
Among the nations of the world what would old England be
But for those battles dearly won by her children on the sea,

How would you get your luxuries, will you just tell to me,
Unless these men from foreign lands brought you sugar, coffee and
    tea?
And when the merry Christmas comes how would your pudding
    taste
Unless these men from foreign lands brought you spices, fruits and
    grapes?

Say you are invited to the boons and many more,
To the common British sailor that seeks the foreign shore,
Young ladies of our country too you should our calling bless,
For the foreign silks and satins of which you make your dress.

To be admired by gentlemen undoubtfully you do,
Then don't despise such gallant men that bring such dainties to
    you;

    reply] apply   boons] ?

And lads that like the fragrant weed, while smoking at your ease
Just think upon those sleepless nights we spend upon the seas.

And all of you that slight us so I'd have you go and try
One night upon the stormy sea when raging winds are high;
Amidst the driving, blinding snow, the pelting hail and rain,
It would be a tempting circumstance if they caught you there again.

But we ask not for your pity, but give to us our due;
Respect us in proportion for the good things that we do,
And the good things that you ask us for we will faithfully procure.
It shall be brought without delay unto your very door.

Excuse our little awkwardness. We are not perfect, quite.
Our heads, I own, are sometimes wrong, but I hope our hearts are
    right.
I hope the time will soon be past
When folks on shore despise a man who sails before the mast.

And lastly this wholesome track by nobody be forgot,
With lords and dukes and all the highest folks must share our
    common lot.

☞ This is another of the songs preserved by Richard Cotten (for whom, see 129
above). The tune and chorus have kindly been supplied by Stan Hugill, who
learned the song from his father.

131   *The Grimsby Fisherman*

I'm a rarem tarem fisherman that sails from Grimsby town,
And in the *Lion* and *Kitchen* I've had many [an] up and down;
But when I've spent my stocker-bait and had a little spree,
Then away I crack on board a smack to plough the stormy sea.

Then watch us, twig us, we're a popular juba jue.
Give her sheet and let her rip, we're the boys to put her through.
You ought to see her rally and the wind a-blowing free
On the passage from the Fisher Bank to Great Grimsby.

Our skipper's a shanghai rooster that loves a drop of good ale;
Our second addition's a rip-stone pippin that's seen the inside of a
gaol;
Our third hand's been a bushranger; the dickey has come from the
Di[a]les;
And to judge from his looks I am certain the cook is a native of
African wilds.

From the captain down to the caili cook we're a Vanderdecken
crew,
A Liverpool Irish packet-rat and a son of a kangaroo;
We've got one of the forty thieves, a bendigo Birmingham hoop,
And in every ringtail monkey man you'd recognize our cook.

[Red] *Lion* and [Hell's] *Kitchen*] Grimsby public houses   stocker-bait] money
made by fishing crews over and above their wages by selling surplus fish   popular
jubajue] ? proper jovial crew   Fisher Bank] Great Fisher Bank in the North Sea,
some 60 miles east of Grimsby   shanghai] shangie: thin, meagre   second
addition] first mate   rip-stone pippin] Ribston pippin, a Yorkshire apple, hence:
? Yorkshireman   dickey] deckie, deckhand   Di[a]les] Seven Dials, London
caili] cailing, weakly   Vanderdecken] doomed (see 106)   bendigo
Birmingham hoop] fur-capped Birmingham braggart

When we get a trip on board for Grimsby town we steer;
The only thing that's in our head is Mrs Sargeant's beer.
We crack on all the canvas, boys, and battle through every gale
Until the Spurn is left astern and then we take in sail.

Sailing over the Dogger Bank, isn't it a treat?
And the wind being from the east-nor'-east we had to give her
    sheet.
We were running wing and wing until we sighted Cleethorpes pier,
And when the voyage is ended we're the boys to gobble beer.

We are the boys to make a noise when we come home from sea;
Like pell mell swells we booze the girls and cause a jubilee.
We'd dance and shout and halloo out and roll about the floor
Until our rent is all spent and then we look for more.

☞ This seems to be an English parody, said to be by a blind fisherman-fiddler, of a
song of the North American lakes, 'The Cruise of the *Bigler*'. (This in turn
derived from, or gave rise to, 'The Knickerbocker Line', which deals with a man
robbed of his watch on the tram, probably in New York.) The Grimsby variant,
sometimes entitled 'The Dogger Bank', seems to have been confined to the
eastern seaboard, save for 'Littlehampton Collier Lads', an adaptation dealing
with the sailing colliers of the south coast. The text given here is from a
broadside without imprint, and the tune from Jack Smith (b. 1883) of Hull, a
former sailor in square-rigged coasters.

132 *The Young Sailor Cut Down in his Prime*

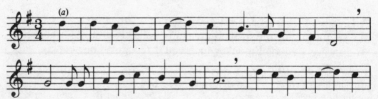

131 Mrs Sargeant] a Mrs Hannah Sargeant is listed in a directory of 1880 as the
landlady of the *Mariners' Tavern*, Victoria Street, Grimsby, close to the fish docks.
Pell mell] Pall Mall   jubilee] celebration   Cleethorpes Pier] built in 1872

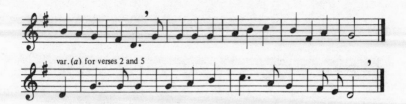
var. (a) for verses 2 and 5

One day as I strolled down by the Royal Albion,
Dark was the morning and cold as the grave.
Who should I spy but one of my messmates,
All wrapped in a blanket, much colder than clay?

So beat the drums o'er him and play the pipes merrily,
Play the dead march as they carry him along.
Take him to the graveyard, fire three volleys o'er him:
He's a young sailor cut down in his prime.

At the corner of the street you will see two girls standing;
One to another they whisper and sigh;
'There goes a young sailor whose money we squandered,
There goes a young sailor cut down in his prime.'

Now all ye young sailors take heed and take warning,
All ye young sailors take warning from me.
Don't go a-courting flash girls in the city;
Flash girls in the city were the ruin of me.

So beat the drums o'er him and play the pipes merrily,
Play the dead march as they carry him along.
Take him to the graveyard, fire three volleys o'er him:
He's a young sailor cut down in his prime.

☞ The 'Royal Albion' is a corruption of the Royal Albert, a London dock which
first opened in 1880. The song is very widely known, with different protagonists
(trooper, soldier, marine, cowboy, gambler, even maiden) and locations (Port
Arthur, Laredo, St James' Infirmary). The earliest text seems to be the
eighteenth-century 'Buck's Elegy', set in Covent Garden, in which the
onlooker's grief is compounded by the realization that he has contracted the
same disease as his comrade, from the same woman: 'Had I but known what his
disorder was, Had I but known it, and took it in time, I'd took pila cotia, all sorts
of white mercury, But now I'm cut off in the height of my prime.' (Pill of cochia
and salts of white mercury were early remedies for venereal disease.) The
version given here was sung as recently as 1980 by Bill Hingston (for whom, see
101).

flash girls] showy prostitutes

Tiger Bay

'Twas early in 'eighty-two, and I think on March the twentieth day,
So I thought I'd have a little cruise from the Well Street Home
   down Tiger Bay.
I had not then been long at sea when I was met by a pretty maid;
She had on a rare red dress and around her neck a tartan plaid.

     Whack for the lura the lura laido, whack for the lura lura lay.
     Whack for the lura the lura laido the pilots down to Tiger Bay.

Now when we set sail it was the hour of ten at night,
And we never tauted a tack or sheet till we got to the house of
   Mother Wright;
And I was shown a cosy room, and there reserved to stop next day;
I gave her ten bob for me harbour dues and she piloted me down to
   Tiger Bay.

Now in the morning I awoke, I found myself in the doldrum
   grounds,
And I didn't think I'd let her go until that day I'd spent ten pounds.

ten bob] ten shillings

Said to meself: 'This'll never do. I'll quit this barque without delay.'
So I made a tack for the Well Street Home from the rocks and
   shoals of Tiger Bay.

Now when I arrived at the Well Street Home I met my chum in the
   smoking room;
For he yells out: 'Jack, where have you been? You seem to be in
   ballast trim.'
I hung me head, not a word did say, but I got another ship that day;
And if ever I get to London again I'll have a good cruise in Tiger
   Bay.

Now all you young men in this room I just got a word to say:
Now whenever you meet a pretty little girl, lead her gently on the
   way;
For many's the ups and downs in the world, and many's the pretty
   girls down the highway,
But the prettiest one that e'er I met was me pilot down to Tiger
   Bay.

Now all you young girls in the room I've only got a word to say:
Oh whenever you meet a sailor hard up, oh give him a leg up by
   the way;
For if you do you'll never rue, for Jack'll have more money some
   other day,
And he'll pay you back when he hoists his jack for a pilot down to
   Tiger Bay.

☞ Wellclose Square, near London docks, was known as Tiger Bay, a sobriquet
also applied to districts in Cardiff and Belfast. The song, which appears to be
unique, was recorded by James Carpenter in the 1920s from John Gerries, a
seaman from South Shields. The tune is a variant of 'The Spanish Lady'.

134   *The* Balena

133 the highway] perhaps Ratcliffe Highway

Oh the noble fleet of whalers out sailing from Dundee,
Well-manned by British sailors to work them on the sea;
On the western ocean passage none with them can compare
For there's not a ship could make the trip as the *Balena*, I declare.

    And the wind is on her quarter and her engine working free,
    And there's not another whaler a-sailing from Dundee
    Can beat the aul' Balena, *and you needn't try her on,*
    For we challenge all both large and small from Dundee to St John's.

And it happened on a Thursday three days after we left Dundee,
Was carried off the quarter boats all in a raging sea
That took away our bulwarks, our stanchions and our rails,
And left the whole concern, boys, a-floating in the gales.

There's the new-built *Terra Nova*, she's a model, with no doubt;
There's the *Arctic* and the *Aurora* you've heard so much about.
There's Jacklin's model mailboat, the terror of the sea,
Couldn't beat the aul' *Balena* on a passage from Dundee.

Bold Jacklin carries canvas and fairly raises steam,
And Captain Guy's a daring boy goes ploughing through the
    stream;
But Mallan says the *Eskimaux* could beat the bloomin' lot,
But to beat the aul' *Balena*, boys, they'd find it rather hot.

And now that we have landed, boys, where the rum is mighty cheap
We'll drink success to Captain Burnett, lads, for gettin' us over the
    deep,
And a health to all our sweethearts an' to our wives so fair;
Not another ship could make that trip but the *Balena*, I declare.

    Terra Nova] launched in 1884, and remained in the Dundee fleet until 1903.
Arctic] launched 1875; lost 1887.   *Aurora*] launched 1876; left the Dundee fleet in
1894.   Jacklin's model mailboat] ? nickname for a ship   *Eskimaux*] launched
1865; left the Dundee fleet in 1900.

By the 1870s steam-assisted whaling ships from Dundee were travelling every March to St John's, Newfoundland, to engage in sealing. In April they went north to hunt the right-whale off the north-west coast of Greenland, then returned home in the early autumn. The trade gradually declined, until by 1900 no Dundee ships went sealing, and only about five a year, whaling. The song referred originally to the *Polynia*, a name which is retained in one Newfoundland version. This was a 472-ton ship launched in 1861 and lost thirty years later, crushed between ice floes in the Davis Strait. From 1883 until 1891 she was commanded by Captain William Guy, who later took over the *Balena*, which was in the Dundee fleet from 1891 until 1914. This vessel seems to have inherited the song, which seems from its references to other ships to have been first sung between 1884 and 1887. The singer of this version was Bruce Laurenson of Lerwick in the Shetlands.

135 ## The Smacksman

Once I was a schoolboy and stayed at home with ease;
Now I am a smacksman and I plough the raging seas.
I thought I'd like seafaring life but very soon I found
It was not all plain sailing, boys, when out on the fishing ground.

> *Coil away the trawl warp, boys, let's heave on the trawl.*
> *When we get our fish on board we'll have another haul.*
> *Straightway to the capstan and merrily heave her round,*
> *That's the cry in the middle of the night: 'Haul the trawl, boys,*
> *   haul.'*

Every night in winter as reg'lar as the clock
We put on our old sou'westers likewise our oilskin frock,
And straightway to the capstan and merrily spin away,
That's the cry in the middle of the night: 'Haul the trawl, boys,
     haul.'

When we get our fish on board we have them all to gut;
We put them into baskets and down the ice-locker put.
We ice them down, we size them, we ice them all quite well;
We ice them and keep them safely like an oyster in his shell.

☞ Sam Larner (1878–1965) of Winterton, Norfolk, whose song this is, started
going to sea occasionally at the age of eight, and four years later signed on as a
cabin boy. He worked on sailing luggers fishing for herring for nine years, then
on steam drifters from 1899 until 1933. He was a fine singer, and also the
inspiration for a song, 'The Shoals of Herring' (154).

136   *The Dockyard Gate*

Come all you married seamen bold, a few lines to you I'll write,
Just to let you know how the game do go when you are out of sight;
Just to let you know how the lads on shore go sporting with your
  wives
While you are on the rolling seas and venturing your sweet lives.

It's now our ship is outward bound and ready for to sail;
May the heavens above protect my love with a sweet and pleasant
  gale,
And keep him clear all from the shore and never more return
Until his pockets are well lined, and then he's welcome home.

A last farewell she takes of him and she begins to cry,
A-taking out her handkerchief to wipe her weeping eyes.
'My husband's gone to sea', she cries; 'how hard it is my case,
But still on shore there's plenty more: another will take his place.'

Then she goes unto her fancy man, these words to him did say:
'My husband he is gone to sea; tomorrow is half-pay day,
And you must wait at the dockyard gate until that I come out,
For that very day we'll sweat his half-pay and drink both ale and
  stout.'

That day they spent in sweet content till the half-pay was no more,
Then, 'Never mind, my dear', she cries, 'he's working hard for
  more.
Perhaps he's at the masthead, a-dying with the cold,
Or perhaps he's at his watch on deck; our joys he can't behold.'

And now our ship she's homeward bound, brought up in Plymouth
  Sound.
She hears the gun: 'My husband's come, to him I must go down.'
She goes unto her neighbour's house: 'One thing of you I crave.
Lend me your gown for mine's in pawn. It's the only one I have.'

the gun] fired to signal the arrival of a ship

Then she goes down unto the Sound and tries for to get in;
She so loudly for her husband calls and runs and kisses him,
Saying: 'How happy we shall be, my dear, now you are safe on
    shore.
You shall sit at home with me, my love, and go to sea no more.'

☞ This is an elusive song, of which only four versions (three fragmentary) have
been published. Frank Kidson obtained one verse in 1895 from a Whitby
woman who had learned it from her sailor-father, and commented: 'I look upon
it as one of a type of song which is produced even today, on shipboard. It is here
that real sailors' songs are invented and occasionally passed on to shore people,
where a generation or two of singers form them into folk-songs pure and
simple.' The only full text of the song was taken down in 1907 from a seventy-
two-year-old singer in Portsmouth Workhouse, though it was not published
until 1965. It is reprinted here. Three and a half verses from Sam Larner
appeared on a record in 1961. Perhaps the long reticence was because of the
sanguine, not to say cynical, attitude displayed in this 'real sailors' song'.

137   *A Great Favourite Song, entitled*
       The Sailor's Hornpipe
       in Jackson Street

Good people pay attention and listen to my song;
I'll sing to you a verse or two, I won't detain you long.
I came home from sea the other day, a fair lass I did meet;
She asked me to go along with her and dance in Jackson Street.

'Jack, as you can't dance too well, will you then have a treat?
Will you have a glass of brandy or something you may take?
At nine o'clock this evening I'll see you at the train,
And if ever you come this road, Jack, you will give us a call again.'

When the dinner was over the whisky did come in,
[And when all hands had got their fill the dancing did begin].
When round the floor with Maggie I danced the merry tune,
And the other couple they did dance double-shuffle round the room.

When the supper was over I prepared and went to bed;
I shortly fell asleep, the truth I do declare.
When I wakened in the morning nothing could I spy
But a woman's shift and apron that at the foot of the bed did lie.

The daylight was past and the night coming on,
I put on the shift and apron, to the quay I did run;
And when I got my foot aboard the sailors they did say:
'By my word, Jack, you have caught the clock since you've been
    away.

'Is that the new spring fashion they've got upon the shore?
Where is the shop they sell them? Do you think there are any
    more?'
Says the captain to me: 'Jack, I thought you were for Newry bound;
You might have got a better suit than that for less than three
    pounds.'

'I met a girl in Heyberry Street. She asked me away to dance.
She stole away my heart with her roguish Irish glance.
She danced to my destruction; I suffered so complete
I take my oath I'll go no more to dance in Jackson Street.'

Come all you jolly seamen, a warning take by me,
Be sure to choose a comrade before you get on the spree.
Be sure and keep out of Jackson Street or you will rue the day;
With a woman's shift and apron you will have to go to sea.

[*The last line of each verse is repeated*]

Nicholson, Printer, Cheapside Song House, 26 Church Lane, Belfast

☞ Under a variety of titles, including 'Jack All Alone' and 'Woman's Shift and
Apron', and in various different settings, including Peter Street (Liverpool) and

Barrack Street (Halifax, Nova Scotia), this cautionary tale for seamen was widely sung, though seldom printed. Nicholson of Belfast was in business from 1888 until 1919. The tune, which is reminiscent of 'The Common Sailor', (130), is from Stan Hugill.

138   *Three Score and Ten*

And it's three score and ten boys and men were lost from Grimsby
    town;
From Yarmouth down to Scarborough many hundreds more were
    drowned.
Our herring craft, our trawlers, our fishing smacks as well.
They longed to fight that bitter night to battle with the swell.

Methinks I see some little craft spreading their sails a-lee
As down the Humber they do glide all bound for the northern sea.
Methinks I see on each small craft a crew with hearts so brave
Going out to earn their daily bread upon the restless wave.

Methinks I see them yet again as they leave the land behind,
Casting their nets into the sea the fishing ground to find.
Methinks I see them yet again and all on board's all right,
With the sails flow free and the decks cleared up and the side-lights
    burning bright.

October's night was such a sight was never seen before:
There was masts, there was yards; broken spars came floating to
  our shore.
There was many a heart of sorrow, there was many hearts so brave;
There was many a hearty fisherlad did find a watery grave.

☞ 'In Memoriam of the poor Fishermen who lost their lives in the Dreadful Gale
from Grimsby and Hull, Feb. 8 & 9, 1889' is the title of a broadside produced by
a Grimsby fisherman, William Delf, to raise funds for the bereaved families. It
lists eight lost vessels, the last two from Hull: *Eton, John Wintringham, Sea
Searcher, Sir Fred. Roberts, British Workman, Kitten, Harold, Adventure,* and *Olive
Branch.* In addition the names of some of the lost sailors are given, and there is a
poem in eight stanzas. This passed into oral tradition, and in so doing lost six
verses and acquired a new one (the last, in which an error of date occurs),
together with a chorus and a tune. The oral version was noted from a master
mariner, Mr J. Pearson of Filey, in 1957, and has subsequently, with some
further small variations, become well known in folk-song clubs.

139 *I am an Ancient Mariner*

I am an ancient mariner, I've sailed o'er many a sea;
I'm skipper of a little smack, she's called the *Nancy Lee.*

  *Blow, shiver my timbers, splice my jib, blow, stormy winds, blow,
  blow.
  She's a gallant clipper smack and it's all right, Jack, heave-o, heave-
  o, heave-o.*

275

We lowsed fae Portabella pier, all on the Firth of Forth;
Bound for the distant land of Fife we steered nor'-east by north.
I bade my old sweetheart farewell in case I never came back;
She answered with a heaving sigh: 'It's all right, Jack'.

We had not sailed a hundred miles till loud the winds did blow;
The little dog and the cabin boy were asleep in their bunks below.
'All hands on deck, reef tops'ls quick, and gather in the slack',
When through the din shouts Bill the boy: 'It's all right, Jack.'

I caught the little cabin boy and punched his little head;
I bound him to the jigger-mast and bade him throw the lead.
The dog began tae howl: I gie'd him sic'n a whack;
He howled and he growled and he snarled and he yowled: 'It's all
    right, Jack.'

Oh was there e'er a mariner in sic a plight before?
All hands in open mutiny a thousand miles from shore,
A school of sharks and Greenland whales all in the vessel's track,
And a bloomin' old mermaid yelling out: 'It's all right, Jack.'

The gale came to a hurricane; the mermaid bounded on deck;
She threw her slimy, scaly tail and her arms around my neck.
She bore me down to the coral cove, full fifty fathoms deep,
So rich, so rare, 'twould make the eyes of fifty misses weep.

'If you will promise to marry me I'll bear ye to your smack.'
It's up, by Jove, and away we go: it's all right, Jack.

☞ With its parody of the heroic manner and its guying of nautical terms, this song
was widely known not only to sailors but to canal boatmen under titles as diverse
as 'The Fish and Chip Ship', 'While going round the Cape', 'Captain Nipper',
and 'The Walloping Window Blind'. The version given here was sung in the late
1960s by two cousins from South Ronaldsway in the Orkneys, John ('Jock') Dass
(b. 1905) and James Henderson (b. 1903). The song probably dates from the
late nineteenth century.

lowsed fae] cast off from

The Merchant Shipping Act

Come all you focsle lawyers that always take delight
By brooding o'er your troubles to set all matters right,
Well versed in every paragraph, in every word and fact,
Of the law that often makes you swear, the Merchant Shipping Act.

> *Then what's the use of growling when you know you get your whack,*
> *Limejuice and vinegar, according to the ac'?*
> *Then what's the use of growling when you know you get your whack,*
> *Exactly what you sign for in the Merchant Shipping Ac'?*

Now follow me attentively and as I go along
I'll tell you of your grievances and sing them in my song;
And after all your only plan is to wait till you get back,
And bear things patient like an ass, as intended by the ac'.

By day and night at every call, as well as Sundays too,
You must spring up whene'er they bawl, like an obedient crew;

And if you're cursed and swore at you must not answer back,
Because you know by doing so you'd be breaking of the ac'.

Now duteous and respectful you must at all times be,
Whether in a foreign port or on the stormy sea;
And though you're starved on rotten grub you know you get your
  whack,
Which is all that you have signed for in the Merchant Shipping Ac'.

Oh, if some noble, well-fed lord by fairy chance could steal
Across the seas and watch poor Jack devour his scanty meal,
'Twould make his manly heart to bleed, and he'd spread abroad the
  fact
How a class of men are daily starved by the Merchant Shipping
  Act.

Or view those dark and noisome dens where seamen go to rest,
A damp and stifling place below, not fit for pigs at best;
Fit places such for foul disease, but then what matters that,
As long as you've the space required by the Merchant Shipping
  Act?

Around the sides and overhead, through half-caulked, leaky seams,
From bitts and pawlpitts to knightheads it's pouring down in
  streams;
It soaks your bedding through and through—again, what matters
  that?
For leaky seams don't come within the meaning of the Act.

If sickness shakes his robust frame and tortures him with pain,
If he lays up he's lazy, they bid him work again;
With threats and jeers remorseless drove he crawls around the deck;
Racked with grief and anger he feels a hopeless wreck.

Curtail all tyrant captains' power and aid us in our cause.
We ask the British Parliament to give us better laws,
Afford their seamen proper dues and treat 'em more like men,
'Twould help to man their merchant ships and be the wiser plan.

We do not want your foreigners to aid us in our toil,
But all true British seamen brought up on British soil.
The Mistress of the Seas, my boys, a tar shall never lack,
Though food and treatment are so bad according to the ac'.

Death comes at last and shipmates gaze on his expiring form;
'Tis then the seamen's hardy hearts in righteous anger warm.
In mute despair they do not dare to cast reproaches back,
Because they know by doing so they'd be breaking of the ac'.

☞ Fifty years of maritime legislation were consolidated in the Merchant Shipping
Act of 1894, but this was not well received by seamen, and gave rise to two songs
in which sarcasm mingled with indignation. The first is given here from
Clements, who writes that 'It was highly popular at sea, and the first four lines of
the chorus passed almost into a proverb and were quoted with philosophical
acceptance on all sorts of occasions when an element of irritation obtruded
itself'. It seems to have lasted in oral tradition for only a few decades, whereas
the second song, 'The Limejuice Ship', continued to circulate at least until the
Second World War, and was favoured not only by merchant seamen (with a
chorus ending in the words: 'God bless the navy, but a merchant ship for me'),
but by navy men who substituted: 'Damn and bugger the navy, boys, a merchant
ship for me.'

141   *On Board the* Leicester Castle

It was early in the month of cold December
When me money it was all spent and gone, and so it is now,
And I thought that I would take a quiet ramble,
And down to the shipping office went.
On the day there'd been a great demand for sailors
To take a trip to China or Japan,
When I shipped aboard the *Leicester Castle*,
And I came home with a month's money in advance.

> And I said: 'Let her come back, heave in your slack.
> Heave away your capstan, gain a port, gain a port.
> About ship. At your station, boys, be handy.
> Raise your sheets, your slacks, and mains'l haul.

Now when I arrived aboard the *Leicester Castle*
Such lovely sights I'd never seen before.
There were ragamuffins there from every nation,
And, golly, how me poor heart felt so sore.
Down in me chest I knew I had a bottle:
I seen the shipping master put it there;
And I thought I'd go and quench me thirsty throttle,
To drive away dull sorrow and all care.

gain a port] gain a pawl   slacks] tacks

Down upon me hands and knees I went a-groping,
A-groping like a pig into his trough;
And with my surprise and wonder
I found it was good medicine for me cough.
Now I wish I was with the jolly sailors
Down in Blaxhall *Ship* a-drinking beer,
And when the singing and dancing it was all over
We raised our ports and sang out with good cheer.

☞ One of the many ships mentioned in different versions of this song was the *Hotspur*, which was at sea in the 1830s. Bone says that 'The Liverpool Song', as he calls it, was popular as a forebitter in 1900, though he had not heard it subsequently. Hugill records it, under the title of 'Paddy lay back' as a capstan shanty. George Ling (1904–75), a Suffolk bricklayer whose trade no doubt accounts for some nautical uncertainties in the chorus, sang this version to Keith Summers in 1974–5.

142   *The Bargeman's ABC*

141 ports] ? glasses of port   Blaxhall *Ship*] public house in the village of
Blaxhall, Suffolk

A is for the anchor we carry on the bow,
B is for the boltsprit that we lower down;
C for the cathead where the anchor is stowed,
D is for the davits where our boat is hove.

So merrily, so merrily, so merrily are we,
There's none so blithe as a bargeman at sea.
Sing high, sing low, a-sailing along;
Give an old barge a breeze and you cannot go wrong.

Oh E is for the ensign that flies at the peak,
F is for the focsle where all the hands sleep;
G is for the gaskets we pass round and round,
H is for the halliards we haul up and down.

Oh I is for the irons that go round our hold,
J is for the jib we set up so bold;
K is for the kelson so long and so straight,
L is for the lamps that we light up at night.

Oh M is for the mainmast abaft our fore-horse,
N for the needle that shows us our course;
O is for the oars that row our small boat,
And P is for the pumps that do keep us afloat.

Oh Q is for the quarterdeck where the skipper do walk,
R is for the rigging so stout and so taut;
S is for the stays which must be set tight,
T is for the truck on our topmast so bright.

Oh U is for the uprights around our ship's wend,
V for the vangs on our sprit's joggle-end;
W is for the wheel where we all take a turn,
And X Y and Z is the name on our stern.

☞ Bob Roberts (1907–82) was born in Dorset, lived mainly in Suffolk, and retired to the Isle of Wight. He first went to sea at the age of fifteen in the Fowey barquentine, *Waterwitch*, but his main career was in spritsail barges, and he was skipper of the *Cambria*, the last working sailing vessel to fly the red ensign. He wrote several books about his experiences and also made two records of songs. His large repertoire included items for bargemen, fishermen and sailors in general. See also 116, 143 and 144.

Stormy Weather, Boys

We were laying in Surrey Dock one day.
The mate knew that it was time to get under way.

Stormy weather, boys, stormy weather, boys,
When the wind blows our barge will go.

He's homeward bound but he's out of luck
'Cause the skipper's half drunk in the *Dog and Duck*.

Then the skipper came aboard with the girl on his arm.
He's going to give up barging and take a farm.

So the mate ran forrard and the cook fell in the dock,
And the skipper caught his knackers in the mainsheet block.

The mate's at the wheel and he gybed her twice
'Cause the skipper's got his knackers in a bowl of ice.

At last we're off down Limehouse Reach,
When our leeboards knocked on Greenwich Beach.

The barge went ashore and scared our whore.
She said: 'Chuck this, I'm off ashore.'

We shoved her off and away we go,
But the skipper's got a bottle of beer below.

143 Surrey Dock] at Rotherhithe, London

She fills away and she sails like heck,
But there ain't no bargemen up on deck.

There's a crash and a bump and she's ashore.
The mate says: 'Christ, we're on the Nore.'

Then up comes a mermaid covered in mud.
The skipper says: 'I think we're on the Whittaker Spit.'

Then up comes another one covered in slime,
So we took her down the focsle and had a good time.

On the top of the tide the barge did fleet,
When the mate sees a ghost on the tops'l sheet.

So away we go and the ghost did steer,
And the cook drank the dregs of the old man's beer.

We laid close-hauled round Orford Ness,
When the wind backed round to the south-sou'-west.

We reached our port all safe and sound
And tied her up in Yarmouth Town.

So after all our fears and alarms
We all ended up in the *Druid's Arms*.

☞ This racy and ribald account of a voyage from London to Great Yarmouth
comes from Bob Roberts (for whom, see 142 above), who pieced it together
from three different sources. He believed it to be the only song peculiar to the
spritsail bargemen of the east coast.

144   *The Candlelight Fisherman*

143 the Nore] off the mouth of the Thames   Whittaker Spit] sandbank off the
Essex coast   fleet] sail (the word is first recorded in this sense in *Beowulf*.)   Orford
Ness] headland on the east coast, just south of Aldeburgh

My dad was a fisherman bold and he lived till he grew old,
Till he opened the pane and popped out the flame
Just to see how the wind do blow.

He often said to me: 'You'll be wise before you go.
Do you open the pane and pop out the flame
Just to see', &c.

When the north wind roughly blow then I lay right down below
And I open the flame and pop out the flame
Just to see, &c.

When the wind comes from the west it will blow hard at the best,
So I open, &c.

Now a wind that's from the east, it's n' good to man nor beast,
So I open, &c.

My wife she said to me: 'We shall starve if you don't go.'
So I open, &c.

So all you fishermen bold, if you'd live till you grow old,
Do you open the pane, &c.

☞ If the candle blows out, there's too much wind, and if not, too little: the sly advice to fishermen is from Bob Roberts (for whom, see 142 above).

145   *Swell my Net Full*

Out on the ocean, dreary and cold,
I lead the life of a fisherman bold.
So swell me net full, swell me net full,
Mack'rel for Monday, swell me net full.

Wind from the south'ard, wind from the west,
Plenty of fishes will come to your mesh.
So swell me net full, swell me net full,
Sea trout for Tuesday, swell me net full.

Wind from the north'ard, wind from the east,
Many a haul but never a feast.
So swell me net full, swell me net full,
We'll fish for Wednesday, swell me net full.

God is our master, the weather he willed,
But it's with herring our bellies are filled.
So swell me net full, swell me net full,
Herring for Thursday, swell me net full.

Stay in the harbour, look o'er the foam,
For Friday's the day the devil doth own.
So swell me net full, swell me net full,
Nothing for Friday, swell me net full.

Stand to your nets with needle and twine,
Whether the weather be stormy or fine.
So swell me net full, swell me net full,
Sand-dabs for Saturday, swell me net full.

When I do die and life in me fails,
Build me a tombstone of herring back scales.
So swell me net full, swell me net full,
Sole is for Sunday, swell me net full.

☞ By contrast with the previous song the advice here is serious and practical, with
homely wisdom for each day of the week. Friday was thought unlucky for any

new enterprise because of its association with the crucifixion. Bob Roberts'
song, which has not previously appeared in print, may have been used to
accompany rowing or net hauling, as well as for the pleasure of singing.

146 *The Mail Boat*, Leinster

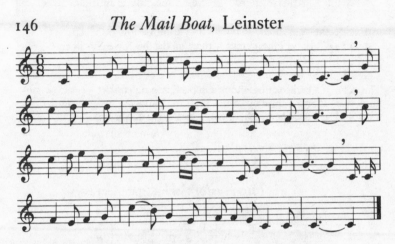

You feeling-hearted Christians all in country or in town,
Come listen to my doleful song which I have just penned down.
'Tis all about that German act, that awful tragedy,
When the Dublin mail boat, *Leinster*, was sunk in the Irish Sea.

On the tenth day of October, nineteen eighteen the year,
The mail boat on her passage went, I mean to let you hear;
With six hundred and ninety passengers and seventy of a crew
She sailed away from Kingstown Quay and for Holyhead bound to.

In pride and stately grandeur did the *Leinster* plough her way,
And all on board were of good cheer with spirits light and gay;
Not fearing that the U-boat lay hid beneath the wave
That would send them soon unto their doom, and give a watery
      grave.

The German monster came on them when they did least expect
And fired torpedoes at the boat, which quickly took effect.
Her boilers burst; the flames ascend with fury to the sky;
'Mid the echo of the deafening din you could hear the women cry.

Oh the *Leinster* now is sinking fast, she's going down by the head,
And many, too, while in their bunks are numbered with the dead.

The passengers, their lifebelts on, unto the boats repair,
While cries for help do rend the skies in sad and wild despair.

Now to conclude and finish, my doleful lines to close;
May the Lord have mercy on their souls and grant them sweet
    repose.
Beside the mail boat, *Leinster*, they quietly now do sleep
In the cold and changeless waters of the Irish Sea so deep.

☞ This echo in a corner of Ireland of a great European conflict was sung almost
thirty years after the event by Patrick Doyle of Curracloe, near Wexford, to the
tune of 'The Poulshone Fishermen', a local song dating from 1863.

147   *The Sailors' Wives*

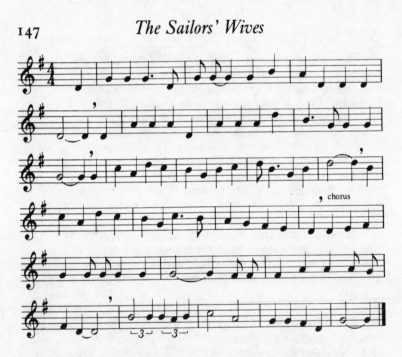

The first one was the gunner's wife and she was dressed in green,
And in one corner of her hat she stowed the magazine;
She stowed the magazine, my boys, the powder and the shell,
And in the other corner was a nine point four as well.

288

*And she'd a dark and a rolling eye and her hair hung down to her
   ankles;*
She was one of the best girls out of Pompey town.

The next one was the stoker's wife and she was dressed in brown,
And in one corner of her hat was a bunker upside down;
A bunker upside down, my boys, the shovels and the rakes,
And in the other corner was a bunch of boiler plates.

The next one was the bunting's wife and she was dressed in black,
And in one corner of her hat she stowed the Union Jack;
She stowed the Union Jack, my boys, and ensigns by the score,
And in the other corner was the starboard semaphore.

The next one was the bosun's wife and she was dressed in red.
And in one corner of her hat she stowed the deep sea lead;
She stowed the deep sea lead, my boys, a loose lead line as well,
And in the other corner was a matelot doing cells.

The last one was the coxswain's wife and she was dressed in blue,
And in one corner of her hat she stowed the cutter's crew;
She stowed the cutter's crew, my boys, the rowlocks and the oars,
And in the other corner were battalions forming fours.

☞ This is very much a Royal Navy song, based on 'The Fire Ship' (101), but
drawing on the modern terminology of steam power and gunnery. It is also
known as 'The Captain's Ball'. This version was sung to Clare Clayton of
Sussex by her father, who served in the Royal Navy during the First World War
and who pointed out that the capacious hat was something quite different in the
original. The word 'ankles' was also a euphemism.

148 *Looking for a Ship*

147 Pompey] Portsmouth

I went down dock the other day,
Went for a ship, didn't you hear me say?
Couldn't get a ship, couldn't get a sub,
So I went down dock on the old woman's lug.
Singing, I'm going to look, I'm going to look,
I'm going to look for a wes'ly ship,
I'm going to look.

I went down dock the very next day, &c.

God made man, man made money,
Deckies did the work and skipper drew the money.
Men worked for ever in the floating bin.
Singing, I had a look, I had a look,
I had a look for a wes'ly ship,
I had a look.

☞ Harry Aisthorpe of the G. F. Sleights Fishing Company, Grimsby, wrote this
chirpy little song, probably in the 1920s. The tune seems to be based on that of
the shanty, 'Johnny Booker', and the last verse echoes a traditional rhyme: 'God
made bees, bees made money. Poor man does the work and the rich man gets the
money.'

149   *The Sinking of the* Graf Spee

148 wes'ly] westerly   sub] advance of wages   lug] ear   deckie] deckhand

Oh there was a jolly ship built in Nazi Germany,
And the name of that ship was the *Admiral Graf Spee*,
And she looted merchantmen of every nationality
As she sailed upon the rolling, bowling,
As she sailed upon the rolling sea.

She met three cruisers of the British army,
And to stop them she knew would put Berlin on the spree.
Their commander laughed aloud: 'Now merry game there'll be,
For I'll sink them 'neath the rolling, bowling,
For I'll sink them 'neath the [rolling] sea.'

She fired her mighty guns, did the *Admiral Graf Spee*,
Her captain laughed aloud, and hugged himself with glee,
But he swore a hasty oath as the little cruisers three
Came dashing over the rolling, bowling,
Came dashing over the rolling sea.

'To the helm, quick,' he cries, 'and turn face right merrily,
Or our Führer's small moustache we never more may live to see.'
With his tail between his legs, in his ear a lively flea,
He went scurrying through the rolling, bowling,
He went scurrying through the rolling sea.

Yes, the 'bear' he went to cover where his wounds the world could
     see,
For the British bulldog bite had hurted painfully,
And the foeman speeding forward knew the fight that he had seen
Would end beneath the rolling, bowling,
Would end beneath the rolling sea.

Yes, and this was the end of the *Admiral Graf Spee*,
And perhaps it was for this that a pocket ship was she,
For in Davy Jones's pocket, scuttled most ingloriously,
She rusts beneath the rolling, bowling,
She rusts beneath the rolling sea.

army] navy

☞ In December 1939 the German pocket battleship, *Admiral Graf Spee*, was attacked by three British cruisers, *Ajax*, *Achilles*, and *Exeter*, off the River Plate in South America. The *Exeter* was soon driven out of the action but the *Graf Spee* was damaged enough to need to take refuge in Montevideo. When the time allowed in a neutral port had elapsed the German captain, who had been bluffed into believing that a considerable British force lay waiting for him, took his ship out into the estuary and scuttled her. The news was rapturously received in Britain, and inspired several songs. One celebrated the return of *Achilles* to her home port in New Zealand and another was made up by sailors to the tune of a popular song of the day, 'South of the Border'. A local newspaper in County Armagh printed the text given here, which is based on a sea song of almost three hundred years earlier, 'The Spanish Galley' (for which, see 22). It was noted by Robin Morton from Dick Bamber of Tandragee, who 'remembered singing this song in pubs during the war and not having to buy a drink because of it'.

150   *The* Jervis Bay

It was a bleak November morning
With a convoy under way
When they sighted a German raider
From the tops of the *Jervis Bay*.

'Clear the decks for action'
Was the order of the day,
And that gallant Captain Fegen
Then sailed into the fray.

She was only a merchant cruiser
Against a battleship,
But she took that noble action
Just to let the convoy slip.

On her decks lay dead and dying,
For them the day was won;
When they heard the convoy scattered
Then they knew their job was done.

Why do we weep, why do we pray?
Those sailors sleep so far away.
They gave their lives that November day,
Those heroes of the *Jervis Bay*.

☞ In a curious echo of the privateers of old, the *Jervis Bay* was a passenger liner converted by the addition of seven guns into an armed merchant cruiser. On 5 November 1940 she was escorting a convoy of 37 homeward-bound ships in the North Atlantic when she was confronted by the German pocket battleship, *Admiral Scheer*. Captain Fegen of the *Jervis Bay* ordered the convoy to scatter, then suicidally engaged the enemy ship. The thirty minutes which elapsed before the *Jervis Bay* was sunk enabled most of the convoy to escape. Captain Fegen was posthumously awarded the Victoria Cross, and he and his crew were commemorated in songs and poems spontaneously written by ordinary sailors. 'The *Jervis Bay*' was widely sung in the navy, with slight variations in text, and to various tunes, including 'Suvla Bay' and 'Kevin Barry'. It has been suggested that the authorities frowned upon it as bad for morale, and I have not seen it in print. CPO Ray Maries of Birmingham sang the version given here in 1984.

151 *Deep Sea Tug*

Oh the trawler wharf in Aberdeen
It's a bonnie place to be
When a force eight gale is blawin'
Oot apon the wild north sea;
And the wee tug battles fiercely
On a course that's hard to find,
With a floating dock that pitches
On a tow rope far behind.

Aye it's cauld, bloody cauld,
On the gie dreich watters o'
The north-east Scottish coast.

Pounding seas come in frae starboard
And the wee tug slews to port,
And the tow rope breaks a stay wire
In the storm's deadly sport.
On the deck an able seaman
Fell down dead before he knew
What it was come oot the dark nicht,
And it sliced his head in two.

There's nae time to help a shipmate;
Though his blood has stained the sea
It's all hands tae fix the stay wire
And tae keep the tow rope free;
For she's dragging by the stern
And we're shipping water green,
And the risk o' being washed awa'
It's the worst I've ever seen.

It was up to Invergordon
We were headed wi' oor tow.
Thank the Christ we didna have to sail
North aboot tae Scapa Flow.

gie] very (pronounced 'guy')   dreich] drear

As ye curse yer damp and heavy clathes
Oh your tired mind starts to dream
Of the comforts at the trawler wharf
In the port of Aberdeen.

☞ Harry Robertson, who wrote this song, served as a Royal Navy reservist on a tug
in 1945. Apart from bringing 'broken ships' into port, the tug was required from
time to time to tow a floating dock north from Rosyth. The dock, which was used
for repairing RAF rescue launches, had no keel, and towed 'like a shoebox'. The
tow rope was supported by two stay wires, which were under very heavy strain.
Because of the danger of their parting, the after part of the tug was roped off and
out of bounds, but on one occasion a sailor strayed into the forbidden area and
paid a heavy penalty. Harry Robertson originates from Barrhead in Scotland,
but soon after the Second World War he emigrated to Australia. He now lives in
Queensland. He has written several songs about his experiences on whaling
ships in the Antarctic.

152 *The Kola Run*

Tune, 'Unfortunate Miss Bailey'

Now gather round, you stroppy Jacks who serve the peacetime
    Andrew,
That's always swinging round the buoy—there ain't much else it
    can do—

While I tell you a tale of the Kola run, a yarn of the Russian
  convoys,
By one who sailed in Arctic gales before you came along, boys,
Came along, boys, before you came along, boys.

It was the good ship '*Orrible*', one of six destroyers;
Her skipper was a tyrant and her crew were mess deck lawyers;
And Number One was a Dartmouth man who bleated in derision:
'God save us from these green ODs of Devonport Division,
'Port Division, of Devonport Division.'

The year was nineteen forty-two, the month it was December,
When we sailed out of Scapa Flow, how well I do remember.
While Hitler raved in Germany and Neptune came to mock us
We braved those hyperborean seas to fill Joe Stalin's lockers,
Stalin's lockers, to fill Joe Stalin's lockers.

On Christmas Eve we took our leave of Iceland's barren station;
No Christmas cheer or cans of beer, Murmansk our destination.
The sin-bosun he prayed aloud; the crew thought of tombola
And cursed the day they ever joined a vessel bound for Kola,
Bound for Kola, a vesssel bound for Kola.

Now east-nor'-east our course was set and the weather hit us
  squarely;
The kye froze in old stripey's cup, the ship was iced-up fairly;
The matelots from their hammocks crept like ancient
  barrack-stanchions,
And jolly Jack wished he was back safe home in Jago's Mansions,
Jago's Mansions, safe home in Jago's Mansions.

The oggin heaved and broke aboard in icy Arctic samples;
The lower deck was a sodden wreck, the heads they were a
  shambles;
The sprogs did vomit pusser's peas until no more would come,
  mates,
And even old three-badge ABs were sea-sick in their rum, mates,
In their rum, mates, were sea-sick in their rum, mates.

The skipper spoke to Number One who spoke unto the buffer:
'Now get you down to the lower deck and make the sailors suffer.

Kola] the Kola Peninsula lies between the Barents and White Seas.   tombola]
game, now usually known as bingo

This ship is in a sorry state, it simply will not do;
The gates of hell are open wide and we are sailing through,
Sailing through, and we are sailing through.'

On New Year's Eve in the Barents Sea the enemy were sighted;
Their big ships hove up warily, the skipper was delighted:
'Now we'll attack—to hell with Jack,' said he, bent on promotion;
On bended knee to the admiralty he offered his devotion,
His devotion, he offered his devotion.

So all day long did battle sound with many an unsung hero;
The dance of death went round and round in temperatures
    sub-zero.
We chipped the ice from off the guns, the Hun we did confound,
    lads,
And so we brought the convoy through to Kola safe and sound,
    lads,
Safe and sound, lads, to Kola safe and sound, lads.

Now listen, all you modern tars what draw the mid-day potion,
Good kids, no doubt, in harbour bars, but, blimey, on the ocean:
The Russkies took the blooming lot, then said: 'It's not enough,
    Jack,'
And that was all the thanks we got for spewing up our duff, Jack,
Up our duff, Jack, for spewing up our duff, Jack.

☞ At the age of twenty-one, D. S. Goodbrand joined HMS *Obdurate* at Scapa Flow
in 1942, and served aboard her as a wireless operator for two years, which were
partly spent in escorting convoys to the Soviet port of Murmansk, on the Kola
Peninsula. He wrote the song in 1961 to show young sailors what service in the
navy was like, twenty years earlier.

153   *Diesel and Shale*

152 mid-day potion] rum issue (discontinued in 1970)

On the fifth of November in 'fifty-three
The big man at *Dolphin* he sent for me:
'I brought you here, boy, 'cause I want you to know
We've booked you a berth in the water below,
With the diesel and shale, diesel and shale,
We've booked you a berth with the diesel and shale.'

Well, when I protested: 'I'm no volunteer',
He said: 'We ain't had one in many a year,
But that's a wee secret between you and me;
There's many a pressed man down under the sea,
With the diesel and shale, diesel and shale,
Down under the sea with the diesel and shale.'

'Oh doctor, dear doctor, I don't think I'm well.'
'Well, never mind, sonny, we'll very soon tell.
Try holding your breath while I count up to three.
There, that proves that you're fit to go down in the sea,
With the diesel and shale, diesel and shale,
To go down in the sea with the diesel and shale.'

I went to the storeroom to gather me rig;
They gave me a sweater ten sizes too big.
I crawled down the boat like an old polar bear,
And I says to meself: 'There's a smell in the air,
And it's diesel and shale, diesel and shale,
There's smell in the air and it's diesel and shale.'

A push on the klaxon and a ring on the gongs,
And then I was down where no mortal belongs,
Where the egg's going bad and the bread's getting stale,
And they mix you a nightcap of diesel and shale,
Diesel and shale, diesel and shale,
They mix you a nightcap of diesel and shale.

Dolphin] the Gosport headquarters of the submarine service

'Keep walking, keep walking, you foolish young man,
You know that I never would give you my hand.
Your hair is too thin and your face is too pale,
'Cause you spend too much time with your diesel and shale,
Diesel and shale, diesel and shale,
You spend too much time with your diesel and shale.'

We circled the Med. for a summer or two,
Where the sun is so warm and the water so blue.
Well, that's what they tell me, but I wouldn't know,
'Cause the view ain't so good when you're stuck down below,
With the diesel and shale, diesel and shale,
When you're stuck down below with the diesel and shale.

Then the big man at *Dolphin* he told me at last:
'It's time you went back to a ship with a mast.'
I feel like a Jonah a-leaving the whale
'Cause I'm saying goodbye to the diesel and shale,
The diesel and shale, diesel and shale,
I'm saying goodbye to the diesel and shale.

Oh Crabby, dear Crabby, I bid you adieu,
And Synagogue Dick and the Black Mamba too.
I'll do all me travelling by road and by rail,
And you know what to do with your diesel and shale,
Diesel and shale, diesel and shale,
You know what to do with your diesel and shale.

☞ Songs about the submarine branch of the navy are rare. This was written by
Cyril Tawney (b. 1930), whose naval service from 1946 to 1959 included several
years in submarines. He was surprised to discover, contrary to the general belief,
that not all submariners were volunteers. One of the lasting memories of his
service was the pervasive smell of diesel fuel and shale oil.

Crabby, Dick, Mamba] nicknames of successive captains

The Shoals of Herring

Oh it was a fine and a pleasant day;
Out of Yarmouth harbour I was faring
As a cabin boy on a sailing lugger
For to go and hunt the shoals of herring.

Oh the work was hard and the hours were long,
And the treatment, sure, it took some bearing;
There was little kindness, and the kicks were many,
As we hunted for the shoals of herring.

Oh we fished the Swarth and the Broken Bank;
I was cook, and I'd a quarter sharing,
And I used to sleep standing on me feet
And I'd dream about the shoals of herring.

Oh we left the home grounds in the month of June
And to canny Shiel's we soon was bearing
With a hundred cran of the silver darlings
That we'd taken from the shoals of herring.

Now you're up on deck, you're a fisherman,
You can swear and show a manly bearing;
Take your turn on watch with the other fellows
While you're searching for the shoals of herring.

In the stormy seas and the living gales
Just to earn your daily bread you're daring;

Swarth] Swarte Bank, a North Sea fishing ground   Broken Bank] another
fishing ground in the North Sea   Shiel's] North and South Shields   cran] 28
stones (392 pounds) weight

From the Dover Straits to the Faeroe Islands
As you're following the shoals of herring.

Oh I earned me keep and I paid me way
And I earned the gear that I was wearing;
Sailed a million miles, caught ten million fishes:
We were sailing after shoals of herring.

☞ Ewan MacColl (b. 1915) wrote this song in 1960, basing it on the life of a
Norfolk fisherman, Sam Larner (for whom, see 135). It was included in a
documentary radio ballad, 'Singing the Fishing', by Ewan MacColl, Peggy
Seeger, and Charles Parker, and later issued on a record. The programme won
an Italia prize and the song became widely popular, especially in Ireland, where
it was quickly accepted into traditional circulation. It now has the feeling of a
valediction, both for a man (Sam Larner died in 1975) and for an industry.

155 *Liverpool John*

When Liverpool John was just sixteen he went away to sea,
Working as a deckhand for the Brocklebank Company.
He saw the sights of India from a bar-room in Bombay,
On the morning after wished he'd never went away.

And he tries to settle down, he tries to stay on shore;
But every time he gets itchy feet and he's off to sea once more.

He met a girl from Scotty Road, he tried to settle down,
Working for her father on a window-cleaning round.
Adverts in the paper caught his eye one day,
And he sailed on a coaster bound for Liverpool Bay.

He jumped ship in Boston; there he learned to sing
In a travelling rock and roll show which lasted till the spring.
Playing by the Hudson he felt the salt winds blow,
And signed as a bosun for the Gulf of Mexico.

He nearly froze to death one night in winter 'sixty-three;
Heading home from Rotterdam he vowed he'd leave the sea.
Working on the night shift, spending days in bed,
Longed to see the sun again, so he sailed from Birkenhead.

☞ Phil Colclough spent six years at sea with the Elder Dempster Line, shuttling
between Liverpool and West Africa or the United States. He wrote the song
with his wife, June.

156 *The Grimsby Lads*

Here's to the Grimsby lads out at the trawling,
Here's to the lads on the billowing deep,
Shooting their nets and heaving and hauling,
All the night long, and the landsmen asleep.

They sail in the cold and the grey of the morning,
Leaving their wives and their families behind;
Following the fishing, fulfilling their calling,
Their charts are all ready the shoals for to find.

Away to the north where they know will be waiting
Frost and black ice and the lash of the gale,
Trawling and hoping and anticipating
A ship bumper-full and safe homeward to sail.

From Scotland's grey shore to the cold coast of Iceland
Through White Sea and Faeroe they're working their way,
Through Dogger and Forties to stormy Bear Island:
Eighteen long hours is the fisherman's day.

The nets are inboard and the catch lies a-gleaming;
There's gutting and washing and packing below.
Ten days of fishing and home they'll be steaming:
A thousand miles gone and a thousand to go.

On Humber's brown water the new sun is gleaming;
To the fisherman's prayer the breeze sings the amen.
The smoky grey town in the stillness is dreaming;
Her sons from the waters return once again.

☞ Distant water fishing has greatly declined since 1966 when John Conolly and Bill Meek wrote this song, but the skill and hardiness of trawlermen remain the same. Both writers were brought up within smell of Grimsby Docks. Conolly, born in 1941, had a grandfather who was a local shipwright. Meek was born in 1937, and his father worked on the docks as a 'lumper' (fish-handler). They set out to write of the trawling industry since they felt that 'the men who did the most dangerous job in the world deserved to be celebrated in song'.

White Sea] north of Archangel in the Soviet Union   Forties] part of the
North Sea, between Scotland and Norway   Bear Island] to the south of Spitsbergen

Fiddler's Green

As I roved by the dockside one evening so rare
To view the still waters and take the salt air
I heard an old fisherman singing this song:
'Oh take me away, boys, my time is not long.

Dress me up in my oilskins and jumper,
No more on the docks I'll be seen.
Just tell my old shipmates I'm taking a trip, mates,
And I'll see you some day in Fiddler's Green.

'Now Fiddler's Green is a place, I've heard tell,
Where fishermen go if they don't go to hell,
Where the weather is fair and the dolphins do play
And the cold coast of Greenland is far, far away.

'The sky's always clear and there's never a gale,
And the fish jump on board with a flip of their tail.

You can lie at your leisure, there's no work to do,
And the skipper's below, making tea for the crew.

'And when you're in dock and the long trip is through
There's pubs and there's clubs and there's lasses there too.
The girls are all pretty and the beer is all free,
And there's bottles of rum growing on every tree.

'I don't want a harp nor a halo, not me,
Just give me a breeze and a good rolling sea,
And I'll play my old squeezebox as we sail along
With the wind in the rigging to sing me this song.'

☞ Fiddler's Green was the generic name for sailortown, the district in large ports
which catered for the sailor's needs by providing boarding houses, dance halls,
public houses, brothels, and seamen's homes. By extension it was the sailor's
ideal world, Eden, Utopia, Paradise. In 1966 John Conolly wrote the song
which, like Ewan MacColl's 'Shoals of Herring', is often paid the compliment by
those who do not know its origin of being considered traditional. It has travelled
all over the world, and is especially popular in Ireland, where it is said to have
been sung in every pub in the country.

158   *The Loss of the* Evelyn Marie

It's mournful to tell you a story so sad;
It's about a new trawler and the equipment it had.
It was fitted with rudder and lifeboats for the sea,
It was blessed for the ocean, the *Evelyn Marie*.

There was six gallant fishermen, men of the sea,
Qualified skippers, her nets to set free.
They'll fish the wild ocean at any degree
In this beautiful trawler, the *Evelyn Marie.*

They fished the wild ocean, north, east and west,
They sold off their catches at the port that was best;
So they then were happy going right back to sea
In this beautiful trawler, the *Evelyn Marie.*

They guided this trawler for one year and some days.
What ill fate befell them within the freak waves.
A call to their comrades: 'Mayday at the sea.
Assist us this moment with the *Evelyn Marie.*'

'Assistance now coming, *Summer Star* and its crew',
Saying, 'With God's help we'll make it, their trawler is new'.
A disaster it was then; they just saw her stern
As she sank near the rocks outside Rathlin O'Beirne.

Come all you good people, I ask one and all.
Pray for the fishermen are on Donegal;
Pray for the six skippers who are lost out at sea
In this ill-fated trawler, the *Evelyn Marie.*

☞ The *Evelyn Marie* was on a herring fishing voyage from Killibegs in Donegal on 7
January 1975 when she ran on to rocks west of Rathlin O'Beirne Island and sank
within seconds. All six of the crew were lost. It is interesting to see so late a
product of the tradition of disaster ballads.

159   *The Final Trawl*

158 skippers] seamen   Rathlin O'Beirne] (pronounced 'Overn') an island off
south-west Donegal   fishermen are on Donegal] ? fishermen of old Donegal

Now it's three long years since we made her pay,
Sing haul away, ma laddie, O,
And we can't get by on the subsidy,
And sing haul away, ma laddie, O.

So heave away for the final trawl;
It's an easy pull for the catch is small.

Now it's stow yer gear, lads, and batten down,
Then I'll take the wheel, lads, and turn her round.

And we'll join the *Venture* and the *Morning Star,*
Riding high and empty beyond the bar.

For I'd rather beach her on the Skerry Rock
Than see her torched in the breaker's dock.

And it's when I die you can stow me down
In her rusty old hold where the breakers sound.

Then we'll make the haven and the Fiddler's Green
Where the grub is good and the bunks are clean.

For I fished a lifetime boy and man,
And the final trawl scarcely makes a cran.

☞ The song is the work of Archie Fisher (b. 1939), who wrote it in 1979.

Skerry Rock] between Peterhead and Aberdeen   cran] 28 stones (392
pounds) weight

ACKNOWLEDGEMENTS

For advice and assistance I should like to thank: Peter Freshwater, Steve Gardham, Keith Gregson, John Holloway, Stan Hugill, the late Gale Huntington, Peter Kemp, Emily Lyle, John Moulden, Pat Palmer (musical advice), Frank Purslow, Steve Roud, Ian Russell, Leslie Shepard, Hugh Shields, A. W. B. Simpson, Tish Stubbs and Sam Richards, Cyril Tawney, Katharine Thomson (invaluable transcriptions), Steve Turner, John Winton, Martyn Wyndham-Read, and Mike Yates.

I should also like to thank all the singers, collectors, editors, authors, and staffs of institutions listed in the sources, and in addition: Bristol Central Library; Cornwall County Library; Cumbria County Library; Department of Communications, Dublin; Dundee Central Library; Eyemouth Museum; Grimsby Public Library; Hampshire County Library; Library of Congress, Washington DC; Museum of Science and Engineering, Newcastle upon Tyne; National Maritime Museum, Greenwich; Naval Historical Library; *Navy News*; Plymouth Central Library; Queen's University, Belfast; John Rylands Library of the University of Manchester; Sydney Public Library; Vaughan Williams Memorial Library at Cecil Sharp House (Malcolm Taylor and Janet Bowcott).

For permission to include copyright material I should like to thank the following:

University of Aberdeen, University Studies Committee: 'Sally Munro' from P. Shuldham Shaw and E. B. Lyle, *The Greig-Duncan Folk Song Collection 1981–4* (AUP, 1984).

American Antiquarian Society: 'Captain James' (text).

Norman Buchan and Peter Hall: 'The Balena' from *The Scottish Folk-Singer* (Collins, 1983).

Chappell Music Limited: 'The Dockyard Gate' from *Marrowbones*, ed. F. Purslow (1965).

Clare Clayton: 'The Sailors' Wives' from *Folk Song Today*, No. 5, ed. T. Wales (1971).

Phil and June Colclough: 'Liverpool John'.

Bob Copper: 'Bold *Princess Royal*' from *Early to Rise* (1976).

Mrs Olive Craig: 'The Banks of Newfoundland' (I) from the Sam Henry Collection.

Helen Creighton: 'Ye Gentlemen of England' (tune) and 'George Jones' from *Songs and Ballads of Nova Scotia* (1932); 'On Board the *Victory*' (tune) and 'The Dreadnought' (under the title of 'The Banks of Newfoundland') from *Maritime Folk Songs* (ed. Helen Creighton, 2nd rev. edn., Breakwater Books, Canada, 1981).

Helen Creighton and National Museum of Man, Canada: 'Captain James' (tune) from *Folk Songs from Southern New Brunswick* (Nat. Museum of Man, 1981).

William Main Doerflinger: 'The First of the Emigrants' from *Songs of the Sailor and Lumberman* (New York: The Macmillan Co., rev. ed., 1972). Copyright © 1951, 1972 by William M. Doerflinger.

Philip Donnellan: 'The Smacksman'.

English Folk Dance and Song Society: 'Captain Every' (tune); 'Jackie Tar' (tune) from *Folk Music Journal* (1970); 'Homeward Bound' (tune); 'Ratcliffe Highway' and 'Rounding the Horn' (verses 2 & 3).

Archie Fisher (Kettle Music): 'The Final Trawl'.

Steve Gardham: 'Three Jolly Fishermen', 'The Grimsby Fisherman' (tune) and 'Looking for a Ship'.

D. S. Goodbrand: 'The Kola Run'.

N. A. Hudleston: 'Three Score and Ten'.

Stan Hugill: 'Roll, *Alabama*, Roll' from *Shanties from the Seven Seas: Shipboard Work-Songs and Songs Used as Work-Songs from the Great Days of Sail*, ed. Hugill (Routledge 1961); 'The Common Sailor' (tune); 'The Sailor's Hornpipe' (tune, under the title of 'Jack All Alone') from *Spin* (1969).

Dick James Music Ltd.: 'Diesel and Shale' by Cyril Tawney. © 1966 Gwyneth Music Ltd. Dick James Music Ltd., London W1 for all countries of the world. All rights reserved. Reproduced by kind permission of the publishers.

Bill Leader and John Zollman: 'Grace Darling'.

The Library of Congress: 'Blow the Man Down' (second version), 'Tiger Bay' and 'The Merchant Shipping Act' (tune) from the James M. Carpenter Collection.

Mrs Charlotte Lloyd: 'Blow Ye Winds' (text) from A. L. Lloyd, *The Singing Englishman* (1944); and 'Off to Sea Once More'.

Ewan MacColl: 'Shoals of Herring' from *Folk Music* (1965).

March Music: 'Fiddler's Green' by John Conolly, © 1968 March Music/Hedley Music Group.

University of Massachusetts Press: 'A Sea Song' from *A Sailor's Songbag: An American Rebel in an English Prison, 1777–1779* by George C. Carey (Amherst: Univ. of Massachusetts Press, 1976). Copyright © The University of Massachusetts Press 1976.

Maypole Music: 'The Grimsby Lads' by John Conolly and Bill Meek, © 1985 by Maypole Music Limited, London NW11 0SA for all countries of the world. All rights reserved. Reprinted by kind permission.

Douglas Miller: 'Rolling Sailor' (tune).

Robin Morton: 'The Sinking of the *Graf Spee*' from *Folk Songs Sung in Ulster* (1970).

National Maritime Museum: 'The Sailor's Christmas Day' (text), 'The Common Sailor' (text).

Oxford University Press: 'Come All You Bold Britons' (tune) and 'The Rambling Sailor' (tune) from *Cecil Sharp's Collection of English Folk Songs*, ed. M. Karpeles (1974).

Sam Richards and Tish Stubbs: 'The Fire Ship' and 'The Young Sailor Cut Down', sung by Bill 'Pop' Hingston.

Anne Roberts and Jill Bennett: 'The Fishes' Lamentation' (tune), 'Rolling Home', 'Stormy Weather, Boys', 'The Candlelight Fisherman' and 'Swell my net full'. All © 1986 by Anne Roberts and Jill Bennett; 'The Bargeman's ABC' first appeared in 1970, © Anne Roberts and Jill Bennett.

Harry Robertson: 'Deep Sea Tug'.

School of Scottish Studies, University of Edinburgh, Dr Alan Bruford and John
   Dass: 'I am an ancient mariner' from *Tocher* (1977).
Keith Summers: 'On Board the *Leicester Castle*'.
Cyril Tawney: 'Paddy West'.
Mrs Ralph Vaughan Williams: 'Duke William' (tune) and 'Fare ye well, my
   lovely Nancy' from R. Palmer, *Folk Songs Collected by Ralph Vaughan Williams*
   (Dent, 1983).
Mike Yates: 'The Sailor's Alphabet' and 'The Wreck of the *Northfleet*'.

Unless specified otherwise permission has been granted for text and tune.

The illustrations in this book are taken from *1800 Woodcuts by Thomas Bewick
and His School*, ed. Blanche Cirker and *Catchpenny Prints. 163 Popular Engravings
from the Eighteenth Century*, both published by Dover Publications, Inc.
   The woodcut on the title-page, by Benjamin Fawcett, was used on street
ballads printed by Forth of Pocklington, Yorkshire.

SOURCES AND NOTES

Abbreviations

BL   British Library

Carpenter James M. Carpenter Collection, Library of Congress, Washington DC (Copy at Cecil Sharp House)

Crampton Crampton Ballads, BL 11621 h 11

Crawford Lord Crawford's Collection of English Ballads, John Rylands Library of the University of Manchester. (See *Bibliotheca Lindesiana: Catalogue of English Broadsides, 1505–1897*, 1898, for list of contents)

Douce   Douce Collection, Bodleian Library

Euing   Euing Collection, Glasgow University Library. (Published as *The Euing Collection of English Broadside Ballads*, with an introduction by John Holloway, Glasgow, 1971)

Firth Bodl. C. H. Firth Collection, Bodleian Library

Firth Sheff. C. H. Firth Collection, Sheffield University Library. (Catalogue: P. W. Carnell, *Ballads in the Charles Harding Firth Collection of the University of Sheffield*, Sheffield, 1979)

Harding Harding Collection, Bodleian Library

Henry   Sam Henry Collection, Belfast Public Library. (For a published selection, see under Moulden in bibliography)

JFS   *Journal of the Folk Song Society*, 1899–1931

Johnson John Johnson Collection, Bodleian Library

Kendrew York Publications (mainly printed by J. Kendrew), BL 1870 c 2

Madden Madden Collection, Cambridge University Library

Pepys Coll. Pepys Ballad Collection, Magdalene College, Cambridge. (For a published selection, see under Rollins in bibliography)

St Bride St Bride Printing Library, London

Thomas Isaiah Thomas Collection of Ballads, American Antiquarian Society, Worcester, Mass. (For a catalogue, see W. C. Ford, 'The Isaiah Collection of Ballads', pp. 34–112 in *Proceedings of the American Antiquarian Society*, April, 1923)

Other sources listed in abbreviated form can be found under the author's name in the bibliography (pp. 327–32). The notes first give details of the source of a song, then document quotations and allusions in the commentary. Finally, there are references to the major classifications of Child, Laws, Wehse and, in the case of shanties, Hugill.

SONGS

1. *John Dory.* Text: Ravenscroft, *Deuteromelia*, 1609. Tune: C. Simpson, p. 399, from *The Second Book of the Pleasant Musical Companion*, 1686. Chappell, p. 67. Child 284.

2. *Lustily, lustily.* T. Brooke (ed.), *Common Conditions*, 1925, ll. 1125–64 (facsimile of original edition of 1576).

3. *Upon Sir Francis Drake's Return.* Pinto and Rodway, p. 63, from Ashmole MSS, Bodl.

4. *In Praise of Seafaring Men.* Halliwell, p. 14, from Sloane MSS, BL.

5. *Another of Seafarers.* Ibid., p. 16.

6. *A Joyful New Ballad.* Text: Mann, p. 468, from a broadside in the BL. Original in 16-line stanzas. Tune: C. Simpson, p. 495, from a lute book of *c.* 1600. Stationers' Register: see Rollins, *An Analytical Index.* Camden: quoted in Palmer, *Ballad History*, p. 11.

7. *Sir Francis Drake.* Text: Halliwell, p. 18, from Harleian MSS, BL. Tune: C. Simpson, p. 392, from an early seventeenth-century lute book. 'New Ballet': Mann, p. 479.

8. *The Sailor's Only Delight.* Quarto Rawlinson 566, fol. 183, Bodl. 'Probably the work. . .': Stone, p. 202 (note by Admiral Sir Cyprian Bridge). Child 285. Laws K33.

9. *The Winning of Cales.* Mann, p. 367, from Deloney's *Garland of Goodwill*, 1631. Original in 12-line stanzas. Masefield: *Garland*, p. xiv. 'Spanish Lady's Love': Mann, p. 375. Ebsworth: in Chappell and Ebsworth, VI, 403.

10. *The Famous Sea Fight.* Euing, No. 108. ' 'Twas when the seas': C. Simpson, p. 720. Child 287. Bronson 287.

11. *The Praise of Sailors.* Chappell and Ebsworth, IX, lxxxi*, from Pepys Coll., I, 418. There are later editions of 1663–74 (Euing, No. 267) and 1684–6 (Douce Ballads, 2). John Wright was out of his apprenticeship in 1610 and dead in 1646. It is possible that the man in question was John Wright, Junior, for whom the same dates are 1634 and 1658.

12. *The Honour of Bristol.* Euing, No. 142. Original in 8-line stanzas.

13. *Sailors for my Money.* Text: Pepys Coll, I, 420. Tune: C. Simpson, p. 769, from a song sheet of *c.* 1735. Ebsworth: Chappell and Ebsworth, VI, 797. Shepherds: Palmer, *Country*, p. 28.

14. *A Song of the Seamen and Land Soldiers.* Halliwell, p. 36, from Sir John Mennes et al., *Wit and Drollery: Jovial Poems*, 1656.

15. *The Famous Fight at Malago.* Text: Pepys Coll., IV, 204. Original in 8-line stanzas. Tune: Karpeles, No. 288, sung by Joseph Jackson (b. 1839), Bourne Workhouse, Lincolnshire; noted by Cecil Sharp, 25 April 1911. Mountagu: J. Thurloe, *A Collection of State Papers*, 7 vols, 1742: V, 257.

16. *The Seaman's Compass.* Text: Euing, No. 325. Original in 12-line stanzas. Tune: C. Simpson, p. 60, from an arrangement for virginals of 1628.

17. *A Net for a Night Raven.* Firth, *American*, p. 54, from Quarto Rawlinson 566, fol. 165, Bodl. Original in 8-line stanzas. Luttrell: I, 187 and 375. 'Woman outwitted': Euing, No. 396. 'Scolding wife': Greig, No. LXXVII, and JFS V, 114.

18. *The Seamen and Soldiers' Last Farewell.* Text: Euing, No. 328. Original in 8-line stanzas. Tune: d'Urfey, VI, 43. 'Our captain cried': JFS II, 202; cf. Palmer, *Vaughan Williams*, p. 42.

19. *Captain Mansfield's Fight.* Broadside without imprint, Madden 4/120. Oral version: JFS V, 167.

20. *A Song on the Duke's Late Glorious Success.* Halliwell, p. 62, 'from a broadside in the possession of Mr Rimbault'.

21. *The Benjamins' Lamentation.* Chappell and Ebsworth, VII, 529. Hammond: JFS III, 93. 'Dudley Boys': Palmer, *Poverty*, p. 58.

22. *Sir Walter Raleigh Sailing in the Lowlands.* Euing, No. 334. Ashton, p. x. Bullen, p. 35. Child 286.

23. *The* Caesar's *Victory.* Text: Rollins, *Pepys*, III, No. 143, from Pepys Coll., IV, 198. Tune: C. Simpson, p. 288, from a broadside of 1684.

24. *The Golden Voyage.* Text: Rollins, *Pepys*, III, No. 149, from Pepys Coll., IV, 199. Tune: C. Simpson, p. 421, from *Apollo's Banquet*, 1687.

25. *The Boatswain's Call.* Chappell and Ebsworth, III, 463. Original in 8-line stanzas.

26. *The Sea Martyrs.* Text: Rollins, *Pepys*, VI, No. 344, from Pepys Coll., V, 375. Tune: C. Simpson, p. 121, from a manuscript of the time of Shakespeare. Luttrell, II, 144 and 174.

27. *An Excellent New Song.* Pepys Coll., VI, 380.

28. *England's Great Loss by a Storm of Wind.* Text: Ashton, p. 40. Tune: Creighton, *Nova Scotia*, p. 136. Marryat, *Poor Jack*, ch. XVII. Laws K2.

29. *The Sea Fight.* D'Urfey, III, 45. The tune is credited as 'set by Mr Akeroyde'. Macaulay, p. 475. Other ballads: Rollins, *Pepys*, VI, Nos 387 and 390.

30. *The Seamen's Wives' Vindication.* Firth, p. 145, from Pepys Coll., IV, 185.

31. *The Sailor's Complaint.* Text: Douce Ballads 3, p. 85. Tune: C. Simpson, p. 358, from a broadside of *c.* 1710.

32. *A Copy of Verses composed by Captain Henry Every.* Text: Rollins, *Pepys*, VII, No. 484, from Pepys Coll., V, 384. Tune: sung (with one verse of text) by John Hatch, Winchester, Hants.; noted by G. Gardiner, June 1907 (Hammond MSS H.706, at Cecil Sharp House). 'Villainy Rewarded': Rollins, *Pepys*, VII, No. 485. Eighteenth-century broadside: Holloway and Black, I, 36.

33. *Captain Kid's Farewell.* Text: Firth, p. 134, from Crawford, No. 843. Tune: C. Simpson, p. 673, from d'Urfey, VI, 251. Cf. tune in *Journal of the English Folk Dance and Song Society*, III, 169, from W. Walker's *Southern Harmony*, 1854. Luttrell, V, 53. Masefield, *Garland*, p. xviii. Colcord, p. 69. Laws K35.

34. *Cordial Advice.* Madden, Garlands, p. 164. Issue of 1709–12: Douce Ballads I, p. 37.

35. *The Death of Admiral Benbow.* Text: Madden 23/689. Tune: Fielding's *Vocal*

Enchantress, 1783, p. 108. Campbell, IV, 257–86. 'Admiral Benbow': Firth, p. 149. Clements, p. 41.

36. *The Greenland Voyage.* Text: Evans, III, 172. Original in 10-line stanzas. Tune: d'Urfey, VI, 197.

37. *The Sailor's Lamentation.* Text: Madden 6/92. Tune: Chappell, p. 293. Ship's log: quoted Firth, p. 351. 'Cavendish's Distress': St Bride, No. 17. Aberdeenshire: Shaw and Lyle, I, No. 35. Laws K3.

38. *English Courage Displayed.* Text: broadside without imprint, Madden 4/252. Tune: Chappell, p. 658. Sailor's letter: quoted Kemp, *British*, p. 75.

39. *The Disappointed Sailor.* Text: Logan, p. 29. Tune: C. Simpson, p. 295, from *Youth's Delight on the Flageolet, c.* 1690, under the title of 'He that loves best', which was an alternative for 'I love you dearly'. 'Seaman's Complaint': Chappell and Ebsworth, VIII, 433. Laws M1.

40. *The Valiant Sailor.* Palmer, *Valiant*, p. 45: text from Ashton, p. 36, adapted, and collated with version sung by Mrs Cranstone, Billingshurst, Sussex; noted by George Butterworth, July 1909, and published in JFS IV, 290. Ashton's text is close to that in *The Irish Boy's Garland*, which was 'printed and sold in Swan Close, a little below the Cross Well, North side of the street', Edinburgh (Harding, Garlands A1).

41. *Disconsolate Judy's Lamentation.* Firth, p. 193, from a broadside without imprint in Madden 4/223.

42. *A New Song on the* Blandford. Slip-song without imprint in Madden 5/316. Bristol privateering: see Powell. Liverpool privateering: see Williams. *Resolution*: 'Captain Barber, a New Song' (Madden 4/254). 'The *Polly* Privateer': Ashton, p. 28. *Amazon*: 'A New Song Called the Spanish Snow' (Kendrew, p. 80). *Antigallican*: Stokoe and Reay, p. 158.

43. *The Lucky Sailor.* Madden 5/156. *Gentleman's Magazine*: 1744, p. 616. Clowes, III, 125 ff. See also Heaps.

44. *New Sea Song.* Firth, p. 239, from Madden 4/258.

45. *A Sea Song.* Carey, p. 63. Other ballads: Firth, pp. 204–5.

46. *Admiral Byng.* Text: Greig, Song CLI, communicated by Miss Bell Robertson, 1908. Tune: Christie, II, 260, 'as sung by the editor's paternal grandfather'. 'Rueful story': Firth, p. 209. 'Address': Palmer, *Ballad History*, p. 62.

47. *The Wreck of the* Rambler. Sung by Mr Bell at the Eel's Foot, Eastbridge, Suffolk; recorded by E. J. Moeran, 7 November 1947. *Gent. Mag.*, 1760, p. 100. Laws K1.

48. *Captain Barton's Distress.* Slip-song without imprint in Madden 4/257. Victory ballad: 'Bold Sawyer' (Ashton, p. 13).

49. *The Jolly Sailor's True Description.* Douce Ballads 3, p. 47. Later edition: Holloway and Black, II, 167.

50. *The Seamen's Distress.* Text: Child 289A, from *The Glasgow Lasses' Garland*, Newcastle, *c.* 1765, BL 11621 *c.* 3(68). Tune: sung by James Herridge (b. 1839), Twyford, Hants.; noted by E. T. Sweeting, 1906 (JFS III, 47).

51. *The* Dolphin's *Return.* Text: Firth, p. 243, from Madden 4/230. Tune: No. 580 (p. 221) in a volume of dance music without a title page (Vaughan Williams Memorial Library, Cecil Sharp House).

52. *Captain James.* Text: Thomas, No. 35. Original not divided into verses. Tune: Creighton, *New Brunswick,* p. 185, from William Ireland, Elgin, New Brunswick. Logbooks: Huntington, pp. 54–9. 'A Copy of Verses made on Capt. Elder's Cruelty': Madden. 'Captain's apprentice': Palmer, *Vaughan Williams,* p. 84. Murders: *Gent. Mag.,* 21 June 1764 and 17 April 1766.

53. *William Taylor.* Text: in the logbook of the ship *Nellie* (Old Dartmouth Historical Society, New Bedford, Mass.); communicated by Gale Huntington. Tune: JFS I, 254, noted from Mrs Agar of Whitby by Frank Kidson. Hannah Snell's song: Firth, p. 200. Woman privateer: Williams, p. 118. Garland: Douce PP.183. Laws N11.

54. *Spanish Ladies.* Text: Marryat, *Poor Jack,* ch. XVII. Tune: Chappell, p. 737. Capstan shanty: Hugill, p. 385. Whalermen: as 'Talcahuano Girls' on the record, *Leviathan* (Topic 12T174, 1967). *Nellie*'s logbook: as in No. 55. *Pequod: Moby Dick,* 1851, ch. 40. *White Jacket:* ch. 74. Stone, p. 209. Clements, p. 79.

55. *A New Song, called the Frolicsome Sea Captain.* Houghton Library, Harvard University. Cf 'Tit for Tat; or, the Merry Wives of Wapping' in Chappell and Ebsworth, VIII, 438, and IX, xciii***. Wehse 355.

56. *Captain Glen's Unhappy Voyage.* Text: from a garland of the same title, without imprint, in the Houghton Library, Harvard University. Cf. 'An Excellent New Song, entitled Captain Glen', in Chappell and Ebsworth, VIII, 141. Tune: Kidson, *Garland,* p. 110. 'William Grismond': Masefield, *Garland,* p. 234. 'Banks of Green Willow': Palmer, *Vaughan Williams,* p. 51. Masefield writes: ibid., p. xxi. Child 57. Laws K22, A and B.

57. *Bold* Princess Royal. Copper, *Early,* p. 244, from John Copper (1817–98) of Rottingdean, Sussex. Colcord: p. 148. Roberts: note on sleeve of the record, *Breeze for a Bargeman* (Solent SS054, 1981). Laws K29.

58. *Jack Tar.* From *Tibby Fowler,* a garland without imprint (Douce S.370, 17). Original in 8-line stanzas. Herd, II, 223.

59. *The Man-of-War's Garland.* From the garland of the same name, without imprint but 'Entered according to Order, 1796' (Harding Garlands A 15, 19).

60. *On the Late Engagement in Charles Town River.* Ashton, p. 15, from *The Shepherd's Garland,* 11621 c.1, 7, BL. 'New War Song': Moore, p. 135.

61. *The Silk Merchant's Daughter.* Sharp I, 381: sung by Mrs Mary Sands, Allanstand, North Carolina; noted by Cecil Sharp, 31 July 1916. Tim Connor's version: Carey, p. 69. Eighteenth-century broadside: 'The Constant Lovers, or the Valiant Young Lady' (Douce Ballads 4). Cannibalism: see A. W. B. Simpson. Laws N10.

62. *The Yankee Man-of-War.* Luce, p. 56. Cf. Colcord, p. 61; C. F. Smith, p. 87. Second campaign song: see 'Paul Jones' (Baring-Gould, *West,* no. 108).

63. *The Greenland Men.* Firth, p. 249, from *Portsmouth Jack's Garland* (11621 c.2, 58, BL). The date on the original sheet is 17780, which is presumably a mistake either for 1778 or 1780. Pressgang incidents: 'The Press Gang in the Northern Counties', *Monthly Chronicle*, January 1891, pp. 1–4. I am indebted to Keith Gregson for these references.

64. *The Rolling Sailor*. Text: first two verses from Gardner, p. 16, and remainder from a garland, *Three Excellent New Songs*, Edinburgh, n.d. (Harding Garlands, A. 1). Cf. 'The Sailor Laddie' (Ashton, p. 35) and 'The Rolling Sailor' (Madden 6/1631). Tune: from the Desmond McMahon Collection, which is in the possession of Mr Douglas Miller. Tailors: William Shield, *The Lord Mayor's Day* (ballad opera, 1782). Colliers: Boardman, p. 18. Fishermen: Stokoe and Reay, p. 103. Oral tradition in Britain: Dawney, p. 12; in America: Sharp, II, 279.

65. *Jackie Tar*. Text: broadside without imprint in Firth Bodl., c.12, 61. Original in 4-line stanzas. Tune: quoted (p. 16) in G. S. Emmerson, 'The Hornpipe', pp. 12–34 in *Folk Music Journal*, 1970. Oral versions: Shaw and Lyle, I, No. 59. Cf. No. 60, a related and perhaps derivative song, beginning 'Come ashore, Jackie Tar an' yer trousers on', which is an oral version of 'The Loving Girl's Invitation to a Young Sailor in his Trowsers' (Chappell and Ebsworth, VIII, 436).

66. *The Ship is all Laden*. Cuthbert Sharp, p. 68.

67. *Duke William*. Text: Madden 18/1058. Tune: Palmer, *Vaughan Williams*, p. 168: sung by Henry Burstow (1826–1916), Horsham, Sussex; noted by Ralph Vaughan Williams, November 1905. Wehse 490.

68. *The Fisher Lad of Whitby*. Forshaw, p. 86.

69. *The Ship in Distress*. JFS IV, 13: sung by Mr H. Akhurst, Lower Beeding, Sussex; noted by George Butterworth, June 1907. 'The words were noted in Shropshire': note by Butterworth. Cf. text in Ashton, p. 44. Further oral version: Karpeles, No. 293.

70. *The Fishes' Lamentation*. Text: Holloway and Black, 1, 100, from Madden 4/613. Tune: sung by Bob Roberts on the record, *Songs from the Sailing Barges* (Topic 12TS361, 1978). Kipling: ch. IV; Whall: p. 96.

71. *A Sailor's Life*. JFS I, 99: sung by Henry Hills, Lodsworth, Sussex; noted by W. P. Merrick, 1899. Australian version: under the title of 'The Lost Sailor' on the record, *Martyn Wyndham-Read* (Leader LER 2028, 1971). Broadside: Madden 18/853. Laws K12.

72. *The Greenland Whale Fishery*. JFS VIII, 279: sung by Harry Cox (1885–1971), Potter Heigham, Norfolk; noted by E. J. Moeran, 1924. (A recording of Cox singing the song can be heard on the cassette, *Jack on the Rocks*, Folktracks FSA 60–033, 18 Brunswick Square, Gloucester). Early versions: Masefield, *Garland*, p. 206; Baring-Gould, *Garland*, No. XXVI; Ashton, p. 265; Whall, p. 99. Laws K21.

73. *The Tars of the Blanche*. Dixon, p. 236. Naval historian: James, I, 282. Printings: Williams, Portsea, 1823–47 (BL 1876 e 3); Fordyce, Newcastle, 1829–37 (Firth Sheff., B131); Wood, Birmingham 1806–39 (Birmingham Reference Library); Pitts, 6 Great St Andrew Street, London, 1819–44 (Broadwood Broadside Collection, Cecil Sharp House); Kendrew, p. 170. See also Firth, p. 274.

74. *Song.* Public Record Office, ADM. 1/727. Other ballads: Gill, pp. 389–90, Firth, p. 277 ff., Palmer, *Valiant*, p. 28 ff., Holloway and Black, I, 44.

75. *President Parker.* Christie, II, 102. Original in 8-line stanzas. 'A New Song': Firth, p. 282. 'Commonest of all': Firth, p. xcix. Oral versions: JFS VIII, 188, Baring-Gould, *West*, No. 23. Tune: Clare MSS, published in G. Deacon, *John Clare and The Folk Tradition*, 1983, p. 346.

76. *A New Song on the Total Defeat of the French Fleet.* Broadside without imprint (Derby Broadsides, 8672, Derby Public Library).

77. *The Boatie Rows.* James Johnson, *Scots Musical Museum*, V (1799), No. 427, p. 438. J. Turnbull and P. Buchan, *The Garland of Scotia*, Edinburgh, 1841, p. 25. Broadside: Madden 18/811. Oral version: sung by Jessie Murray of Portnockie, Banffshire, on the record, *Sailormen and Serving maids*, Topic 12T194, 1969.

78. *Second of August.* Text: Kendrew, p. 37. Tune: Stokoe and Reay, p. 178.

79. *Distressed Men of War.* Firth, p. 228, 'from a broadside in the possession of the editor'. Gardner, p. 235.

80. *Nelson's Death and Victory.* Kendrew, p. 233. Tune: p. 9 in A. G. Gilchrist, 'Some old Westmorland Folksingers' pp. 5–14 in *Journal of the Lakeland Dialect Society*, No. 4, Nov. 1942. Cf. Palmer, *Valiant*, p. 47. 'Bold Sawyer': Firth, p. 212. Other Nelson songs: Palmer, *Valiant*, p. 44, and *Ballad History*, p. 88.

81. *A New Song called the* Victory. Text: A Collection of Ballads Printed at Various Places in the Provinces, 1876 e 3, BL. Tune: Creighton, *Maritime*, p. 42, sung by Mr Grace Clergy, East Petpeswick, Nova Scotia; noted by Helen Creighton, August 1951. Such sheet: Kidson Broadsides, Mitchell Library, Glasgow.

82. *Pleasant and Delightful.* As 47 above except sung by Mr Willie Miller. Jennings sheet: Old Street Ballads, p. 41, in Liverpool Record Office, Brown, Picton and Hornby Library, Liverpool. Later broadside: H. P. Such sheet in Bolingbroke Collection, Norwich Public Library. Oral version: Purslow, *Marrowbones*, p. 80.

83. *The Servant of Rosemary Lane.* Text: Johnson, Box 4. Tune: JFS VI, 2, sung by Henry Burstow (for whom, see note on 67 above); noted by Lucy Broadwood, 1893. 'Bell-bottomed Trousers': Gardham, p. 33. Laws K43.

84. *A Copy of Verses on Jefferys the Seaman.* Madden 8/2. For Lake's court-martial, see Naval Chronicle, XXIII, Jan.–June 1810, p. 261.

85. Shannon *and* Chesapeake. Text: Firth, p. 311, 'a traditional version supplied by Sir J. K. Laughton'. Original in 8-line stanzas. Tune: 'Peggy of Darby O' 'from a music sheet' in F. Kidson, 'Notes on Old Tunes', articles in the *Leeds Mercury Weekly Supplement*, 1886–7. 'The *Constitution* and *Guerrière*': Shaw and Lyle, I, No. 43; Firth, p. 309; Colcord, p. 65; Thomas, Nos 4, 171, and 183. 'On Board the *Shannon* frigate': sung by Jack Goodban of Sussex on the record, *Green grow the laurels*, Topic 12TS285, 1976; cf. Firth, p. 312. Hughes, *Tom Brown's Schooldays*, 1856, ch. VI. Whall, p. 61. Laws J20.

86. *The* Flying Cloud. Colcord, p. 73. Doerflinger, p. 334. Beck: see bibliography. Aberdeenshire: Shaw and Lyle, I, No. 44.

87. *The North Country Collier.* Masefield, *Garland*, p. 321. 'A Sailor for me': Firth Bodl., b.25, 186. 'Molly's Lamentation': in a garland, *The Rural Felicity, or, the Young Men and Maidens' Choice Delight*, 1781 (Harding Song Books and Garlands, 000398).

88. *Homeward Bound.* Text: Stone, No. XVIII, 'from a slip song in the possession of C. H. Firth'. Tune: sung by W. Bolton, Southport (for whom, see note on 94 below); noted by Anne Gilchrist, February 1906 (MS G.212, 43, Cecil Sharp House). Whall, p. 9. Hugill, p. 40.

89. *The Smuggler's Victory.* BL 1876 e 3.

90. *Sally Munro.* Shaw and Lyle, I, No. 23A, sung by Mrs Mackenzie, 1908. Greig: Song LXXIV. Laws K11.

91. *The Banks of Newfoundland* (I). Henry, No. 569. 'The words contributed by John Henry Macaulay, Bog Oak Shop, Ballycastle'; source of tune unspecified. Additional verses from Madden 21/425. Cannibalism: see A. W. B. Simpson. Shetland: *Tocher*, No. 26, 1977, p. 91. N. America: see for example E. Fowke, *Traditional Singers and Songs from Ontario*, Hatboro, 1965, p. 24.

92. *The Rambling Sailor.* Text: Crampton, VIII. Tune: Karpeles, No. 298A, sung by George Wyatt, West Harptree, Somerset; noted by Cecil Sharp, 14 April 1904. Soldier: BL 1876 e 3, to the tune of 'The Rambling Sailor'. Miner: Firth Bodl., b.26, 133. Suiler: Henry, No. 183. 'Female Rambling Sailor': Kidson Broadsides, Mitchell Library, Glasgow. 'Jolly Sailor': Kendrew, p. 74.

93. *Fare ye well, lovely Nancy.* Palmer, *Vaughan Williams*, p. 53: sung by George Lovett (b. 1841), Winchester, Hants.; noted by Ralph Vaughan Williams, January 1909. 'Adieu, my lovely Nancy': Harding Quarto Sheets, No. 38. 'Undaunted Seaman': Chappell and Ebsworth, VII, 551. 'Undaunted Mariner': Pepys Coll., V, 304. Laws K14.

94. *Ratcliffe Highway.* Sung by William Bolton, Southport, Lancashire; noted by Anne Gilchrist, 19 June 1906 (Gilchrist MSS, G.211, 57 and 216, 45, Cecil Sharp House) Pitts' catalogue, probably published in 1831–2, is in Madden 9. On the singer, see M. Yates, 'The Best Bar in the Capstan: William Bolton, Sailor and Chantyman', pp. 10–11 in *Traditional Music*, No. 7, 1977.

95. *Loss of the* Amphitrite. Crampton, IV, 125. Cf. sheets by Fordyce, Newcastle (Johnson, Box 13), Ford, Sheffield (Selbourne Irish Ballads, Birmingham University Library) and Livsey, Manchester (Houghton Library, Harvard University). *Anford-Wright*: Cox, p. 303. Laws K14.

96. *Bold Adventures of Captain Ross.* Madden 14/16.

97. *The Female Cabin Boy.* Text: BL 1876 e 3. Tune: Palmer, *Rambling*, p. 163, from John Clare MS. Karpeles, No. 217. Laws N13. Wehse 101.

98. *The Fancy Frigate.* Text: Ashton, p. 78*, from BL 1871 f 32. Tune: Whall, p. 17. Oral versions: Masefield, *Garland*, p. 217; Firth, p. 362 n. Dress: Dickens, p. 5. Hugill, p. 462.

99. *Three Jolly Fishermen.* Sung by Thomas Calvert, Runswick Bay, North Yorkshire; noted by Steve Gardham, 1971. Cf. version from a Whitby singer in Dawney, p. 30. Sharp: MS No. 1750. Broadside: BL 1876 e 3. Nairne song: R.

A. Smith, *The Scottish Minstrel*, 5 vols, Edinburgh, 1821–4: V, 18. Gow music: sheet in Kidson Collection, Mitchell Library, Glasgow. For a children's version, see I. and P. Opie, *The Singing Game*, Oxford, 1985, p. 386.

100. *Grace Darling*. Sung by Walter Pardon of Knapton, Norfolk, on the record, *Our Side of the Baulk* (Leader LED 2111, now Highway Records); recorded by Bill Leader, 1974. McGlennan song: now in its 150th edition; available from the R.N.L.I. and the Grace Darling Museum, Bamburgh, Northumberland. Street ballads: Madden 18/1026, Crampton, IV 20, Sharp Broadside Collection, Cecil Sharp House. Oral versions: Australia: Edwards, p. 285; Ireland: Ranson, p. 86; East Anglia: Palmer, *British Ballads*, p. 121.

101. *The Fire Ship*. Sung by Bill ('Pop') Hingston (b. 1914) of Dittisham, Devon; noted by Sam Richards and Tish Stubbs, 1979. Hingston can be heard singing the song on the cassette, *Hingston's Half-hour* (People's Stage Tapes 03, available from 6 South Street, Totnes, Devon). Text supplemented from broadside, 'Black and Rolling Eye', printed by Jackson and Son (late Russell), 21 [Moor] Street, Birmingham (Folder marked 'Songs', Birmingham Reference Library). Cf. Madden 18/746. Shanty: Hugill, p. 171. See Sam Richards, 'Bill Hingston, a Biography in Song', pp. 24–46 in *Oral History*, X, No. 1, 1982.

102. *Liverpool Girls*. Bone, p. 118. Hugill, p. 400.

103. *Leave her, Johnny*. Bone, p. 135. Hugill, p. 293. Bullen, p. xiii. Colcord, p. 58.

104. *George Jones*. Creighton, *Nova Scotia*, p. 238: sung by Mr Ben Hennebery, Devil's Island, Nova Scotia.

105. *Heave away, my Johnny*. L. A. Smith, p. 54. 'Yellow Meal': Moulden, p. 153. Hugill, p. 302. Coleman, p. 80.

106. *The* Flying Dutchman. Ranson, p. 45: sung by Jack Murphy, Broadway, 1943, 'to the air of "The Banks of Newfoundland" ' (ibid., p. 118). Boughton: p. 51. Original song: Baring-Gould, *Minstrelsie*, I, 88. Laws K23.

107. *The Sailor's Alphabet*. Sung by Johnny Doughty on the record, *Round Rye Bay for More* (Topic 12TS324, 1977); recorded by Mike Yates, 1976. 'A was an archer': I. and P. Opie, *The Oxford Dictionary of Nursery Rhymes*, Oxford, 1977 edition, No. 2.

108. *Blow the Man Down*. First version James H. Williams, pp. 77–8. Second version Carpenter, Tape 21, Side B, No. 420. Carpenter article, 'Chanteys that "Blow the Man down" ', pp. 10–11 in *The New York Times Magazine*, 26 July 1931.

109. The City of Baltimore. Ranson, p. 54 (3 lines wanting): 'Words from Mary White. Air from Jos. White, Ballyhack'. Cf. Creighton, *Nova Scotia*, p. 117; Peacock, III, 860.

110. *The First of the Emigrants*. Doerflinger, p. 149, from Captain Patrick Tayluer.

111. *Whip Jamboree*. Sung by Mr John Short, Watchet, Somerset; noted by Cecil Sharp, 12 May 1914 (MS No. 2923), and published by him in *Capstan Chanteys*, n.d., p. 1, with verse 2 added, probably from Terry. 'Jenny, get your hoe cake done': copy in Harding, Songs, Box 170. The date, '1840', is written on the cover. I am indebted for this reference to Mike Pickering. 'Whoop Jamboree': quoted in Carpenter thesis, p. 433.

112. *Lady Franklin's Lament.* Madden 18/343. Tune: Palmer, *Love*, p. 74, from Henry, No. 815. Cannibalism: Owen Beattie, Canadian anthropologist, reported in *The Guardian* of 2 July 1983. Oral versions: Ireland: Henry, No. 815; Scotland: Shaw and Lyle, I, No. 16; N. America: Laws K9. Sea versions: Colcord, p. 158; J. Faulkner, *Eighteen Years on a Greenland Whaler*, New York, 1878, p. 73.

113. *Paddy West.* Sung by Timothy Walsh, Devonport, Devon, on the record, *Sailormen and Servingmaids* (Topic 12T194, 1969); recorded by Cyril Tawney. Stories: Bernard, p. 432; Lubbock, pp. 98–9; Boughton, pp. 23–4; Hugill, p. 334; Clements, pp. 94–7.

114. *The* Dreadnought. Creighton, *Maritime*, p. 140, under the title of 'Banks of Newfoundland': sung by Mr Berton Young, West Petpeswick, Nova Scotia; noted by Helen Creighton, August 1951. Samuels: pp. 264–5. Kipling: ch. IV. Cf. Hugill, pp. 120 ff.

115. *Andrew Rose.* Colcord, p. 81. Cf. Clements, p. 63.

116. *Rolling Home.* Sung by Bob Roberts (1907–82); communicated by his daughters, Anne Roberts and Jill Bennett. Bob Roberts can be heard singing the song on the record, *Breeze for a Bargeman* (Solent SS054, 1981). Masefield: 'Sea Songs', p. 79. Mackay text in *The Poetical Works of Charles Mackay*, n.d. (1876), p. 610. Hugill, p. 181 ff.

117. *The Wreck of the* Royal Charter. Palmer, *Strike*, p. 54: version sung by James Sutton, Winterton, Norfolk; noted by E. J. Moeran, July 1915 (JFS VII, 6); supplemented from broadside without imprint (Collection of Street Ballads, p. 23, Brown, Picton and Hornby Library, Liverpool).

118. *Blow Ye Winds.* Text: A. L. Lloyd, *The Singing Englishman*, n.d. (1944), p. 66. This may be an anglicization of the text in Colcord, whose tune, from p. 103, is given here. 1859 text: Huntington, p. 42. Hugill, p. 223.

119. *The Banks of Newfoundland* (II). JFS V, 300: sung by Harry Perrey (b. 1854) on board the American liner, *St Paul*; noted by Cecil Sharp, 23 July 1915. Anecdote: Karpeles, *Cecil Sharp, his Life and Work*, 1967, p. 131. Hugill, p. 412. 1844 version: Ranson, p. 118. Laws K25.

120. *The Leaving of Liverpool.* Heard by Roy Palmer in England and Ireland; derives from Doerflinger, p. 104.

121. *Execution of Five Pirates for Murder.* Johnson, Box 3. Original in 8-line stanzas.

122. *Roll, Alabama, Roll.* Hugill, p. 159. Broadside: C. Hindley, *Curiosities of Street Literature*, 2 vols, 1871: I, 104. 'Cumberland's Crew': Luce, p. 138.

123. *Strike the Bell.* Palmer, *Strike*, p. 60, from Roy Harris, who sings it on the record, *The Bitter and the Sweet* (Topic 12TS217, 1972). This version probably derives from Hugill, *Shanties and Sailors' Songs*, 1969, p. 165.

124. *Off to Sea Once More.* Sung by A. L. Lloyd on the record, *Leviathan* (Topic 12T174, 1967); learned from Ted Howard of Barry, Glamorgan, 1954. Cf. another notation of the same song, without chorus, in A. L. Lloyd, p. 284. Hugill, p. 582. Shanghai Brown: Hugill, *Sailortown*, p. 221. 1909: Bernard, p. 434.

125. *The Holy Ground.* Heard by Roy Palmer in England and Ireland. Hugill, p. 431.

126. *The Wreck of the* Northfleet. Sung by Johnny Doughty (for whom, see 107 above) on the record, *Round Rye Bay*. Street ballads: 'Copy of Verses on the Loss of the ill-fated Emigrant Ship, *Northfleet*' (Buchan, Leeds: Kidson Broadsides, 10, 96); 'The Dreadful Loss of the *Northfleet*' (Crampton, VIII, 18); 'Lines on the Fearful Collision at Sea' (Pearson, Manchester: Firth Bodl., c.12).

127. *Rounding the Horn.* Sung by William Bolton, Southport, Lancashire; noted by Anne Gilchrist, May 1907 (Gilchrist MSS. G.211, 45 and G.216/46, Cecil Sharp House); published, less verses 2 and 3, in JFS V, 165. Noble, p. 211. Cf. Karpeles, No. 290, Moulden, p. 63, Colcord, p. 94, Purslow, *Foggy*, p. 80, Clements, p. 82, Carpenter thesis, p. 272.

128. *The Unseaworthy Ship.* Palmer, *Strike*, p. 58, from broadside No. 774, printed by Pearson of Manchester (Ballads Q 398.8 S9, II, 615, Manchester Central Reference Library).

129. *The Sailor's Christmas Day.* Text: Cotten. Original in 8-line stanzas. Tune: Chappell, p. 716.

130. *The Common Sailor.* Text: Cotten. Original in 76 lines without a break. Tune: from tape of his own singing communicated by Stan Hugill, July 1984.

131. *The Grimsby Fisherman.* Text: broadside without imprint (Kidson Broadsides 5, 148). Tune: sung by Jack Smith (b. 1883), Hull; noted by Steve Gardham. 'Cruise of the *Bigler*': Creighton, *Maritime*, p. 141. 'Knickerbocker Line': Kennedy, No. 323. 'Littlehampton Collier Lads': Richards and Stubbs, p. 12; cf. W. H. Gill, No. 4.

132. *The Young Sailor Cut Down.* As for 101 above, except: noted, 1980. 'Buck's Elegy': Holloway and Black, I, 48. Laws Q26.

133. *Tiger Bay.* Sung by John Gerries, South Shields; recorded by James M. Carpenter (Carpenter, Tape 20, Side A, No. 397). One of three versions recorded in England by Carpenter in 1928. See his thesis, p. 154.

134. *The* Balena. Buchan and Hall, p. 125. Original in 4/4 time. Newfoundland version: Fowke, p. 48.

135. *The Smacksman.* Sung by Sam Larner (1878–1965) of Winterton, Norfolk, on the record, *A Garland for Sam* (Topic 12T244, 1974); recorded by Philip Donnellan, 1958–9. Verse 2 was known to Sam Larner, but not sung on the occasion of the recording.

136. *The Dockyard Gate.* Purslow, *Marrowbones*, p. 26: sung by Frederick Fennemore (b. 1830), Portsmouth Workhouse; noted by J. F. Guyer, August 1907. Kidson: JFS II, 265. Larner: record, *Now is the time for fishing* (Folkways FG3507, 1961).

137. *The Sailor's Hornpipe.* Text: Belfast Public Library. I am indebted to John Moulden for this reference. In the original the title concludes: 'in Caxon Street'. Tune: sung by Stan Hugill, and published in *Spin*, Vol. 7, No. 2, 1969, p. 14. Liverpool version: Hugill, p. 376 ('Jack All Alone'). Halifax, Nova Scotia: Creighton, *Nova Scotia*, p. 22 ('Barrack Street'). Laws K42.

138. *Three Score and Ten.* Sung by Mr J. Pearson, Filey, Yorkshire; noted by N. A. Hudleston, 1957–8, and kindly communicated by him. Delf broadside: Grimsby Public Library. Cf. Palmer, *Ballad History*, p. 156.

139. *I am an Ancient Mariner.* Sung by Jack Dass, 'with some help from James Henderson'; recorded by Alan Bruford (School of Scottish Studies, Edinburgh University, SA 1967/117 A4 and SA 1969/47 A; published in *Tocher*, No. 26, 1977, p. 84). 'Fish and Chip Ship': Bob Roberts, on the record, *Songs from the Sailing Barges* (Topic 12TS361). 'While going round the Cape': Doughty record, *Round Rye Bay* (Topic 12TS324). 'Captain Nipper': Becket, p. 12.

140. *The Merchant Shipping Act.* Text: Clements, pp. 84–8. Original in 8-line stanzas. Tune: sung under the title of 'The Limejuice Act' by Rees Baldwyn, Barry Docks, S. Wales; recorded by James M. Carpenter, 1928 (Carpenter). See also Carpenter thesis, p. 244 ff. 'Limejuice Ship': Clements, p. 91. Hugill, p. 58.

141. *On Board the* Leicester Castle. Sung by George Ling (1904–75) on the record, *The Ling Family* (Topic 12TS292, 1977); recorded by Keith Summers, 1974–5. The original has verses in 8, 12, and 4 lines. Bone, p. 139. Hugill, p. 320 ff.

142. *The Bargeman's ABC.* Sung by Bob Roberts (1907–82); communicated by his daughters, Anne Roberts and Jill Bennett. Books: see bibliography. Records: *Songs from the Sailing Barges* (Topic 12TS361, 1978) and *Breeze for a Bargeman* (Solent SS054, 1981).

143. *Stormy Weather, Boys.* As 142 above. Bob Roberts can be heard singing the song on the record *Sailing Barges*.

144. *The Candlelight Fisherman.* As 143 above. Cf. Kennedy, No. 219.

145. *Swell my Net Full.* As 142 above. Bob Roberts can be heard singing the song on the record *Breeze*.

146. *The Mail Boat*, Leinster. Ranson, p. 35: sung by Patrick Doyle, Curracloe, to the tune of 'Poulshone Fishermen' (ibid., p. 102).

147. *The Sailors' Wives.* T. Wales (ed.), *Folk Songs of Today*, No. 5, 1971, p. 7.

148. *Looking for a ship.* Sung by Garfield Everitt (b. 1904), trawlerman, Grimsby; recorded by Steve Gardham, 1970. 'Johnny Booker': Hugill, p. 289.

149. *The Sinking of the* Graf Spee. Morton, p. 51: sung by Dick ('Dixie') Bamber, Tandragee, Co. Armagh; noted by Robin Morton at Lurgan, 1965–6. 'The *Achilles*' (song): words by David W. Fraser; music by Claude M. Haydon (copy preserved aboard the present HMS *Achilles*, for information about which I am indebted to Communications Yeoman R. Cooksley).

150. *The* Jervis Bay. Sung by CPO R. W. Maries, Birmingham; recorded by Roy Palmer, 13 September 1984. I have another version sent by Mr W. A. York of Bournemouth, and a poem sent by Mr S. A. Culverhouse of Bedhampton.

151. *Deep Sea Tug.* Sung by Harry Robertson on a tape recording made in 1983 by Martyn Wyndham-Read, and kindly communicated by him. A performance of the song by Steve Turner can be heard on his record, *Jigging One Now*, Fellside FE 030, 1982. Harry Robertson sings his own whaling songs on the cassette, *Whale-chasing Men*, Larrikin Records of Australia, LRCO49, 1980.

152. *The Kola Run.* Written by D. S. Goodbrand in 1961 to the tune of 'Unfortunate Miss Bailey'.

153. *Diesel and Shale.* Written in 1958 by Cyril Tawney, who sings it on the record, *Cyril Tawney in Port* (Argo ZFB28, 1972).

154. *The Shoals of Herring.* Written in 1960 by Ewan MacColl, and published in *Folk Music*, Vol. 1, No. 11, 1965, p. 15. It appears on the record, *Singing the Fishing* (Argo DA142, 1967).

155. *Liverpool John.* Written by Phil and June Colclough.

156. *The Grimsby Lads.* Written by John Conolly and Bill Meek, and first published in *Folk Music, Ballads and Songs*, No. 4 (New Series), n.d. (?1966).

157. *Fiddler's Green.* Written by John Conolly.

158. *The Loss of the* Evelyn Marie. Sung by an unnamed Irish woman on a tape communicated via Katharine Thomson by Mrs Cait Mulkerrins of Ballydavid, Co. Kerry.

159. *The Final Trawl.* Written in 1979 by Archie Fisher. Sung by Cilla Fisher on the record, *Songs of the Fishing* (Kettle Records, KOP–11, 1983, The Post House, Kingskettle, Fife).

BIBLIOGRAPHY

[W. L. Alden] 'Sailors' Chanties and Sea-songs', pp. 794–6 in *Chambers' Journal*, 1869
J. Ashton, *Real Sailors' Songs*, 1891
N. Ault, *Elizabethan Lyrics*, 1966, 4th ed.
Avery, The Life and Adventures of Captain John, 1709 and Los Angeles, 1980
S. Baring-Gould, *English Minstrelsie*, 8 vols, Edinburgh, 1895–7
—— *A Garland of Country Song*, 1895
—— *Songs of the West*, 1905 ed.
R. Barker, *The Log of a Limejuicer*, ed. J. P. Barker, 1934
H. Baynham, *Before the Mast*, 1971
—— *From the Lower Deck*, 1969
—— *Men from the Dreadnoughts*, 1976
R. Beatson, *Naval and Military Memoirs of Great Britain from 1727 to 1783*, 3 vols, 1790
H. P. Beck, 'The Riddle of the *Flying Cloud*', pp. 123–33 in *Journal of American Folklore*, Vol. 66, 1953
C. Beckett, *Shanties and Forebitters*, 1914
D. H. Bernard, 'Sea Songs and Chanties', pp. 431–5 in *Nautical Magazine*, Vol. LXXV, 1906
H. and L. Boardman, *Folk Songs and Ballads of Lancashire*, London and New York, 1973
D. W. Bone, *Capstan Bars*, Edinburgh, 1931
G. P. Boughton, *Seafaring*, 1926
G. Stewart Bowles, *A Gun-room Ditty-box*, 1898
B. H. Bronson, *The Singing Tradition of Child's Popular Ballads*, Princeton, New Jersey, 1976. (This is a selection from the same writer's *Traditional Tunes of the Child Ballads*, 4 vols, Princeton, New Jersey, 1959–72).
R. Brown, *Spunyarn and Spindrift: a Sailor Boy's Log*, 1886
R. Curtis Brown, 'Sailors' Shanties', pp. 294–9 in *Nautical Magazine*, Vol. XCVII, 1917
J. C. Bruce and J. Stokoe, *Northumbrian Minstrelsy*, 1882
N. Buchan and P. Hall, *The Scottish Folksinger*, London and Glasgow, 1973
F. T. Bullen and W. F. Arnold, *Songs of Sea Labour*, 1914
A. Burton, *The Past Afloat*, 1982
D. Butcher, *The Driftermen*, Reading, 1979
—— *Living from the Sea*, Reading, 1982
J. Campbell, *The Lives of the Admirals*, 4 vols, 1742–4
G. G. Carey, *A Sailor's Songbag: an American Rebel in an English Prison, 1777–9*, Amherst, Mass., 1976.
J. M. Carpenter, *Forecastle Songs and Shanties*, unpublished Ph.D. thesis, Harvard University, 1929
—— 'Lusty Chanteys from Long-dead Ships', pp. 12–13, 12 July 1931; 'Life before the Mast: a Chantey Log', pp. 14–15, 19 July 1931; 'Chanteys that

"Blow the Man down"', pp. 10–11, 26 July 1931; 'Chanteys in the Age of Sail', p. 6, 30 October 1938: all in the *New York Times Magazine*.

W. Chappell, *Popular Music of the Olden Time*, 1859

W. Chappell and J. W. Ebsworth, *The Roxburghe Ballads*, 9 vols, Hertford, 1871–99

J. Charnock, *Biographia Navalis*, 6 vols, 1794–8

F. J. Child, *The English and Scottish Popular Ballads*, 5 vols, Boston and New York, 1898

J. Choyce, *The Log of a Jack Tar*, 1891

W. Christie, *Traditional Ballad Airs*, 2 vols, Edinburgh, 1876 and 1881

R. Clements, *Manavilins: a Muster of Sea-songs*, 1928

W. Laird Clowes, *The Royal Navy*, 7 vols, 1897–1903

J. Colcord, *Roll and Go: Songs of American Sailormen*, Indianapolis, 1924

T. Coleman, *A Passage to America*, Harmondsworth, 1974

J. Conolly and B. Meek, *The Singing River*, Hull, 1985

W. Durrant Cooper, 'Smuggling in Sussex', pp. 69–94 in *Sussex Archaeological Collections*, Vol. X, 1858

Bob Copper, *Early to Rise*, 1976

—— *A Song for Every Season*, 1971 .

R. Cotten, Manuscript diary and book of poems and songs in National Maritime Museum, JOD 119.

J. H. Cox, *Folk-songs of the South*, Cambridge, Mass., 1925

H. Creighton, *Folk Songs from Southern New Brunswick*, Ottawa, 1971

—— *Maritime Folk Songs*, Toronto, 1961

—— *Songs and Ballads from Nova Scotia*, New York, 1932

W. J. Dakin, *Whalemen Adventurers*, Sydney, 1934

W. Darling, *Journal*, 1866

M. Dawney, *The Iron Man: English Occupational Songs*, 1974

C. Dibdin and others, *Sea Songs and Ballads*, 1863

G. Dickens, *The Dress of the British Sailor*, 1957

Dillon's Narrative, ed. M. A. Lewis, 2 vols, 1963 and 1966

J. H. Dixon, *Ancient Poems, Ballads and Songs of the Peasantry of England*, 1846

W. M. Doerflinger, *Shantymen and Shantyboys: Songs of the Sailor and Lumberman*, New York, 1951

W. I. Downie, *Reminiscences of a Blackwall Midshipman*, 1912

J. W. Ebsworth, *The Bagford Ballads*, 2 vols, Hertford, 1878

R. Edwards, *The Overlander Song Book*, London and Adelaide, 1972

R. England, *Schoonerman*, 1981

Fairburn's *Naval Songster for 1819* (copy in Birmingham Reference Library)

Fairburn's *Old Casket of Mirth, c.* 1825 (copy in Birmingham Reference Library)

S. Festing, *Fishermen*, Newton Abbot, 1977

C. J. Finger, *Frontier Ballads*, New York, 1927

C. H. Firth, *An American Garland*, Oxford, 1915

—— *Naval Songs and Ballads*, 1908

C. F. Forshaw, *Holroyd's Collection of Yorkshire Ballads*, 1892

E. Fowke, *The Penguin Book of Canadian Folk Songs*, Harmondsworth, 1973

—— *Sea Songs and Ballads from Nineteenth Century Nova Scotia*, New York and Philadelphia, 1981

S. Gardham, *An East Riding Songster*, Lincoln and Hull, 1982
J. A. Gardner, *Above and Under Hatches: Naval Recollections*, ed. R. V. Hamilton
    and J. K. Laughton, 1906, and C. Lloyd, 1955
C. Gill, *The Naval Mutinies of 1797*, Manchester, 1913
W. H. Gill, *Songs of the British Folk*, 1917
P. Gosse, *The History of Piracy*, 1934
S. F. Gradish, *The Manning of the British Navy during the Seven Years' War*, 1980
W. Graham, *The Spanish Armadas*, 1972
R. P. Gray, *Songs and Ballads of the Maine Lumberjacks*, Cambridge, Mass., 1924
G. Greig, *Folk Songs of the North-east*, Peterhead, 1914
H. E. Hale, *New England History in Ballads*, Boston, Mass., 1903 and 1940
J. Hall (ed.), *The Poems of Laurence Minot*, 1886
J. O. Halliwell, *The Early Naval Ballads of England*, 1841
D. Hammond, *Songs of Belfast*, Skerries, Co. Dublin, 1978
T. A. Hampton, *The Sailor's World*, 1971
M. Hay, *I saw a ship a-sailing*, 1981
J. N. Healy, *Irish Ballads and Songs of the Sea*, Cork, 1967 and 1983
L. Heaps, *Log of the 'Centurion'*, 1974
D. S. Henderson, *Fishing for the Whale*, Dundee, 1971
D. Herd, *Ancient and Modern Scottish Songs*, 2 vols, 1776
H. W. Hodges and E. A. Hughes, *Select Naval Documents*, Cambridge, 1922
J. Holloway and J. Black, *Later English Broadside Ballads*, 2 vols, 1975 and 1979
J. W. Holmes, *Voyaging*, 1965
D. Howarth, *Sovereign of the Seas: the Story of British Sea Power*, 1974
S. Hugill, *Sailortown*, 1967
—— *Shanties from the Seven Seas*, 1979, 3rd ed.
G. Huntington, *Songs the Whalemen Sang*, New York, 1964
G. Jackson, *The British Whaling Trade*, 1978
T. S. Jackson, *Logs of the Great Sea Fights, 1794–1805*, 2 vols, 1899–1900
W. James, *The Naval History of Great Britain*, 6 vols, 1837
C. Johnson [Daniel Defoe], *A General History . . . of the Most Notorious Pirates*,
    1724
J. Johnson, *Scots Musical Museum*, 6 vols, Edinburgh, 1787–1803
M. A. Jones, *Destination America*, 1976
T. Jones, *Heart of Oak*, 1984
M. Karpeles (ed.), *Cecil Sharp's Collection of English Folk Songs*, 2 vols, 1974
P. Kemp, *The British Sailor*, 1970
—— *The Oxford Companion to Ships and the Sea*, 1976
P. Kennedy, *Folk Songs of Britain and Ireland*, 1975
F. Kidson, *A Garland of English Folk Songs*, n.d. (1926)
R. Larn, *Shipwrecks of Great Britain and Ireland*, Newton Abbot, 1981
L. G. Carr Laughton, 'Shantying and Shanties', pp. 48–55 and 66–74 in
    Mariners' Mirror, Vol. IX, 1923
G. M. Laws, *American Balladry from British Broadsides*, Philadelphia, 1957
C. C. P. Lawson, *Naval Ballads and Sea Songs*, 1933
R. C. Leslie, *A Sea Painter's Log*, 1886
M. Lewis, *The Navy of Britain*, 1948
A. L. Lloyd, *Folk Song in England*, 1967

C. Lloyd, *The Slave Trade*, 1949
—— *English Corsairs on the Barbary Coast*, 1981
—— *The British Seaman*, 1968
W. H. Logan, *A Pedlar's Pack of Ballads and Songs*, Edinburgh, 1869
J. A. and A. Lomax, *American Ballads and Folk Songs*, New York, 1934
A. B. Lubbock, *The Western Ocean Packets*, Glasgow, 1925
S. B. Luce, *Naval Songs: a Collection of Original, Selected and Traditional Sea Songs*, New York, 1902, 2nd ed.
E. Lucie-Smith, *Outcasts of the Sea: Pirates and Piracy*, New York and London, 1978
N. Luttrell, *A Brief Historical Relation of State Affairs, 1678–1714*, 6 vols, Oxford, 1857
Lord Macaulay, *The History of England*, Harmondsworth, 1979 (abridged ed.)
E. MacColl and P. Seeger, *The Singing Island*, 1960
—— *Travellers' Songs from England and Scotland*, 1977
W. R. Mackenzie, *Ballads and Sea Songs from Nova Scotia*, Cambridge, Mass., 1928
J. P. W. Mallalieu, *Very Ordinary Seaman*, 1956
F. O. Mann, *The Works of Thomas Deloney*, Oxford, 1912
G. J. Marcus, *Heart of Oak: a Survey of British Sea Power in the Georgian Era*, 1975
—— *A Naval History of England*, 2 vols, 1961 and 1971
J. Masefield, *A Sailor's Garland*, 1906
—— 'Sea Songs', pp. 56–80 in *Temple Bar*, 1906
M. Mason, B. Greenhill and R. Craig, *The British Seafarer*, n.d.
P. McCutchan, *Tall Ships*, 1976
A. McKee, *The Golden Wreck*, 1961
B. Meek, *Songs of the Irish in America*, Skerries, Co. Dublin, 1978
A. Moffat, *English Songs of the Georgian Period*, n.d. (?1907)
F. Moore, *Songs and Ballads of the American Revolution*, New York, 1856
S. E. Morison, *John Paul Jones, a Sailor's Biography*, Toronto, 1959
R. Morton, *Folk Songs Sung in Ulster*, Cork, 1970
J. Moulden, *Songs of the People: Selections from the Sam Henry Collection*, Belfast, 1979
L. H. Neatby, *The Search for Franklin*, 1970
F. F. Nicholls, *Honest Thieves: The Violent Heyday of English Smuggling*, 1973
Sam Noble, *'Tween Decks in the 'Seventies*, 1925
C. O'Boyle, *Songs of County Down*, Skerries, Co. Dublin, 1979
J. Ogilby, *Africa*, 1670
J. Ord, *The Bothy Songs and Ballads*, Paisley, 1930
R. Palmer, *A Ballad History of England*, 1979
—— *Everyman's Book of British Ballads*, 1980
—— *Everyman's Book of English Country Songs*, 1979
—— *Folk Songs Collected by Ralph Vaughan Williams*, 1983
—— *Love is Pleasing*, Cambridge, 1974
—— *Poverty Knock*, Cambridge, 1974
—— *The Rambling Soldier*, Harmondsworth, 1977 and Gloucester, 1985
—— *Strike the Bell*, Cambridge, 1978
—— *The Valiant Sailor*, Cambridge, 1973

C. Northcote Parkinson, *Britannia Rules*, 1977
E. Parry, *Memoirs of Rear-admiral Sir W. Edward Parry*, 1857
J. Paxton and J. Wroughton, *Smuggling*, 1971
K. Peacock, *Songs of the Newfoundland Outports*, 3 vols, Ottawa, 1965
G. Peters, *The Plimsoll Line: a Biography of Samuel Plimsoll*, 1975
G. Petrie, *The Complete Collection of Irish Music*, ed. C. V. Stanford, 3 vols, 1902–5
D. Phillipson, *Smuggling*, Newton Abbot, 1973
J. A. Picton, *Memorials of Liverpool*, 2 vols, Liverpool, 1903
V. de Sola Pinto and A. E. Rodway, *The Common Muse: an Anthology of Popular British Poetry*, Harmondsworth, 1965
D. Pope, *Life in Nelson's Navy*, 1981
J. Damer Powell, *Bristol Privateers and Ships of War*, Bristol and London, 1930
F. Purslow, *The Foggy Dew*, 1974
—— *Marrowbones*, 1965
J. Ranson, *Songs of the Wexford Coast*, Wexford, 1948 and 1975
S. Richards and T. Stubbs, *The English Folksinger*, Glasgow and London, 1979
Bob Roberts, *Coasting Bargemaster*, 1949 and Lavenham, 1984
—— *Last of the Sailormen*, 1960
—— *Breeze for a Bargeman*, Lavenham, 1981
—— 'Bargeman', ed. Dave Arthur, pp. 11–13 in *English Dance and Song*, Vol. 44, No. 1, 1982, and pp. 12–15 in id., No. 2.
J. Robinson, 'Songs of the Chantyman', pp. 38–44, 66–72, 96–102 and 123–8 in *The Bellman*, Minneapolis, July–August, 1914
W. Robinson, *Jack Nastyface: Memoirs of a British Seaman*, 1973
W. Rogers, *Life Aboard a British Privateer in the Time of Queen Anne*, 1894
H. E. Rollins, *An Analytical Index to the Ballad Entries (1557–1709) in the Registers of the Company of Stationers of London*, North Carolina, 1924
—— *The Pepys Ballads*, 8 vols, Cambridge, Mass., 1929–32
W. Runciman, *Collier Brigs and their Sailors*, 1926
H. Russell, *One Hundred Songs*, 1856
S. Samuels, *From the Forecastle to the Cabin*, New York, 1887
W. Saunders, 'Folk Songs of the Sea', pp. 984–5 in *Musical Opinion*, July, 1927
—— 'Sailor Songs and Songs of the Sea', pp. 1102–4 in id., August, 1926
B. B. Schofield, *The Russian Convoys*, 1984
J. A. Scott, *The Ballad of America*, New York, 1972
[Cuthbert Sharp], *The Bishoprick Garland*, 1834 and Newcastle, 1969
C. J. Sharp, *English Folk Chanteys*, London and Taunton, 1914
—— *English Folk-songs from the Southern Appalachians*, ed. M. Karpeles, 2 vols, 1932
J. Shaw, *Alongside Bristol Quay: Songs from an Old English City*, n.p., n.d.
A. Shewan, *The Great Days of Sail*, 1927
H. Shields, *Shamrock, Rose and Thistle: Folk Singing in North Derry*, Belfast, 1971
P. Shuldham-Shaw and E. B. Lyle, *The Greig-Duncan Folk Song Collection*, 2 vols (and proceeding), Aberdeen, 1981 and 1984
A. W. B. Simpson, *Cannibalism and the Common Law*, Chicago, 1984
C. Simpson, *The British Broadside Ballad and its Music*, New Brunswick, New Jersey, 1966

C. Fox Smith, *A Book of Shanties*, 1927

L. A. Smith, *Music of the Waters*, 1888

W. H. Smyth, *The Sailor's Word-book*, 1867

G. Sorrell, *The Man before the Mast*, 1928

J. Stokoe and S. Reay, *Songs and Ballads of Northern England*, Newcastle and London, n.d. (?1899)

C. Stone, *Sea Songs and Ballads*, Oxford, 1906

F. W. H. Symondson, *Two Years Abaft the Mast, or, Life as a Sea Apprentice*, Edinburgh, 1876

C. Tawney, 'The Singing Sailor in the Twentieth Century', pp. 6–8, November, 1971, and p. 9, December, 1971, in *Folk and Country*

R. R. Terry, *The Shanty Book*, 2 parts, 1931

H. Thompson, *Body, Boots and Britches*, Philadelphia, 1939

P. Thompson and others, *Living the Fishing*, 1983

C. Thomson, *Autobiography of an Artisan*, 1847

W. R. Thrower, *Life at Sea in the Age of Sail*, London and Chichester, 1972

H. G. Thursfield, *Five Naval Journals, 1789–1817*, 1951

T. d'Urfey, *Pills to Purge Melancholy*, 7 vols, 1719–20

G. Uden and R. Cooper, *A Dictionary of British Ships and Seamen*, 1980

A. Villiers, *Voyaging with the Wind*, 1975

F. W. Wallace, *Wooden Ships and Iron Men*, 1924

A. Walters, 'Songs of the Sea', pp. 485–95 in *Temple Bar*, 1900

O. Warner, *The Navy*, Harmondsworth, 1968

R. Wehse, *Schwanklied und Flugblatt in Grossbritannien*, Frankfurt, 1979

W. B. Whall, *Ships, Sea Songs and Shanties*, Glasgow, 1913, 3rd ed.

G. Williams, *History of the Liverpool Privateers and Letters of Marque, with an account of the Liverpool Slave Trade*, 1897

J. H. Williams, 'The Sailor's Chanties', pp. 76–83 in *The Independent*, New York, 1 July 1909

O. E. Winslow, *American Broadside Verse from Imprints of the 17th and 18th Centuries*, New Haven, 1930

A. Winston, *Pirates and Privateers*, 1972

J. Winton, *Hurrah for the Life of a Sailor*, 1977

R. L. Wright, *Irish Emigrant Ballads and Songs*, Ohio, 1975

GLOSSARY OF NAUTICAL TERMS

abaft, point nearer the stern of a ship than another

about ship, to go about, change tack

aft, towards the stern

a-lee, 'helm's a-lee' is the response of the helmsman after putting the helm down in order to tack

Andrew, Royal Navy

bar, wooden bar used to push round the capstan after inserting it in socket; shoal running across the mouth of a river

barque, three-masted sailing vessel, square-rigged on mainmast and fore and aft rigged on mizen

barquentine, vessel resembling a barque, but square-rigged on foremast only

barrack stanchion, sailor in comfortable post on shore

belay, stop; make fast

belaying spin, bar of wood or iron to which running gear is made fast or belayed

biscuit, ship's bread: flat, hard dough-cakes

bloody flag, large square red flag hoisted by British warships to indicate that they were going into battle

Blue Peter, rectangular blue flag with white rectangle in the centre: signal that a ship is about to sail

boatswain, pron., and often written, 'bosun': warrant officer in charge of sails, rigging, anchors, and of all work on deck

boltsprit, bowsprit which pivots on a bolt, so that it can be raised

boom, spar used to extend the foot of a sail

bouse, stall (confinement)

bower, the best bower anchor was stowed on the starboard bow

bowline (or bowling), rope made fast to the leech or side of a sail to pull it forward

bowse, to haul with a tackle to produce extra tightness

bowsprit, sprit projecting from the bow of a ship

brail, to furl a sail by pulling it in towards the mast

braces, ropes fastened to the yardarms to move them about

brig, originally an abbreviation of 'brigantine', but later a two-masted, square-rigged vessel in her own right

brigantine, two-masted vessel, square-rigged on foremast and fore and aft rigged on mainmast

bring to, check the movement of a ship by arranging the sails in such a way that they counteract each other and keep her stationary

buffer, chief bosun's mate: regulating petty officer in charge of discipline

bulwarks, planking or plating along sides of ship round upper deck

bumboat, boat privately selling goods or provisions to seamen on ships in harbours or anchorages

bunting, signaller

cable, large rope

calavances, small beans sometimes used for making soup

capstan, vertical rotating cyclinder used for winding up anchor and other cable

cat, cat o' nine tails

cathead, projection on each bow to which anchors are secured ('catted') after being raised

chains, projections from sides of a ship to which shrouds or rigging of lower masts secured by means of wooden blocks (deadeyes) chained and bolted to ship's side

chain-shot, cannon balls fastened together with chain

clap on, to add a temporary feature: to clap on a sail means to rig an additional sail

clew, lower corner of a square sail; aftermost corner of fore and aft sail

clew gallants or **clew garnets,** ropes running double from nearly the centre of fore or main yard to clews where tack and sheet are fixed; used for clewing up (taking in) the sail

333

clipper, fast sailing-ship

close-hauled, arrangement of trim of ship's sails to allow her to progress in nearest direction possible towards the wind

coaming, raised edge round a hatch

cockpit, space near after hatchway and below the lower gundeck allocated to surgeon and his mates, and used as operating theatre

courses, fore and main sails and driver

cutter, small, decked vessel with one mast; later a clinker-built ship's boat

davits, piece of timber used as crane; small cast-iron crane

driver, large sail suspended from mizen gaff; also called a spanker

fathom, depth measurement of six feet

fid, wooden marline spike

flemish, to coil a rope concentrically in the direction of the sun's movement

fluke, broad part of anchor

fore and aft, lengthways on a ship

forebitter, recreational song which takes its name from its having originally been sung by the forebitts, the bitts being a wooden or iron structure on the deck

forecastle, (pron., and often spelled, 'focsle') foremost part of deck, below which merchant seamen had their quarters; later these quarters themselves

foremast, mast of vessel furthest forward

forward (for'ard), towards the bows

frigate, three-masted, fully-rigged ship with from 24 to 38 guns

furl, to wrap or roll a sail close to the yard, stay, or mast to which it belongs, and to wind a gasket (cord) round to secure it

gaff, spar which holds upper edge of a four-sided fore and aft sail

galley, ship's kitchen; ship powered by oars as well as sails

gasket, piece of rope or cord used for fastening sails when furling

glass, sandglass which indicated the passage of half an hour

going large, advancing freely before the wind (opposite to close-hauled)

ground, sea bottom

gybe, to allow vessel to fall so far off course

that the wind catches her on the opposite quarter and blows all the sails and gear to the wrong side

halliards, rope or tackle for hoisting a spar holding a sail

haul wind, to direct ship's course as nearly as possible in the direction from which the wind is coming

head, forwardmost part of ship

heads, lavatories

heave to, stop

holystone, piece of sandstone used for scrubbing wooden decks

horse, iron or wooden bar running athwart deck on which a sail sheet can travel

jack-flag, flag flying from staff in bows

Jack o' Clubs, first lieutenant

Jago's Mansions, RN barracks, Devonport

jib, triangular sail, normally extending from bowsprit to foremast

jury, makeshift

kelson, timber or iron plate immediately above keel

killick, anchor

knightheads, baulks of timber to which inner end of bowsprit secured

kye, cocoa

lanyard, rope reeved through deadeyes for setting up rigging; any small rope for making anything fast

larboard, old term for port (left)

lead, weight at end of line cast into sea to find depth of water

league, three miles

lee, side away from wind

leeboard, triangular or pear-shaped board fitted instead of a keel to a sailing barge and lowered on lee side to prevent vessel from being blown to leeward when beating against the wind

leeward, (pronounced 'looard') direction to which wind blows

let go and haul, order on tacking square-rigged ship given when the bow has just passed across the wind: 'let go' refers to the forebowline and weather braces, 'haul' to the lee braces

list, lean to one side

luff, forward edge of fore and aft sail; to sail a ship closer to the wind; order to helmsman to steer so as to make the ship sail nearer to the direction of the wind

lugger, two-master sailing vessel with lug-sail (four-sided sail set on lug or yard) rig

mainmast, principal mast

marline spike, pointed steel or wooden tool for opening strands of rope when splicing

master, captain of merchant vessel; originally officer of warship responsible to captain for navigation

matelot (pron. 'matlow'), sailor

messdeck lawyers, know-alls

mess-kid, wooden tub for cooked victuals

midshipman, non-commissioned rank below sub-lieutenant

mizen, or **mizzen,** aftermost mast in three-masted vessel; mast aft of the mainmast in two-masted vessel

nipper, short length of rope used to bind anchor cable to messenger which went round capstan

Number One, second in command (first lieutenant)

OD, ordinary seaman, the lowest seaman rating in the Royal Navy

oggin, sea

painter, length of rope for securing small boat to pier or jetty

peak, uppermost corner of a fore and aft sail

pawl (or **peal**), sort of ratchet on capstan or windlass to prevent its slipping back

pawlpitts, timber construction supporting system of pawls on windlass

pinnace, small two-masted vessel; eight-oared (later sixteen-oared) ship's boat

pipe, order formerly conveyed by boatswain's whistle or call; now by loudspeaker

poop, raised section at stern of ship

port, left; aperture cut in side of ship

purser (pron. 'pusser'), officer responsible for issue of clothing and provisions; by extension, anything supplied by the navy

quarter, part of side of ship nearest the stern

quarterdeck, after end of upper deck

quartermaster, originally the officer appointed to assist the master of a ship in such duties as stowing the hold and coiling cables

quarters, mercy (later known as 'quarter')

reef, to shorten sail by rolling up the bottom section and securing it by tying points (short lines) attached to the sail

rigging, general name for ropes, chains, and wires which hold masts, spars, and yards in place (standing rigging) and which control movement of sails and spars (running rigging)

royal, sail above topgallant

scuppers, holes pierced in deck near bulwarks to allow surplus water to drain off

seizing, line attaching the bottom of a drift net to the warp

shank-painter, chain used to secure shank of an anchor to ship's rail

sheet, line running from the bottom aft corner of sail by which it can be adjusted to the wind

shrouds, standing rigging stretched from the side of a ship to support the mast

sin-bosun, chaplain (cf sky-pilot and Bible-bosun)

skysail, sail above royal

sloop, sailing vessel with fore and aft rigged single mast

smacksman, sailor on smack, a cutter or ketch-rigged sailing vessel, used for inshore fishing

snow, two-masted merchant vessel, rigged as a brig with the addition of a trysail mast

spanker, see **driver**

speegul, ? from speg (peg)

sprit, spar running diagonally upwards from the mast to the aft, upper corner of a fore and aft sail (hence spritsail)

sprogs, raw recruits

squadron, group of warships numbering under ten

square-rigged, rig consisting of four-cornered sails hung from yards set athwartships

335

stanchion, upright support

starboard, right

stargazer, sail set above moonsail, which in turn is set above skysail

start, to hit with rope's end or cane

stay, standing rigging running fore and aft and supporting a mast

staysail, sail hung from stay

stopper, short length of rope secured at one end temporarily to hold part of running rigging

strike, to lower

stripey, long service able seaman (from chevrons worn for long service with good conduct)

studding sail (stuns'l), sail extending beyond side edge of square sail to make the most of light winds

tack, lower, forward corner of fore and aft sail; in square-rigged ships, line controlling forward lower corner of sail; ship's course in relation to the wind (on starboard or port tack according to whether wind is coming from starboard or port)

tackle pron. 'tayckle', purchase of ropes and blocks

tender, small vessel attached to larger ship for harbour duties; the press tender delivered pressed men to ships

top, (as in maintop) platform at masthead of ship

topgallant, sail above topsail

topman, picked man who worked on topsail and topgallant yards

topmast, mast next above lower mast, the second division of a complete mast, the topgallant mast being the third

topsail, sail above mainsail (second in ascending order from deck)

trace up (or **trice up**), order to lift studding sail boom ends, when topmen were out on yards, in preparation for furling or reefing

Trinculo, ? the purser

vang, running rigging securing end of gaff or sprit

waister, seaman employed in waist of ship; untrained or incompetent seaman

warp, rope or cable used to move vessel (hence, 'to warp'); wire or rope used for hauling a fishing net

wear, to change course by turning stern through the wind

weather, side from which wind is blowing; to sail to the windward of something

weigh, to raise

windlass, capstan-like fitting, on a horizontal shaft

windward (pron. 'wind'ard'), direction from which winds blows

yard, spar attached to mast to carry a sail

yawl, four-oared ship's boat or small sailing boat

336

INDEX OF TITLES AND
FIRST LINES

References are to the numbers of the songs

338

339